Architecture in the United States

P9-DGX-395

Oxford History of Art

Dell Upton is Professor of Architectural History at the University of California, Berkeley. His previous books include *Holy Things and Profane: Anglican Parish Churches in Colonial Virginia*; *Madaline: Love and Survival in Antebellum New Orleans*; *America's Architectural Roots: Ethnic Groups That Built America*; and (with John Michael Vlach) *Common Places: Readings in American Vernacular Architecture*.

Oxford History of Art

Architecture
in the United States

Dell Upton

Oxford New York

OXFORD UNIVERSITY PRESS

1998

Oxford University Press, Great Clarendon Street, Oxford OX2 6DP

Oxford New York
Athens Auckland Bangkok Bogota Bombay
Buenos Aires Calcutta Cape Town Dar es Salaam
Delhi Florence Hong Kong Istanbul Karachi
Kuala Lumpur Madras Madrid Melbourne
Mexico City Nairobi Paris Singapore
Taipei Tokyo Toronto
and associated companies in Berlin Ibadan

Oxford is a trade mark of Oxford University Press

First published 1998 by Oxford University Press

British Library Cataloguing in Publication Data
Data available

Library of Congress Cataloging in Publication Data
Data available
0–19–284217–X Pbk
0–19–284253–6 Hb

10 9 8 7 6 5 4 3 2 1

Picture Research by Elisabeth Agate
Designed by Esterson Lackersteen
Printed in Hong Kong
on acid-free paper by
C&C Offset Printing Co., Ltd

720.923
UPT

10/98

Contents

Acknowledgements

For such a short book, this one has accumulated an extraordinary number of debts that I am delighted to acknowledge. Annmarie Adams, Daniel Bluestone, Betsy Cromley, Susan Garfinkel, Marlene Heck, Greg Hise, Zeynep Kezer, Bill Littmann, Richard Longstreth, Bruce Thomas, Abby Van Slyck, and David Vanderburgh all read the original proposal and made such excellent and pointed suggestions that I discarded it entirely. Their comments contributed significantly to giving the book its present shape. So did the students in Architecture 174A in the spring of 1996, who sat through my first attempts to work out these ideas in lectures.

Tom Carter, Betsy Cromley, Paul Groth, and Marlene Heck read the entire manuscript and helped make it much better than it would have been. In addition, Catherine Bishir, Margaretta Lovell, Roger Montgomery, and Christine Rosen read portions, to equally good effect. I am grateful to them all.

Several friends contributed vital bits of information, photographs, and access to buildings, for which I thank Bill Beiswanger, Tom Carter, Meredith Clausen, Jeff Cohen, Galen Cranz, Betsy Cromley, Sam Davis, Dennis Domer, Jim Gregory, Greg Hise, Lynne Horiuchi, Zeynep Kezer, Travis McDonald, Robert St George, Ellen Weiss, and Sibel Zandi-Sayek.

Among the books I have published this has been the one I have enjoyed most by far. Credit goes to the vision and expertise of Simon Mason and Katie Jones at Oxford University Press. Special thanks to Lisa Agate, whose imaginative approach to picture research made an onerous task fun.

In a sense, a book like this is the product of an entire career. I have learned more than I can tell from field trips and discussions I have had with friends and colleagues over the years, in particular Catherine Bishir, Barbara Carson, Cary Carson, Tom Carter, Edward Chappell, Betsy Cromley, Jim Deetz, Henry Glassie, Paul Groth, Bernie Herman, Rhys Isaac, the late Spiro Kostof, Carl Lounsbury, Fraser Neiman, the late Jeff O'Dell, Orlando Ridout V, Stephen Tobriner, Camille Wells, Shane White, and the late Barry Zarakov.

CANADA

Minnesota

Wisconsin

Michigan

Iowa

Chicago

Illinois

Indiana

Cincinnati

Kansas
City

Missouri

St Louis

Detroit

Cleveland

Ohio

Pittsburgh

Kentucky

Tennessee

Arkansas

Mississippi

Alabama

Louisiana

New Orleans

Georgia

Maine

Vermont

New Hampshire

Massachusetts

Boston Providence

Rhode Island

Connecticut

New York

New York

New Jersey

Philadelphia

Baltimore

Delaware

Washington D.C.

Maryland

West
Virginia

Richmond

Virginia

North
Carolina

South
Carolina

St Augustine

Florida

MAP 9

Introduction

Rhys Isaac has described history as an act of telling stories.[1] It is a deceptively straightforward characterization, for *to tell stories* can mean many things. It can simply mean to report information or narrate events. At a more ambitious level, *to tell stories* can mean to make sense of events by explaining, analysing, or myth-making. As we learned from our parents, *to tell stories* can also mean to lie: 'Are you telling me a story?'

Architectural historians routinely report facts, narrate events, explain, analyse, mythologize, and occasionally even stretch the truth. What makes our work interesting is that the buildings about which we spin tales were made and used by men and women with stories of their own to tell. The historian's challenge is to choose which of many possible stories to tell and to decide how to integrate our stories with theirs.

The architecture of the United States is astonishingly diverse, shaped by a dizzying variety of architectural practices, building processes, regional expressions, and cultures, the disparate experiences of class, gender, and ethnicity as well as the idiosyncrasies of personality. As architectural historians have slowly acknowledged this diversity, our discipline has been enriched as well as fragmented. Formerly, histories of American architecture focused on the aesthetic appreciation of a relatively small, predictable canon of monumental buildings. However, as the quintessential art-architect Louis Sullivan observed, 'once you learn to look at architecture not merely as an art more or less well or more or less badly done, but as a social manifestation, the critical eye becomes clairvoyant'.[2] Architecture is an art of social storytelling, a means for shaping American society and culture and for 'annotating' social action by creating appropriate settings for it. Sometimes, but not always or principally, it is also a vehicle of individual aesthetic expression, but there is more to architecture than the pristine two-dimensional image of the architect's drawing or the historian's photograph. So new scholarly attention to such topics as the vernacular (including indigenous, folk, and popular architecture), ethnic traditions, commercial landscapes, and conservative aesthetic movements has challenged the traditional story of American architecture. In addition, many architectural historians now look outside the

Detail of 127

discipline to social and economic history, sociology, anthropology, feminism, colonial and post-colonial studies, material culture, cultural landscape studies, and literary theory for fresh perspectives on architecture that have enriched and in some instances supplanted accepted aesthetic and art-historical interpretations. As a consequence, no history of American architecture, however compact or introductory, can do justice to the field if it confines itself to the familiar canon. It cannot even do justice to the canon.

My approach to American architecture is, as much as possible within the confines of a short book, catholic. I use 'architecture' to stand for the entire cultural landscape, including so-called designed landscapes, urban spaces, and human modifications of natural spaces. I de-emphasize the traditional distinctions between vernacular and high-style (or academic, or monumental) building, for contemporary scholars teach us that high-style and vernacular buildings share many of the same architectural strategies and that their builders and designers share many of the same cultural values. In short, I assume that architecture means all sorts of building, at all scales, made by all Americans, including those whose ancestors lived here before the first Europeans arrived.

I also believe that the history of architecture should account for the *entire* life of a structure from its initial planning to its destruction, and even its afterlife in history and myth. Those who use architecture and those who interpret it are its makers as much as those who draw plans or drive nails. Buildings are changed in construction and they are changed in use. They are used differently from the ways they were intended and they are appreciated or experienced differently from the ways their architects or patrons might have imagined. Criticism, histories, folklore, and even rumours are other parts of architecture's history that deserve attention. So, where appropriate and where the sources permit, I have considered the responses of the users and observers of architecture.

These are brave ambitions for a history of American architecture, particularly since the new work that is reinvigorating the field is unfortunately incomplete and unevenly distributed. Some sub-fields have been radically transformed (vernacular, colonial, and twentieth-century architectural history most prominently), while others, particularly the history of American art-architecture between about 1800 and 1880, remain relatively untouched by the new scholarly currents.

For all these reasons, I have foregone the traditional survey. Despite the obvious advantages of a chronological structure, it is impossible to 'survey' anything as unruly as many centuries' worth of building on a vast continent. Instead, I have chosen a thematic structure that I believe honours the diversity of American architecture and its recent scholarship, even though it cannot encompass them.

The five themes are Community, Nature, Technology, Money, and Art. *Community* examines the ways Americans have used architecture to grapple with issues of inclusion and exclusion in their society. These questions are as old as human building on the continent, but they assumed a new poignancy with the creation of an American republic in the late eighteenth century. Republican citizenship was a novel concept in modern world history and in architectural design. It reopened old debates about the role of political, cultural, and religious authority in the landscape. In the new republic, architecture was asked to shoulder new burdens of communal mythology and historical commemoration that aggravated, rather than resolved, these dilemmas of inclusion and exclusion. The question whether any architecture can represent an entire society remains a live one.

Architecture is a way of defining relationships—of the self to others, of parts of the community to other people, and of people to their physical and cosmic environments. *Nature* takes off from this commonplace observation. Americans have been obsessed with the relationship of architecture to its site as an expression of a dichotomy between humans and the natural world. Whether expressed as a sensitivity to place, a concern for the debilitating effects of civilization on the human psyche, or fear of the damage that urban, technological society visits on ecological systems, nature has played an essentially theological role in American architecture.

Nature and culture are rhetorical antonyms, but they are nearly always entwined in the landscape. *Technology* examines the ways Americans have used building, and particularly spectacular feats of engineering, construction, and invention, to explore what it means to be human. Technologists sought to overcome the limits of the body, making humans equal to the sublimity of their natural surroundings. Equally important, they fashioned, through environmental controls, an artificial climate essential to emerging middle-class social self-definition.

Money explores the political economy and the economic culture of American architecture. Money's power has been given short shrift in architectural history. It is not enough to present architecture as the simple product of economic 'forces': builders respond to the economy as they understand it. Their understanding derives from culturally shaped notions of human psychology and morality more than from the precepts of the dismal science. The most significant aspect of the economic culture of American architecture was the creation of a landscape of consumer citizenship that complemented the landscape of republican citizenship. Builders of the consumer landscape have been as vexed by questions of inclusion and exclusion as builders of the political landscape.

The puzzling attempt to confine the diffuse expressiveness of architecture to the procrustean bed of *Art* can best be understood in the same consumerist context. The assertion that architecture is an art has been an important strategy for adapting building to a republican, consumer society. Specifically, claims for architecture's artfulness supported the efforts of professional architects to claim a place in a building market that had done quite nicely without them. For years architects struggled to define their distinctive contribution to the building process. The notion that the architect is an artist has been an effective strategy, but one fraught with problems of the relationship of the art-architect to the profession at large, the exclusion of women and ethnic minorities from professional practice, and the role of art-architecture in shaping the landscape of a democratic society.

While my history encompasses many aspects of American architecture overlooked in traditional histories, I make no claim that it is more complete or even more true than they were. It is not a survey, nor is it meant to be. Instead, it cuts through American architecture in other directions from the usual ones, telling other stories from the customary ones. I do believe that the particular themes I have chosen, familiar though most of them are to students of American culture, allow me to explain some of what is *distinctive* or *characteristic* about the ways architectural ideas and forms have been used in the United States without falling into the exceptionalist error of treating its architecture or any of its elements as unique phenomena in world architecture.

A final note on dates: the terms BC and AD are derived from the Christian religion and are inappropriate to the disparate cultural origins of American builders. Following the practice of archaeologists, I use the more neutral BCE (Before the Current [or Common] Era) for BC, and CE (Current [or Common] Era) for AD.

An American Icon

1

Americans are obsessed with houses—their own and everyone else's. We judge ourselves and our neighbours by where and how we live. We categorize the poorest members of contemporary society not as hungry, badly dressed, or unemployed, but as 'homeless'. For those people who are able to own homes (never the majority), a house is the largest single purchase that they will ever make, a significant rite of passage as important as marriage or a first child. This has been true for many generations. In the past, it was not uncommon for home-owners to inscribe construction dates on their houses, marking them as mileposts on the road to success [1]. Some included the initials of both husband and wife, to identify the house as a bench-mark in the generations-long progress of an entire family line.

The house owes its importance to its association with the family. All the indigenous and immigrant cultures who have lived in what is now the United States have identified the family as the core institution of their societies, although they have defined it in very different ways. However they are defined, families are complex institutions. Shared values bind them, but internal divisions distinguish their members as individuals and according to their assigned roles, as spouses, parents, children, servants. Equally important, families have histories—gene pools, genealogies, family stories and traditions: they are constellations of memories that surface in surprising ways from one generation to the next.

Houses are equally rich in meanings. They dignify families and help to structure their working lives. They claim a place for the individual and the family in time (history) and space (community) and in the timeless cosmos. Like families, houses are repositories of memories of the ways that families have organized and represented themselves through many generations.

The protean nature of the family through time and across cultures has contributed to the metaphorical power of the family at the same time that it has made for the great variety of American houses. The free-standing, multi-room, single-family house has been a powerful and conspicuous icon of American culture, but it has not been the only kind of American house. Most Americans lived differently. Native

Americans occupied dwellings ranging from caves big enough for only one or two people, such as those surviving in the Bandelier National Monument, New Mexico, to enormous extended-family dwellings such as those built by the Iroquois of the north-east or the Northwest Coast peoples. From colonization until the twentieth century, small one- and two-room buildings housed the majority of rural Americans [2] [3]. Urbanites might squeeze into subdivided single-family houses such as the two that the Carpenters' Company of Philadelphia bought as a site for its new hall in 1768. These were common urban houses with two rooms, one in front of another, on each floor of a main block and two rooms in an ell or 'back building', but each room was rented to a different tenant. A few Americans lived in the communal dwellings of utopian communities such as the Shakers and the Oneidans, while after the 1840s many more lived in purpose-built multi-family rental housing. Some Americans did not live in houses at all, but in schools, penitentiaries, asylums, hospitals, or military barracks, in the attics, cellars, barns, or outbuildings of their employers or owners, or on the streets. Yet despite the diversity it is possible to identify some common themes that create 'family resemblances' among many kinds of American houses.

1

John and Mary Dickinson House, 1754, Salem County, NJ.

Glazed brick was used to pick out the owners' initials and the construction date, along with an elaborate diaper-work pattern, in the gable end.

2

Perkinsons, late 18th century Chesterfield County, Va.

This tiny house is one of the smallest surviving 18th-century American dwellings. The small wing to the right was the original 12-by-14-foot one-room building. The 16-foot-square room to the left was added around 1800, and the porch in the mid-19th century. This was a better-than-average residence by colonial standards.

It should come as no surprise that architects and historians have been fascinated by houses. In addition to their inherent social interest, houses have a particular appeal to those concerned with design. Because notions of domestic life have been stylized quickly and thoroughly in most traditional and modern cultures, houses are paradoxically the building type least constrained by idiosyncratic requirements. By the middle of the nineteenth century, for example, the single-family house had become so ubiquitous, so stereotyped, and so familiar, the social and functional ground rules of middle- and upper-middle-class domestic life so fixed, and the stress on the symbolic character of the house so great, that the programme became in a sense the background or continuo against which architects and clients could play out claims of originality on aesthetic terms. The same constancy in the bourgeois single-family house has served historians as a standpoint from which to make sweeping aesthetic and social comparisons and grand synthetic interpretations.

The iconic status of the house in American culture makes it a particularly rich starting-point for those interested in the history of architecture in the United States, for the themes and values that have shaped the entire landscape are present, in highly condensed form, in its houses. By the same token, the long chains of history and culture that connect houses and families mean that a single house can offer a window on many aspects of American dwellings. Monticello, one of the most famous of American houses, offers just such a starting-point, owing to its excellent state of preservation and to the extensive documentation available for the house and its owner and builder, Thomas Jefferson [4]. The densely layered, half-resolved agglomeration of visual images, social ideas, and spatial relationships that Jefferson created at Monticello ran the gamut of his obsessions, passions, desires, and fears. The result is a rich and fascinating touchstone for exploring the histories of American houses.

Monticello

When he was twenty-five years old, Thomas Jefferson decided to move from his mother's home in Albemarle County, Virginia, to a nearby site on the family's lands, on the lesser of the two peaks of Carter's Mountain. There, in 1768, workers began to construct a house that at first contained only three principal rooms and an entry or 'lodge' on the ground floor [5]. Shortly after he began to build, Jefferson added semi-octagonal spaces at the north and south, called the bedroom and 'north bow-room', respectively. At that time the three original rooms were designated the parlour, dining-room, and dressing-room. Although the house's plan was compact, its appearance was monumental. Both fronts were intended to be embellished with two-storey porticoes. Had they been completed, their pediments would have risen higher than the dome of the present house.

In 1790, Jefferson began to think about enlarging his house. The reconstruction began in 1796, and by 1809 a second file of rooms had been added to the east of the original ones. The old dressing-room became Jefferson's bedroom, the old bedroom his 'cabinet', or private office, and a 'book room' and glazed greenhouse or 'South Piazza' were added to his personal suite of rooms. The old and new sections of the house were separated by longitudinal hallways and a service core that

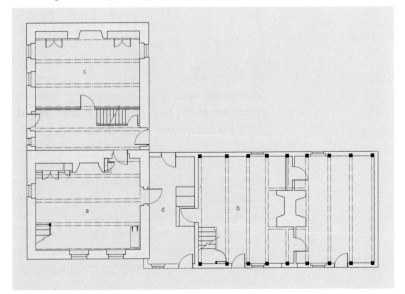

3

Bronck Houses, (a) late 17th century, (b) 1738, (c) 1792, (d) mid-19th-century, Coxsackie, NY.

A one-room Dutch house enlarged over the course of 150 years.

4 Thomas Jefferson

Monticello II, 1796–1809, Charlottesville, Va.

Garden front.

contained privies and service spaces. The stone columns used in the uncompleted east portico of the old house were reused in a colossal pedimented portico on the new one [**6**]. On the west, the two-storey portico was similarly reduced to a single storey supported on plastered brick columns, while a dome was built over the semi-octagonal parlour bow. The long-contemplated subterranean service wings were completed. All this was the product of nineteen years of constant changes of mind. The work had been put up and taken down so many times, visitor Anna Thornton commented, 'that in many parts without side it looks like a house going to decay from the length of time that it has been erected. . . . He is a very long time maturing his projects.'[1]

The Ordinariness of Architecture

The story of any house begins with its ordinariness—its status as a product of labour and money and its accommodation of daily routines. Monticello was a plantation's big house, the headquarters of an economic enterprise. Jefferson had inherited a 5,000-acre plantation from his father and acquired another 11,000 acres in Albemarle and other Virginia counties when he married. In addition, he maintained other enterprises, including several mills, a nailery, and a textile operation, to keep his slaves busy during slack agricultural times. These enterprises paid for the house and its contents, they paid for Jefferson to live the kind of life he did, and they fed the people who were needed to support his way of life.

At its most ordinary, this large, complex house tells a simple story. Monticello is organized according to a series of dichotomous categories that govern the distribution of its house life dynamically along

5

Monticello II.
Ground floor plan with
Monticello I superimposed.

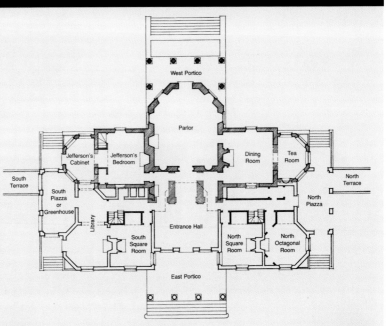

6

Monticello II.
Exterior view from the
south-east. The monumental
entrance portico led into
Jefferson's entrance hall,
or 'Indian Room'. In this
late-19th century view,
the louvred terrace
enclosures survived.

7

Monticello II.
Schematic view showing
axial organization.

8

Henry and Anne Saunders
House, *c*.1795, Isle of Wight
County, Va.

The hall panelling (left
room) of this hall-chamber
(or hall-parlour) house can
be seen in the National
Museum of American
History in Washington.

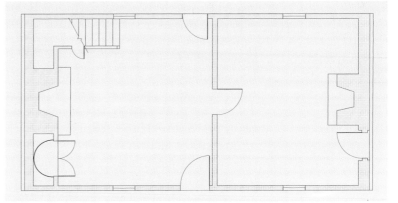

vertical and horizontal axes [**7**]. A vertical axis connects working spaces below ground with 'living' spaces on the ground and upper floors, active spaces in the basement, and places for retirement in the upper storeys. This axis intersects others on the ground floor, where the east-west axis formed by the entrance-hall-and-parlour suite separates Jefferson's private spaces to the south and spaces for visitors to the north. North and south passages (hallways) divide Jefferson's primary working and social spaces to the west from guest and storage rooms to the east. (The north-south axis also connects the domestic work spaces in the south wing to the plantation work and storage spaces in the north wing.)

Jefferson was famously contemptuous of the houses of his Virginia neighbours, calling them 'ugly, uncomfortable, and happily . . . perishable', yet Monticello shared its dualities and axialities with its humbler neighbours and with a multitude of other small vernacular houses in eighteenth-century America.[2] The habit of stringing domestic spaces along a single horizontal axis that ran from better to worse, refined to rough, was deeply engrained in European vernacular architecture. These distinctions are most evident in the two-room houses (meaning houses with two principal rooms on the ground floor) that English, French, German-Swiss, and Dutch colonists built [**3**].

The plans of these houses varied from one ethnic group to another, as did the names and specific uses of the rooms. For example, in Jefferson's Virginia, houses that historians call *hall-chamber* or *hall-parlour* houses incorporated the traditional horizontal axis [**8**]. At what English vernacular builders would have called the 'upper' end, a large, usually square room called the *hall* was the primary living or social space. It contained the main entry and might also function as a kitchen in a particularly small house. A smaller room, traditionally called the *chamber*, opened off it and served as the primary sleeping-room. Just over the Blue Ridge Mountains from Monticello, German-Swiss builders (who settled in the inland valleys from Pennsylvania south to the Carolinas) organized their *Flurküchenhauser* into a narrow *Küche*, or kitchen, which also contained the main entrance, and a square *Stube*, or parlour, that served as the primary formal space [**9**].

In the sixteenth and seventeenth centuries distinctions between the formal and informal, public and private, living and working aspects of household life grew stronger among European builders. Vertical and front-back axes supplementing the old horizontal axis multiplied possibilities for refining interior organization. The late-seventeenth-century Boardman House at Saugus, Massachusetts, is a good example of this type of modern house [**10**] [**11**]. It was built as a hall-parlour house with an upper storey for bedchambers and an underground cellar for food storage. About a decade after its initial construction, the kitchen was moved to a new rear ell, or lean-to.

These axes and the domestic dichotomies that they express linked Jefferson's mansion to the vernacular of his neighbours, however contemptuous he might be of their houses' appearance and solidity. They offer an excellent example of the ways that cultural memory permeates the house, for they are the products of deep-seated, long-standing, barely articulated assumptions about what it meant to live as a civilized householder. They made Jefferson's house familiar and comprehensible to his family and his neighbours, giving scale and significance to his more idiosyncratic gestures. Without such an ordinary fabric to embroider, Monticello would have been a meaningless gesture, a diatribe in an unknown language.

The Domestic Community
One of architecture's most important tasks is to sort out its users, setting them spatially and psychologically into the desired relationships

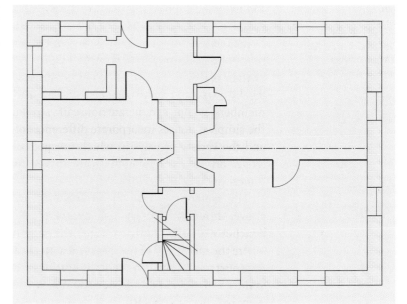

9

Sites House, *c*.1800–10, Rockingham County, Va.

In this two-room *Flurküchenhauser*, the *Küche* is on the left and the *Stube* (divided into two rooms shortly after construction) on the right. Often, there was a third room, called the *Kammer* (chamber) or *Stibli*, behind the *Stube*.

10

Boardman House, 1687, lean-to *c.*1696, Saugus, Mass. The Boardman House was an up-to-date vernacular dwelling organized around three axes: horizontal, vertical, and front-back. Although houses like this are sometimes mislabelled 'medieval', they were 17th-century innovations in Anglo-American vernacular architecture.

with one another. For that reason, it is never possible to speak of 'the' experience of a building: every building is a fragmented space. This is as true of houses as of any other kind of architecture. Conventional categories such as living and working or public and private imply that a house is a unity, made for a nominal owner whose name we attach to it: 'the Thomas Jefferson House'. Even to call Monticello 'the Jefferson House' would imply a single experience of the building by a monad called a family. But a household is a molecule more than an atom. Some members have more control over the house than others, some do more work there than others, and all experience it differently according to their places in the domestic community. Although one person may legally own a house and exercise more control over it than other family members, no one can dictate house life absolutely. Consequently, even the simplest houses incorporate differences of control and experience, and the variety of ways in which unequal relationships are acknowledged and represented in the house makes for much of the diversity in American housing.

For example, within the *Flurküchenhauser* that we encountered above, differences of age and sex were called out [**9**]. A table and benches were commonly built into the outer front corner of the *Stube*, where the male head of the house sat at the head, in the corner, with his wife next to him at the head of the outside bench. The male and female children then lined up on the wall-side and outside benches, respectively, in order of seniority.

Boardman House.

The Boardman House's modern qualities are evident in the ways that activities traditionally performed in or adjacent to the main room have been sorted and moved away. The large fireplace and corner oven show that cooking was once done in the hall (front right room), but was moved to a new kitchen (the centre room of the lean-to), where a new fireplace and oven were constructed. Food storage was pushed back to a milk-house in the lean-to and down into a subterranean cellar, while sleeping spaces have been been moved back into the lean-to and up into second-floor chambers.

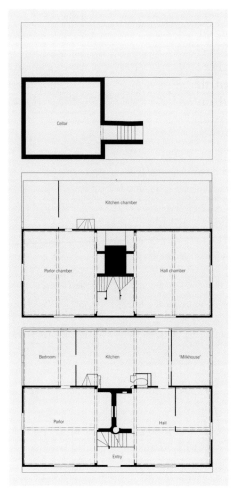

Many indigenous builders followed similar ritual principles of social differentiation. The hogan, an earth, stone, or log (or, more recently, frame-and-plywood) traditional dwelling of the Navajo people of the American South-west, follows a social principle common among a variety of indigenous groups. Inside the single round or polygonal space, an axis leads from the east-facing door to the place of honour opposite it, the seat of the household's elder. On ritual occasions, men are arrayed around the south side and women around the north [12].

Jefferson's Monticello derived from an élite Southern tradition that also acknowledged differences in social roles spatially. Monticello was not Jefferson's residence alone. His employees and their families (sixteen people in 1776), as well as some of Jefferson's relatives, also lived there. Although Jefferson's wife died fourteen years before the rebuilding began, his daughter Martha Jefferson Randolph (who had a home of her own nearby) spent most of her time at Monticello with her daughters. Other relatives stayed for varying lengths of time at

Monticello, as did the numerous visitors, announced and un-announced, who regularly showed up on the mountain. Most of all, Monticello was home to a large contingent of African-American slaves. In 1776, eighty-three lived on the mountain. In 1794, as Jefferson planned the rebuilding of Monticello, there were sixty-four. Even more than for Jefferson, Monticello was the centre of their working and personal lives.

The metaphor of the village commonly used by travellers to describe southern plantations was aptly applied to Monticello, which should be thought of as a heterogeneous community of people of all ages, races, sexes, degrees of freedom, and relationships to the nominal owner. In common with his slaveholding peers, Jefferson preferred to conceive of the Monticello community as a family, a term that encompassed everyone, slave and free, living on the mountain. He meant this in the sense derived from the biblical patriarchy: Jefferson was the rul-

12

Prototypical Navajo conical forked-pole hogan.

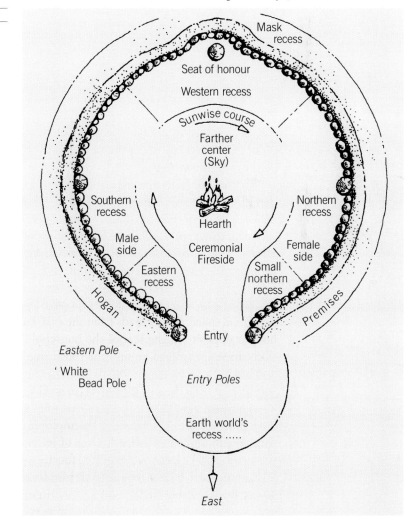

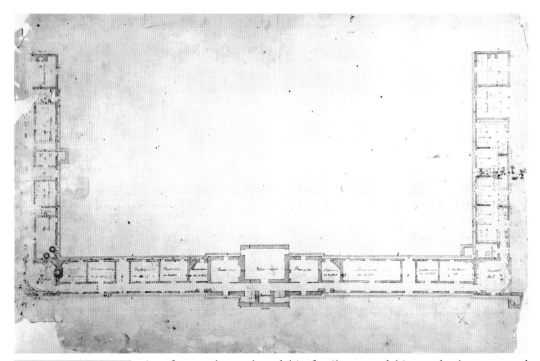

13 Thomas Jefferson

Monticello I, 1772.
Although this plan of the
basement and service wings
was made in 1772, the wings
were not completed for many
years: the north (right) one
in 1799, and the south (left)
one after 1801.

ing figure who gathered his family around him and who governed them absolutely. More than anything, he organized Monticello to convey his sense of himself as the patriarch at the centre of his universe. Within it, the members of the family were ranked and assigned places in the house and grounds.

First of all, Jefferson distinguished his 'indoor' from his 'outdoor' families. The latter, who were primarily slaves, lived along Mulberry Row, a 1,000-foot-long road containing seventeen log, frame, and stone houses, yards, and shops at the lip of the hill. The distinction between living and working further divided the indoor family. Cooking, storage, the clean-outs for the interior privies, and other working spaces that served the bodily needs of the 'indoor' family were located in the basement wings, along with some living spaces for the slaves who performed them [**13**]. The bedchambers on the top two floors of the house were allocated to relatives, children, and guests of the house. Monticello's command centre was the South Square Room on the ground floor, from which Jefferson's daughter Martha ran the day-to-day affairs of the house [**5**]. This left most of the principal, or ground, floor to the patriarch.

Jefferson's Monticello was a dynamic space: residents were sorted and distributed, then brought back into contact with one another along carefully choreographed routes and points of encounter. This was another way in which Jefferson's house was like those of his neighbours. Virginia slaveholders established separate routes through their houses for white and black residents, for outsiders and insiders. Even a

14

Mount Airy, *c.*1754–64,
Richmond County, Va.

The rusticated south façade
is the least formal, in keeping
with its garden view. The dark
stone walls may originally have
been stuccoed.

dwelling as small as the Henry and Anne Saunders House has an end door into the chamber through which slaves would enter from the domestic outbuildings that stood just outside it [**8**]. John Tayloe's Mount Airy (1762), Richmond County, Virginia, observed the same principle on a much grander scale. The main house is flanked by two visually coordinated outbuildings that were originally freestanding but were connected by quadrants at an early date [**14**]. The one on the west was the kitchen, the realm of slaves, that on the east provided auxiliary living quarters for the family. Each group had its own door into the end of the house, while the north door greeted visitors.

Host and Hermit

The ordinariness of architecture means that no house-builder can afford to ignore the facts of daily life and household social relations, yet most strive to transform their house's story from a simple narrative of domestic facts to an interpretive myth of domestic life. At Monticello the simple distribution of architectural decoration, which is confined on the interior to the rooms that Jefferson used, tells us that while the house was home to many people, it was meant to be seen as a portrait of its patriarch.

And a curious, contradictory portrait it is. In some moods, Jefferson wanted to be seen as a public man and Monticello as a public place. The eighteenth-century Virginia élite imagined themselves as heirs to a hospitable aristocratic tradition of open-handed largesse that stretched back to the Middle Ages. In fact, they practised a distinctly eighteenth-century version of hospitality. Where a medieval lord would have entertained any and all comers in a single large room called a 'hall', the company entertained at a Virginia plantation would have been considerably more restricted—to one's neighbours of equivalent social standing—and distributed through a suite of rooms fine-tuned to Virginian forms of entertaining. Monticello's entrance hall, where invited guests were met and where uninvited ones waited to learn whether they would be received, led to the parlour or sitting-room, and then into the dining-room. Jefferson's renowned dinnertime conviviality reflected the centrality of dining in Virginia social rituals and the importance of the dining-table as the altar of the sociable house.

But Jefferson the good host was also Jefferson the recluse. Neighbouring planters surrounded themselves with their family and slaves, but Jefferson constructed his house to allow himself the luxury of the company of family and the services of slaves while denying their presence. He concealed the family rooms up nearly invisible stairs and hid servants behind doors and in passages. Where other planters would have slaves wait at table, build fires in their rooms, lay out their clothes, and empty their chamber-pots, Jefferson installed dumb waiters and lazy susans, built his own fires, constructed a revolving clothes-rack at the foot of his bed to allow him to select his own clothes, and defecated in a *garde-robe*, adjacent to his bedroom, that was cleaned out from the cellar.

The solitary conceit carries outside the house. At a house like Mount Airy, the visually co-ordinated, hierarchical massing and decoration of house and outbuildings proclaimed a model of domestic community that set patriarch, family, and slaves in their appropriate places in a stratified landscape [14]. Jefferson rejected this familiar pattern. He attached wings and dependencies to Monticello, but he used them as retaining walls to support the west terrace, hiding them from view [4]. Furthermore, this large, three-storey house is deliberately made to appear as a small, one-storey house. Just as the slaves' work spaces are hidden by the terrace, the family quarters are concealed behind balustrades. The only storey that we see is the patriarch's. Visually Jefferson's house claims that the home of many people, white and black, is the home of one man. A man surrounded by family and slaves represented himself as a hermit alone on his mountain.

The metaphor of the hermitage was reinforced by Monticello's setting. Jefferson began to think about the grounds at the same time that he planned his house, and the landscaped setting is important for understanding the self-images that Jefferson intended his house to project. Monticello was conceived as a villa, a word that originally referred to a Roman farmstead. During the Renaissance, the villa was recast as an élite farmstead or country estate close to the edge of the city. The eighteenth-century English builders from whom Jefferson drew inspiration understood the Renaissance villa primarily as a sociable retreat. Jefferson planned for his mountain-top villa to be surrounded by a landscaped garden such as the ones that adorned the suburban London villas of English aesthetes like Lord Burlington and Alexander Pope, and those illustrated in the gardening books he read so assiduously. It would be adorned with follies and garden pavilions, including obelisks, temples, even a miniature Pantheon. None of these was ever built, although the domed central bay of the second Monticello might be seen to double as a garden Pantheon.

In many eighteenth-century gardens a rustic hut or grotto, meant to look as though it were unshaped by human artifice, alluded to the stock figure of the hermit. The hermit was a man who had rejected the social contract and chose to live on nature's terms. He embodied a proto-romantic sense of the mysterious in the landscape, of the emotional depths of nature. Jefferson was powerfully attracted to these ideas during his early years on the mountain, making a note to himself in 1771 to 'Choose out for a Burial place some unfrequented vale in the park, where there is "no sound to break the stillness but a brook, that bubbling winds among the weeds; no mark of any human shape that had been there, unless the skeleton of some poor wretch" ', and he planned to shelter a spring in a moss-covered 'cave or grotto'.[3]

As a house and as a landscape, Monticello was both villa and hermitage, a place of sociability and of retreat. At the same time it had a larger purpose. Houses (and their settings) have long been called upon to define the relationship between the family and the cosmos. After the eighteenth century sophisticated builders were more likely to express such ideas in the allusive language of 'nature' than in explicitly theological terms. The landscape gardens of the eighteenth century that Jefferson admired and the romantic language of wild nature that he called on in describing his burial plans were exploratory essays in the connection between the human and the divine. Jefferson was by no means the first or the only American of his time to be intrigued by these ideas, but his is one of the earliest and best-documented landscapes created under their influence, and it illustrates the importance of aesthetic ideas in carrying out Jefferson's purposes.

Design

A French visitor to Monticello in 1782 declared Thomas Jefferson 'the first American who has consulted the Fine Arts to know how he should shelter himself from the weather'.[4] He was determined to use every bit of his great architectural erudition in the construction and re-construction of his house. As he imagined the first Monticello, every room would be decorated in a different classical order, derived from a different precedent. This house was a relatively simple pastiche of formal and visual ideas borrowed from the work of the sixteenth-century Italian architect and treatise-writer Andrea Palladio, filtered through a miscellany of eighteenth-century English architectural books, notably Robert Morris's *Select Architecture* (1755). In short, it was a collection of visual quotations of the kind that amateurs and professionals alike commonly mistake for design.

Jefferson's travels in Europe after the American Revolution showed him French and English neo-classical architecture, from which he absorbed new visual and spatial ideas. In addition, he supplemented his library of Anglo-Palladian treatises with French studies of ancient architecture. He drew on these liberally—especially Roland Fréart de Chambray's *Parallèle de l'architecture antique avec la moderne* (1650; known to Jefferson through a 1766 edition) and Antoine Babuty Desgodetz's *Les Édifices antiques de Rome* (1779)—in embellishing the reconstructed house. The result is a much more complex building than its predecessor, a dense mixture of familiar and novel ideas drawn from several sub-traditions of European classicism, but it was never the smoothly integrated work of art that twentieth-century historians and architects see in it: no building is.

Jefferson's great accomplishment at Monticello and the nearby University of Virginia (another of his projects) have earned him credit as one of the first American architects. In the sense that he took a hand in designing buildings, this is strictly true, but every building is designed by someone. The label architect implies more than this: it implies a particular social relationship to architecture and to clients, as well. It is instructive to compare Jefferson with the first *professional* architect, Benjamin Henry Latrobe, Jefferson's friend and architectural confidant.[5] An English-born and -trained professional who began his career in his home country before coming to the United States in 1796, Latrobe sought to make his living as an architect and engineer in a commercializing society. Lacking a material object to sell, the architect had to establish himself as the product, distinguished as an expert or authority who commanded knowledge qualitatively different from that of the best-educated lay person. Latrobe made his argument on the basis of his long specialized training and his mastery of the latest architectural fashions. Where Jefferson sought access to arcane architectural ideas through books, Latrobe offered arcane architectural ideas drawn from his expertise. For Latrobe, the seller of architecture, architectural ideas were necessarily successive. Each new idea rendered its predecessors obsolete.

Latrobe offered clients the validation of his own personal authority, but Jefferson sought personal validation from cultural authority. For him, architecture was a means of self-improvement, a mode of being, rather than a stock in trade. New ideas supplemented the old, enriching self-definition. To Latrobe this was absurd, a sign of a man who did not understand architectural progress. As architect of the government buildings at Washington during Jefferson's presidency, Latrobe felt cramped by his employer's 'prejudices in favor of the old French books, out of which he fishes everything'.[6] He respectfully tolerated Jefferson's architectural advice, but he privately resented the interference with his professional judgement. 'You and I are both blockheads,' he wrote to his construction supervisor John Lenthall. 'Presidents and Vice presidents are the only Architects and poets, and prophets for ought I know in the United States.'[7]

Consumption

At Monticello, mantels, window sash, wallpaper, and other architectural goods purchased abroad supplemented locally made cornices, orders, mouldings, and other decorations that the workmen derived from architectural books that Jefferson had purchased. These in turn formed a setting for the fine furnishings that filled the public parts of the house. Some were custom-made and locally obtained, but Jefferson also embellished the house over the years with furniture and decorative arts from France and England, original works of art, and copies of Old Master paintings that he obtained from abroad. In short, Monticello is best understood in the context of the broader-based phenomenon of Anglo-America consumer culture, which historians tell us was born during Jefferson's lifetime, and Jefferson as an eclectic consumer of architectural images more than a creator of architecture.

By *consumerism* or *consumption*, historians mean a complex set of social, economic, and psychological phenomena that link objects and marketing strategies with personal identity. The core of the idea of consumption is the issue that we have been examining at Monticello: the role that artefacts play in defining the relationship between the individual and the world. One persuasive argument finds the origins of Euro-American consumerism in Protestant religion.[8] According to sociologist Colin Campbell, one strain of Protestantism emphasized the primacy of personal judgement over the claims of authority. By the eighteenth century personal autonomy had become self-gratification and self-fulfillment. Since Western culture has always had a materialist bent, meaning that westerners believe there is a strong connection between the physical world and human values and behaviour, it is no surprise that the possession of goods has appeared to promise self-fulfillment. To put it another way, consumption is a quest for identity through sensual means. We buy what we think we see in an object, grasping at the physical to get at the intangible, buying the commodity to obtain the unsaleable quality. The catch, however, is that the longing for identity is diffuse, unfocused, and not described by any specific missing quality, so no particular commodity can satisfy it. We desire, we buy, we are inevitably disappointed, and we buy again, and again. Desire and acquisition, the ephemeral moment between wanting and

15

Mount Airy.

The east front was the family's
entrance from its dependency.
Originally one entered a door
in the central arched window.
The covered hyphen to the
right was added early in Mount
Airy's history.

having, are essential to consumption; possession is an afterthought.

Consumption offers an important avenue for understanding the importation of architectural ideas, books, and craft workers in late-eighteenth-century America. The importation of European goods and ideas has customarily been interpreted as simple imitation, the product of a desire to emulate the lives of English gentry as closely as possible. But American clients were looking in the other direction: architecture and other consumer goods were a way of creating an identity within American society, by drawing on reserves of cultural authority available only to a select few. Consider the use of Anglo-Palladian architectural ideas at Mount Airy. With the advice of an Annapolis builder named Edmund Jenings, John Tayloe adapted the plan and main elevations from plates in James Gibbs's *Book of Architecture* (1728). The architectural ordonnance was closely co-ordinated with the system of domestic social differentiation examined above. The austere Tuscan north front, framed by its forecourt of outbuildings, contains a recessed loggia within which visitors could be greeted in appropriate formality, while the south façade is rusticated, as befits its garden view [**14**]. The two end doors are decorated very differently, as befit the status of their principal users [**15**].

Mount Airy is a well-known example of the close copying of published images. However, architectural consumption depended on establishing visual differences from one's surroundings more than it did faithful reproduction of sources, so book-bound houses of this sort were rare in colonial America. Even at Mount Airy, the Anglo-

Palladian visual language annotated the social hierarchy of the house, while its esoteric European provenance emphasized Tayloe's social distance from his neighbours.

As a rich, intelligent, ambitious man born at the fringes of empire, Jefferson sought to cloak himself in the same cultural authority that John Tayloe invoked. The architecture and landscape of the first Monticello were straightforward exercises in the consumption of architecture to fashion a distinctive identity. As he grew older, Jefferson never relinquished his attachment to cultural authority: his identity was too deeply invested in it. Late in Jefferson's life, Latrobe called him 'a man *out of a book*'.[9] But Jefferson's architectural consumption grew more complex later in his life. Because no idea was ever abandoned, his initial allegiance to Palladio—depicted by his Anglo-Palladian sources as the ultimate rule giver—remained with him throughout his life. Jefferson added new, not always compatible, architectural ideas derived from the neo-classicism that flourished in Europe when he travelled there in the 1780s.

The second Monticello is a layered work that incorporates everything Jefferson had learned over the years. Behind a colossal east portico such as one would expect to find on an Anglo-Palladian country house is an equally English hall-saloon (parlour) public suite [5] [6]. In reworking the house, Jefferson used the original rooms as a garden-side sequence with a polygonal central parlour. They were set off from the predominantly private east rooms by a longitudinal hall. These are French neo-classical ideas that intrigued another American visitor to France, Charles Bulfinch, who incorporated them into his Barrell House (1792–3), Charlestown, Massachusetts, and Swan House (1796),

16 Charles Bulfinch

Swan House, 1796, Dorchester, Mass.

The garden-side bedroom and projecting bay, the longitudinal hallway, the dining-room-parlour axis, and the stair location all link the Swan House's spatial pattern to Monticello's.

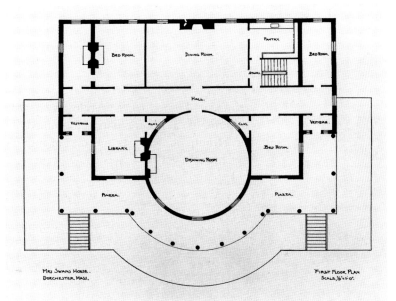

AN AMERICAN ICON 35

Dorchester, Massachusetts. The plan of the Swan House, in particular, is very similar to Monticello's, with a garden-front range set at right angles to a hall-dining-room suite [**16**]. The domed garden front of Monticello resembles a Palladian-garbed version of the Hôtel de Salm (Pierre Rousseau, *c.*1785), under construction in Paris during Jefferson's sojourn there, while the bedroom-office-library suite is equally reminiscent of French hôtel planning [**5**].

Jefferson came of age during the turbulent decade that began with the Stamp Act Crisis of 1765 and ended with the Revolutionary War. In its early years the revolutionary movement was often cast as a crisis of consumption. The Non-Importation Agreements, for example, equated consumer behaviour with political identity. Under the weight of his participation in the Revolution and the formation of a new national government, his reading in Enlightenment philosophy and political theory, and his exposure to neo-classical aesthetic ideas during his service as an envoy to France (appropriately, he was charged with the promotion of commerce), the meanings of architectural consumption and the cultural authority shifted for Jefferson. The consumerist dimensions of Jefferson's relationship to architecture transformed a backward-looking reliance on cultural authority into a forward-looking project of personal reconstruction. Widely known architectural and landscape images and ideas, disseminated commercially through books, appeared to Jefferson to be a tool to remake himself, to declare his individuality, to transform himself from a colonial Virginian to a post-colonial American.

Rethinking the Landscape

As time passed, Jefferson redesigned Monticello's landscape as carefully as he reworked its house. From his initial, rather simplistic plan for an English landscape garden, Jefferson began in 1806 to create a landscape that would combine the useful with the pleasurable. It would be a version of a *ferme ornée*, with productive gardens and animal husbandry integrated with ornamental gardening. The west lawn remained a pleasure garden. Below it, behind Mulberry Row, was an artificial terrace serving as a vegetable garden, with adjacent orchards, vineyards, and groves. Between the second and third 'roundabouts', or circumferential roads, were a series of animal pens and small fields containing various feed grasses, beyond which the surrounding landscape offered a picturesque prospect.

The reworking of the Monticello landscape defined a new human relationship to the cosmos, one that differs from the picturesque and incipient romantic models of the late eighteenth century as much as it did from traditional theological models. The landscape garden that provided the first model for Monticello's grounds (and that was never entirely eradicated from them) was both a didactic construction that instructed its viewers (many English landscape gardens were filled with overt political images, for example) and a transformative one that improved its viewers by exposing them to the delights and the healing effects of nature. The new garden reversed the flow of power. It represented an attempt to dominate nature, to subordinate it to the will and the gaze of the patriarch.

Monticello commands a view of the surrounding lowlands. In turn, the big mountain, Montalto, looks down on Monticello, but since Montalto belonged to Jefferson, as well, he turned the table. At one point, he hoped to put an observatory tower on its summit, as a kind of visual handle or grasping point. Instead he created something more relentless, a landscape insistently focused on himself, with the domed second house at its centre. The dome was the visual pivot around which the entire countryside revolved, the symbolic eye of Jefferson. It has no other function, for it covers a nearly inaccessible third-floor room that was always treated as a left-over space. In the Enlightenment intellectual tradition, surveillance—one-sided vision—was power. The all-seeing eye on the national seal of the new United States is a good example. Jefferson's dome was a kind of eye on the landscape, a surrogate of its owner. It transformed Jefferson into an all-seeing I.

Monticello reminds us how intimately the ideas of nature's beneficial power over humanity and of humanity's power over the natural world have been entwined in American architectural history. Nature and technology are two sides of the same coin. Monticello is famous for its idiosyncratic household technologies. Such devices as multipurpose desks, folding ladders, double-facing clocks, automatic door-closing mechanisms, and a host of other furnishings and architectural devices used the power of human ingenuity to reconstruct Jefferson's material world to suit—and to focus on—himself. Yet it is important to recognize this house as the best-documented (and the only survivor) of a number of similar late-eighteenth-century American houses. One would have found the same sort of ingenious contrivances in the homes of such men as Benjamin Franklin and Charles Willson Peale. These houses were technologies of the self, tools for defining their owners.

The Republican House

In his varied and active household, Jefferson struck the pose of a patriarchal isolate while enjoying a relationship with his immediate family similar to that historians identify with the modern affectionate family. This tension between the individual and the group, this dual emphasis on solitude and sociability, linked Jefferson's domestic life with the concept of republicanism, the central political idea of the new nation that he did so much to foster.

As Monticello did in the domestic arena, the republican philosophy balanced the competing demands of individual and community in the public realm. Among its theoretical underpinnings was the seventeenth-century agrarian or commonwealth philosophy, which identified the landowner as the only upright, politically independent person, incorruptible because he owned the means of his own livelihood and was thus free to do what was right, rather than what was expedient or profitable. In that sense, political 'hermits' made the best citizens. In its hilltop isolation, Monticello fused the romantic hermit age with the commonwealthman's political hermit.

But republicanism also held that such extreme individualism could lead to anarchy without a governor of some sort. They called this governor *virtue*, meaning self-discipline based on shared values. In a republic, public education was indispensable in shaping political virtue. Élite citizens, particularly artists with expressive powers, were duty-bound to instruct their fellow citizens. Jefferson took these duties seriously. The public portions of Monticello were devoted to edifying his neighbours. Visitors to Monticello discovered that the entrance hall or 'Indian Room' was a museum of cultural authority and scientific observation, two key sources of shared values in Jefferson's view. The room was festooned with maps, Native American artefacts, palaeolithic remains, religious paintings, and portrait busts of philosophers and reformers. Instruction continued in the parlour, adorned with fifty-seven works of art to 'improve the taste of his countrymen', including portraits of Isaac Newton, Francis Bacon, Ferdinand Magellan, Christopher Columbus, Benjamin Franklin, and John Locke. The tea-room, in the bow off the dining-room, contained busts of John Paul Jones, Washington, Franklin, and Lafayette.

The private end of the house was devoted to Jefferson's own study and improvement. Yet, in keeping with the republican injunction to the élite to educate their neighbours by exemplary behaviour, this was a privacy intended for public consumption. A glazed door between Jefferson's apartment and the adjacent passageway offered intriguing glimpses of the great man in his cabinet. Even this was too constricting for one visitor, who broke an exterior window so that she might see him better. Assured that his hermitage fulfilled a public function, Jefferson could sit on his mountain top, surveying all but invisible to his neighbours, believing himself to be an active, responsible citizen who cultivated his own virtue and promoted it among his compatriots.

The New American House

At Monticello, Thomas Jefferson assembled a collection of familiar ideas and architectural images into a new kind of American house, one that transcended the accumulated sources of its ideas. It is not that Jefferson invented any particular element or even the republican house,

17
Speculative houses, c.1900, Dayton, Ky.
These houses all share the same plan, as well as comparable but different embellishments—porches, dormers, and bay windows—carefully chosen to give the appearance of individuality while maintaining a uniform price.

but that this particular synthesis did not exist before the end of the eighteenth century. The language and categories of domestic life evident at Monticello by 1809, when the house was as close to complete as it would ever be, have shaped the houses of the American middle- and upper-middle classes ever since.

For example, the belief that the single-family house should be an individualized portrait of its occupants has been articulated at all levels of specificity (and vagueness) ever since Jefferson's time. In his influential *Architecture of Country Houses* (1850), the landscape gardener and domestic theorist Andrew Jackson Downing developed an elaborate theory of personal expression in which every detail of a house was thought to convey something about its owner. Downing had no patience for pretence: the statement should be a truthful one. 'The man of common sense views only, if he is true to himself, will have nothing to do . . . with picturesque and irregular outlines. . . . He will naturally prefer a symmetrical, regular house, with few angles', Downing wrote. Similarly, 'The man of sentiment or feeling will seek for that house in whose aspect there is something to love', while 'men of imagination' will seek houses 'with high roofs, steep gables, unsymmetrical and capricious forms…—any and every feature that indicates originality, boldness, energy and variety of character'.[10] Downing's theory of expressive truthfulness was as rooted in social class as it was in individual personality: the poor should not aspire to individuality, he observed, because their lives are all the same. They should seek tasteful, generic houses.

CEILING

MOULDING AND MEAT BOARD

DISH DRAINER

SINK

LID

FLOUR BARREL DOOR

RYE

CORN MEAL

COARSE FLOUR

TOWELS

SCOURING

SUGAR

SUGAR

MOLASSES

18 Catherine E. Beecher and Harriet Beecher Stowe

Design for an efficient galley kitchen, 1869.

Beecher and Stowe modelled their kitchen on the galleys of ships. Their concern with efficiency of layout and movement anticipated the scientific-management movement in home economics by thirty years.

Not everyone agreed that the house should closely fit its owner. At mid-century Americans were acutely aware of the rapidity of change and the vagaries of economic fortune. Optimistic writers urged clients to go for broke. Progress was so rapid that one's children could never be satisfied with the old-fashioned houses of the current generation, so why not suit oneself? Others feared that the present generation might not live out life in one house: who knew when prosperity might inspire the purchase of a new house, or business reverses might force a sale? An idiosyncratic house would be unsaleable.

Most advocates settled for emphasizing simple differentiation from one's neighbours rather than a detailed character portrait. 'Don't be afraid to introduce breaks, jogs, and angle, the more the better, for an

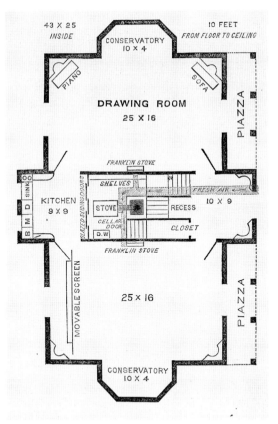

irregular plan breaks the skyline of the roof and lends picturesque beauty to the corners, [and] costs comparatively little', urged George Garnsey, a Chicago architect-builder in 1885.[11] The developers of the first middle-class apartment houses used such devices to allow tenants to pick out their 'own' homes from the street. So did the builders of a late-nineteenth-century row of small speculative houses at Dayton, Kentucky, who carefully balanced individuality against costs [17]. Each house evidently has the same plan, a variation of the common side-passage, two-room-deep urban house. Each has a porch, an elaborate window on the second floor, and a decorative dormer on the roof, but these details are different in each case. The houses were all equal in accommodation and price, but the developers 'individualized' them by manipulating a kit of parts, catalogue millwork, and standardized imagery. They transformed individualism into a saleable consumer good, rather than a portrait of a unique individual.

Like Jefferson, nineteenth- and twentieth-century builders of single-family houses struggled to accommodate diverse household communities. The unity of the family and the conventions of the single-family house were never as certain as they sometimes appeared. For Downing, as for many of his contemporaries, the house's exterior imagery was a portrait of the male head of household, yet Victorian

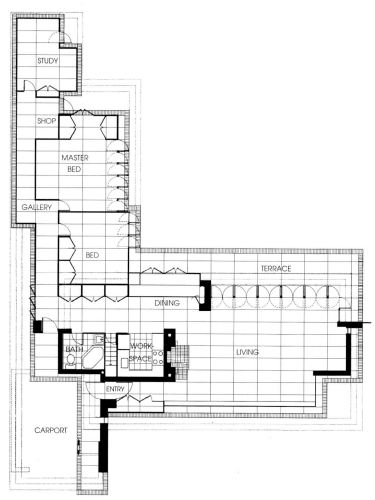

DRAWING BY WILLIAM ALLIN STORRER, USED WITH PERMISSION

20 Frank Lloyd Wright

Herbert Jacobs First Residence, 1937, Madison, Wis.

This house, built for the family of a Madison newspaperman, was the first 'Usonian House', Wright's contribution to recurrent national efforts to develop affordable housing for middle- and lower-middle-class Americans. Wright attempted to control costs by constructing the house of prefabricated panels of insulation sandwiched between exterior and interior sheating and by incorporating radiant heating in a concrete slab that doubled as foundation and floor.

domestic ideology declared the home to be the province of the woman, the place where she exerted her special influence over her family. Women were urged to personalize the interior by furnishing it with goods of their own making or simply of their own choosing. The garden, as well, was often treated as a female domain. The gendered nature of these domestic ideas was often pointed out—most often by women, who responded in varying ways. Some accepted the gendering of household spaces and sought to aggrandize those assigned to women.

In *The American Woman's Home* (1869), Catherine E. Beecher and her sister Harriet Beecher Stowe presented the common mid-nineteenth-century argument that the family was a special institution, the repository of society's moral values, and that the woman's role was consequently central, not marginal, to republican society.[12] To make their point, Beecher and Stowe compared women's domestic spaces and modes of work to male spaces and work in the outside world, particularly to the industrial organization of labour. The housewife charged with the important task of manufacturing citizens should take her job as seriously as a manufacturer of chairs did his, and organize her work as efficiently. The house was her tool, and should be arranged for her convenience. Beecher and Stowe criticized the common domestic kitchen, where supplies and work stations were so spread out that 'half the [woman's] time and strength' were wasted just gathering what she needed. They proposed a design for a kitchen based on the compact galley of a steamship, where all that was needed to cook for hundreds of people was efficiently organized within a small space, and they placed it at a strategic position at the centre-rear of the house from which the industrialist-cook-captain could visually command her domain [18] [19]. Beecher and Stowe gave almost no attention to those aspects of external appearance that Downing thought so essential to (male) 'expression'.

In his 1930s Usonian houses for families without servants, Frank Lloyd Wright moved the kitchen to a location at the intersection of public and private spaces (with the children's bedrooms closest to the kitchen), creating a command-post analogous to Beecher and Stowe's galley kitchen [20]. In both cases, the strategy was to draw women into household life by aggrandizing their roles in the house without altering them. They hark back to Monticello's South Square Room, situated between Jefferson's private suite and the entrance hall, from which Martha Jefferson Randolph ran that house's affairs.

In contrast to those who celebrated women's domestic labour architecturally, some critics of the house argued that women would be freer to inspire their families if they were liberated from all household drudgery. The 'material feminists' of the turn of the century produced schemes for single-family houses that shared communal kitchens, laundries, and bakeries. They promoted apartment hotels with shared cooking facilities. Entrepreneurs started short-lived commercial meal-delivery services. These simply disguised the inequality of the family, rather than abolishing it. As at Monticello, the labour was still performed by an 'outdoor family': the servants who staffed the communal buildings or the employees of the meal-delivery service. Jefferson's dilemma—the unresolved nature of the household community and the ways that the house ought to define and accommodate it—was an enduring one.

Characteristically, eighteenth-century élite tendencies to close off the house to its neighbours received their most emphatic expression in Jefferson's mountain-top retreat. Traditional Euro-American houses were open to the outside. In vernacular farmhouses, the hall was a very public room in which all members of the household, including hired

21 Lamb and Rich
Henry R. Mallory House,
c.1885, Bryam, Conn.

labourers (or, in North America, slaves), gathered and worked. Doors led directly into the hall from the road and the farmyard. In traditional élite houses, the hall was similarly open to all [**8**].

Small open houses were common well into the twentieth century, but just as English colonists arrived in North America, élite builders and prosperous farmers were beginning to buffer the hall and other 'public' rooms with passages, vestibules, entry porches, and similar architectural devices that shielded them from direct access. The Fairbanks House (1637 and later), Dedham, Massachusetts, was built with the traditional hall-parlour plan but with an entrance lobby (as at the Boardman House [**11**]). That is, the oldest surviving English building in North America was an ultra-modern house of a sort that had not existed seventy-five years earlier. Around the beginning of the eighteenth century, the builders of the largest houses began to use central passages (hallways) for this purpose.

Monticello, sited on its mountain top, carries this buffering to an extreme, but it also incorporates an ambivalence about the relationship of the household to its neighbours that has characterized the middle-class house ever since. A tension between domestic privacy and public sociability has always been embedded in genteel houses. In many early-nineteenth-century cities, visitation was an important social ritual. On New Year's Day, for example, urbanites held open house, with men visiting and women remaining home to receive guests. The historian Elizabeth Blackmar describes this kind of household as 'the "public" home'. Rituals of private domesticity were enacted in public view as a sign of personal respectability and republican virtue.[13]

In the mid-nineteenth century, however, domestic advice givers began to urge owners of rural and suburban republican houses to emphasize improving their families over serving as examples to society at large. In her *Treatise on Domestic Economy* (1841), Catherine Beecher rehearsed the rules of hospitality, but she argued that the 'multiplication of a large circle of acquaintances' was an evil that ought to be avoided. The family worked best when its friendships were restricted to 'a few families, united by similarity of character and pursuit'.[14] Architecturally, this new version of republican hermitage was matched by an elaborate visual language of shelter. Houses shielded their faces from the street. They were surrounded with elaborate verandas and

22 John Calvin Stevens

James Hopkins Smith House, 1885, Falmouth Foreside, Me.

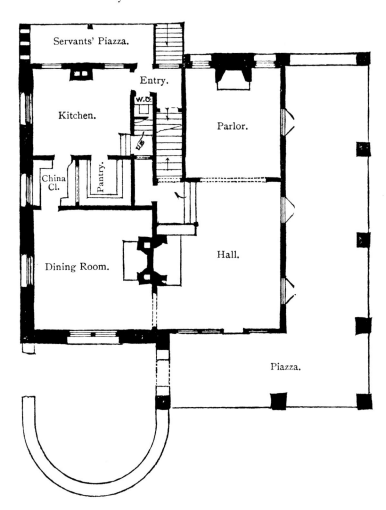

their entrances were concealed by recesses and porticoes [21]. Often the ground floor was made of a heavy stone that made the house appear to be fortified.

Inside, the house was fitted for family life. Mid-Victorian parlours were carefully arranged for moral preparation. A large round centre table around which the family could gather and a piano for the cultivation of refined sensibilities left little room for outsiders. The main public rooms of large late-Victorian houses were often thrown open to promote family togetherness [22]. At the same time, Victorian domestic theorists recognized the need for privacy within the family. Beecher and Stowe urged that each member of the family should have a separate bedroom, while other writers promoted the use of nooks and bay windows that would allow residents a measure of seclusion even when they gathered in the social spaces of the household. The projection of these features on the exterior of the house broadcast domestic privacy to passers-by.

Since the late eighteenth century, Americans at home have touted the good offices of an vaguely defined 'nature', whose mere presence was believed to transform human spirits and morals. Andrew Jackson Downing promoted the country retreat as a refuge from the morally debilitating effects of the city. Even those who could not afford the kind of rural estate that Downing had in mind might, he thought, surround themselves with a bit of greenery.

To bring nature as close as possible, builders of all sizes of houses blurred the bounds between outside and inside. At Monticello, open porches (which Jefferson sometimes called 'Angular Portals') at the

23 Alexander Jackson Davis
Rotch House, *c*.1845–7, New Bedford, Mass.

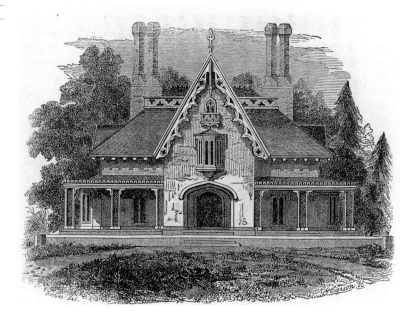

Rotch House.
Like many architectural popularizers of the first half of the 19th century, Davis and his architectural ally Andrew Jackson Downing dressed up traditional spaces in fashionable decoration. The Rotch House's 'Georgian plan' is a spatial type that has been used in large American houses since the beginning of the 18th century.

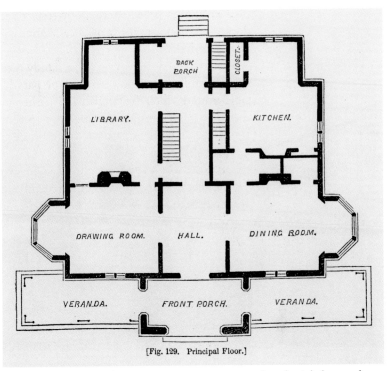

[Fig. 129. Principal Floor.]

south-east and south-west corners were once fitted with louvred en-closures or 'porticles' that were transitional spaces between inside and outside [6]. In addition, a glazed 'South Piazza' between the cabinet and library bays provided Jefferson with a 'greenhouse' whose triple-hung sash permitted many of the windows to function as doors.

It is curious that similar devices characterized small houses after the mid-nineteenth century. Plant-filled bay windows, or 'conservatories', projected from many a parlour and dining-room, bringing a bit of the natural indoors while connecting it visually with the out-of-doors [19, 24]. Verandas served as transitional spaces between the completely open and the completely enclosed. Contact with nature was intended to improve family members, as at Monticello, but the relationship was a passive one. Nature was there primarily to be watched, to be observed from the shelter of the conservatory, the balcony, the veranda, or the pergola, or, in twentieth-century middle-class houses, from behind picture windows and sliding-glass patio doors.

Heirs of Monticello

The domestic themes that shaped Monticello and its successors were idealized images—stories—of family life depicted in bricks and mor-tar. Most Americans lived differently, then as now. It is not possible even to say that those who lived in single-family houses lived as the ar-chitecture implied that they did. Nevertheless, these ideas, worked out differently from era to era and house to house, are woven through the

PHOTO RICHARD BRYANT/ARCAID, LONDON

25 Frank Lloyd Wright
Frederick C. Robie Residence, 1908, Chicago, Ill.

single-family houses that have been so conspicuous an element of the American landscape since Jefferson's day, as three élite houses will illustrate.

Andrew Jackson Downing called the Rotch House (*c.*1845–7) in New Bedford, Massachusetts, a 'cottage-villa', meaning, in his terminology, that it was the country retreat of a wealthy person (a villa), but that it was unpretentious and informal (a cottage) [**23**].[15] The architect, Alexander Jackson Davis, based the plan on the eighteenth-century vernacular plan type that folklorists and geographers call the Georgian-plan house: it is two rooms wide and two rooms deep, with a passageway through the centre [**24**]. The dichotomies and axes observed at Monticello structure the Rotch House as well. The formal public rooms at the front contrast with the 'pleasant and retired' library at the rear (the words are Downing's). The ground-floor rooms are opened up into an interconnected suite, but insulated from the kitchen, the servants' working area, by closets, passages, and back stairs. The simple plan, then, was socially complex.

The front door of the Rotch House was sheltered by an enclosed porch tower that intercepted outsiders, while a veranda and gable-end conservatories opened the house to nature. Downing read the exterior, whose 'Gothic' central gable was as formulaic as its plan, as a Rotch family portrait. The combination of the high gable, the porch, and the 'drooping, hipped roof' characterized the occupants as 'a man or family of domestic tastes, but with strong aspirations after something higher than social pleasures'.[16]

The 'Prairie' houses that Frank Lloyd Wright built for well-to-do Chicago suburbanites in the first decade of the twentieth century looked very different, but incorporated many of the same ideas. Looking back from the perspective of the 1930s, Wright described the Prairie house as an 'enclosure' that opened up inside to outside while providing a sense of shelter and giving the house 'more free space'. [17] His Robie House of 1908 was certainly an enclosure: it might be called Fort Robie for the way it walled off the family from the city [25]. Its high exterior walls and raised living-storey shielded the house from the street. An outer ring of service yards and walls hold outsiders even farther at bay. The carefully controlled interpenetration of outside and inside allowed the residents to see out, but not to be seen. In an élite urban neighbourhood, Wright created a one-way surveillance similar to Jefferson's on his mountain top.

Wright sought 'interior spaciousness' in his houses, a phrase that, like the houses themselves, concealed more than it revealed. The archi-

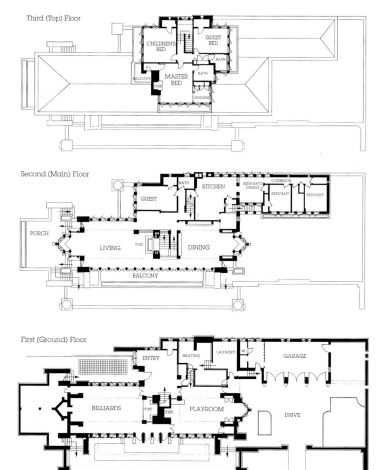

26

Robie Residence.

First- (ground), second- (main), and third-floor plans. Only the main floor has the open plan for which Wright's houses were so famous.

DRAWING BY WILLIAM ALLIN STORRER, USED WITH PERMISSION.

27 Richard Meier

Smith House, 1965,
Darien, Conn.
Entrance front.

tect's sense of domestic community was derived from the Victorian ideal of the family insulated from the outside world but thrown into each other's presence. On the main (second) floor, the living and dining space focused on a central hearth—an emblem of family togetherness in the Victorian tradition—that was open to both rooms, allowing one to see through it, thus creating the illusion of a single open space [26]. From these formal spaces, balconies overlooked the street. However, there is more to the Robie House than this famous room. As at Monticello and its vernacular cousins, the three axes organized the interior. On the ground floor, under the living- and dining-room, were the more active play spaces. These were divided into the traditionally male domain of the billiard-room and a playroom for the children, with no pretence of openness between them. The least active spaces, the bedrooms, were on the third floor.

The Robies employed live-in servants. No longer African-American slaves, they were nevertheless set off in a separate wing as Jefferson's slaves were. In common with Davis, Stevens, and scores of other planners of middle-class Victorian houses, Wright further isolated the servants' working spaces by interposing a stair, a closet, a pantry, and the bulk of a buffet and its contents between service and family spaces, creating an extra layer of insulation between them. In short, the 'openness' of the Robie House, as in all of Wright's Prairie houses, applies to only a small part of a house that incorporated a wide range of social and functional distinctions. Most of the Robie House consisted of the 'boxes beside boxes or inside boxes, called *rooms*' that Wright so often denounced.[18] Moreover, its gendered nature is particularly striking when we note that while there were rooms clearly identifiable as men's, children's, and servants' spaces, none was set aside for the female head of the household. The household community, while apparently comprehensive, was male-oriented.

In explaining his Smith House (1965), Darien, Connecticut, architect Richard Meier wrote of a 'dialectic of open and closed', and of the 'idea of a spatially layered linear system with circulation across and along the layers' [27]. The plan was 'expressive of the programmatic separation of the public and private areas of family life', he noted.[19] Through the laboured professional jargon, the traditional dichotomies shine through. The front-back, up-down axes that have organized the active–passive, public–private categories of European-American domestic life since the Middle Ages were deployed here as expected [28]. The kitchen was below entry level, while the master bedroom and living-room were on the main floor, with secondary bedrooms lifted above them. As at Monticello, a longitudinal axis separated the social spaces along the back of the house from the private and work spaces along the front. Like a Victorian house or one of Wright's, the Smith House romanticized family life. All the bedrooms looked out on the

28

Smith House.

Plans.

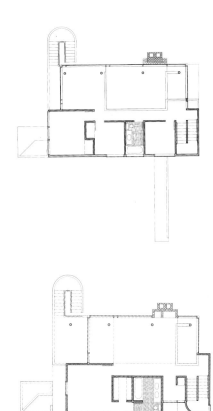

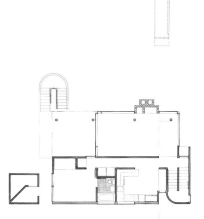

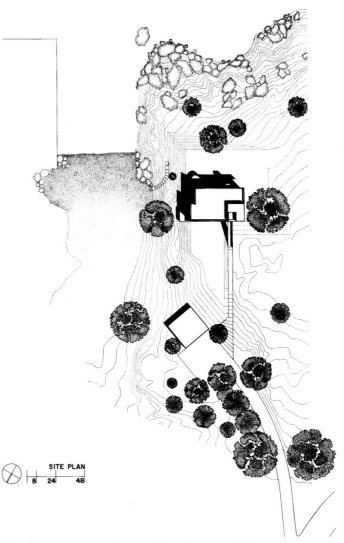

SITE PLAN

8   24   48

two-level living room, whose only architectural feature was a prominent fireplace, a traditional sign of family bonding.

Set between the road and the Long Island Sound, the house served
as a mediator between nature and culture like all the other houses that
we have seen [**29**]. Unable to hide on a mountain top and unwilling to
shield itself with a porch, the house dodged our gaze by the oblique approach and the raised and off-axis entry. The façade deflected attempts
to see what is behind it. Only the entry was at eye level, and that looked
straight through the house and out the back, ricocheting off the chimney. The back wall, on the other hand, was almost entirely glass, making the view of the Sound part of domestic space.

Where Davis and Wright sought individuality through generic languages of shelter and personality, Meier returned to the notion of cultural authority that informed Jefferson's self-fashioning. In this case,

the entrance façade recalled the work of Le Corbusier, as powerful a form-giver and rule-maker in 1965 as Palladio was in 1765. The façade borrowed authority by reminding us of the master's villas of the 1920s, crossed with the fenestration of his Notre Dame de Ronchamp of thirty years later.

But there was an ambiguity in the Smith House: while the domestic organization, the surveillance of nature, and the allusions to cultural authority all remind us of Monticello, client and architect were separated here. If Monticello was a celebration of Jefferson's will, an exercise in self-making, we might ask whose will is being celebrated in the Smith House, Meier's or the Smiths'? The house conveys a double individuality: as one of his first published works, it distinguished the architect as a vendor of images. At the same time, it addressed the clients' desire for personal distinction. The consumerist impulse whose early stages were visible at Monticello in the 1790s is full-blown at the Smith House in the 1960s, where will, desirable imagery, and individual distinction were conferred on those who could pay for them.

Obviously, there are many important ways in which the Rotch, Robie, and Smith houses differ from Monticello, ways that have to do with the specific terms of their historical contexts and the ways their architects understood the fundamental categories we have examined. Two hundred years do make a difference, as the remaining chapters will demonstrate. From the vantage point of the late twentieth century, these categories seem commonsensical, even hackneyed, but they have a history that can be traced to the late eighteenth century. At Monticello, the categories—architecture as a product of the ordinariness of daily life, of its social rituals and economic patterns; architecture as a tool for defining identity in a consumer society; architecture as a vessel of memory of past social spaces and past architectural form; the role of cultural authority—were already in place.

Community

2

On 4 July 1788 a great parade in Philadelphia celebrated the Declaration of Independence and the recent ratification of the Constitution. As the crowds looked on, riders on horseback, individual marchers, military companies, and guilds of craftworkers passed by, carrying banners and riding floats that represented civic virtues and historic dates important to the young republic. Twenty-fourth in the procession was 'The NEW ROOF, or GRAND FEDERAL EDIFICE; on a carriage drawn by ten white horses.' The float, which was over twenty-three feet high, was built for the Carpenters' Company by William Williams and Company from a design by the painter Charles Willson Peale. A statue of Plenty carrying a cornucopia stood on top of a domed rotunda which was in turn supported on thirteen Corinthian columns 'on pedestals proper to that order'. Thirteen stars encircled the frieze while the base was inscribed 'IN UNION THE FABRIC STANDS FIRM.' Three of the columns were unfinished, a reminder that three states had not yet ratified the new frame of government. Four hundred and fifty architects and house-carpenters, led by six of the wealthiest and most prominent of their number, marched behind the float.[1]

The Grand Federal Edifice combined a variety of traditional iconographies, including the dome as a sign of the all-encompassing universality of the heavens and the circle or sphere as an emblem of completeness and perfection. By depicting the states as columns, the float alluded to the republican ideal of self-sufficient sameness. The columns were like the states which were like individual citizens: every column was complete in itself, but every one was like every other one, and all were needed to finish the structure. In common with many Americans of the revolutionary era, the builders of the Grand Federal Edifice evoked a mythical link between the United States and the ancient Roman republic and the legendary virtue of its élite. Rhetorically, the American Revolution had been a revitalization movement, a kind of phenomenon that typically arises during periods of social lassitude and takes the form of a call for a return to fundamental values.[2] The American revolutionaries claimed to be inventing nothing new, but to be restoring the purity of an original order before it had been corrupted. This was an argument that Renaissance classicists, the first to

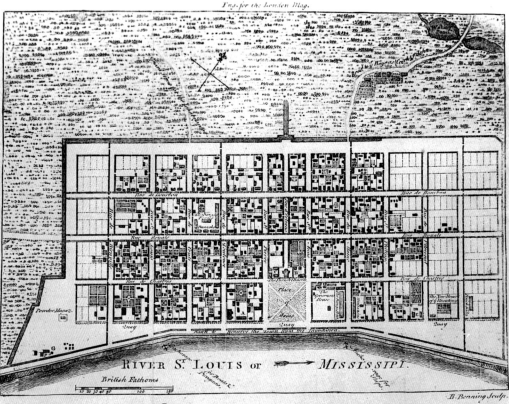

RIVER Sᵗ. LOUIS or ➤ MISSISSIPI.

British Fathoms

B. Benning Sculp.

PLAN OF NEW ORLEANS THE CAPITAL OF LOUISIANA.

30

Plan of New Orleans, the Capital of Louisiana.

This 18th-century plan illustrates the clustering of the institutions of church, state, and military around the riverside *place d'armes* and accurately depicts property boundaries as well.

look back to the Romans, had applied to architecture. In the Grand Federal Edifice architectural and political nostalgia reinforced one another.

Architecture is one of the most ancient and most evocative tools for symbolizing communities and polities. Its metaphorical possibilities are enriched by architecture's complexity. As an artefact comprised of many differentiated parts and spaces, a building can represent the human body (and vice versa), a community, or the cosmos. Consequently, architecture can help people conceptualize relationships among citizens and between citizens and authorities. The seventeenth-century New England Puritans, for example, imagined society as a nested series of patriarchal families ranging from the family proper up to the state and church. At each level, all members of the community were important, but each had been assigned a different degree of power and responsibility by God. The acceptance by each of his or her station created an integrated society. To illustrate these ideas, Puritan divines resorted to architectural metaphors. Richard Mather compared the necessity for integration in a church (meaning the institution) to the structure of a house, which was mere stones and timber 'till they be compacted and conjoyned'.[3] His Connecticut colleague

Thomas Hooker compared the social order to a timber frame: 'if the parts be neither morticed nor braced, as there will be little beauty so there can be no strength. Its so in setting up the frames of societies among men, when their mindes and hearts are not mortified by mutu-all consent of subjection to one another, there is no expectation of any successeful proceeding with the advantage of the publick.'[4]

For all its richness, architectural symbolism raises recurrent questions. One has to do with the legibility of communal symbols. In most instances, it is easy enough to interpret what a monument was intended to mean by its designers or owners, but can we say with confidence what it did mean to its viewers? Second, is there a universal formal language that can be understood even where there are no auxiliary texts to explain intentions? Third is the issue of inclusion and exclusion. Who belongs to the community, and in what capacity? The premiss of monuments, governmental buildings, and other representations of community is that they encompass all of society's members, that they stand for universal values. But architecture necessarily operates at a level of abstraction that is not always legible or satisfying to its users, who may find themselves explicitly excluded, inadequately represented, or co-opted to values that they do not share. It is rarely possible to extract this sort of information from the monuments themselves, but by raising these questions of reception (where it is possible) we can think more insightfully about the way architectural symbols of community work.

Authority

Those who have spent time in any western nation are usually able to 'read' its public spaces easily. Consciously or unconsciously, we recognize a variety of standard techniques for expressing authority, such as monumental size, expensive building materials, distinctive architectural decoration, or imagery that makes extraordinary mythical-historical claims to antiquity or authenticity for authoritative buildings; and their clustering, emphasis by axial approaches, or simple elevation above their surroundings that sets them apart from their surroundings.

A familiar example is the European-American practice of town planning that clusters authority at the centre, often arranging it around a plaza or square, establishing a legible centre-periphery, public-private, or authority-subject relationship. This pattern was endorsed as long ago as 1573 in the *Laws of the Indies*, a set of ordinances to govern town planning in Spanish-American colonies. The authors of the *Laws of the Indies* envisaged a landscape that was socially integrated in the sense that it assigned every inhabitant and activity a place, and that it was to be politically and economically orderly. The colonial town would be both outward- and inward-looking, for it was meant to control both the indigenous inhabitants and the European colonists, who were believed to need as much supervision as the natives. To accomplish these intentions, the *Laws of the Indies* described an ideal town laid out on a grid plan aligned to the cardinal directions and surrounded by fields cultivated by farmers who would live in town. The headquarters of church and state would flank a large central plaza that was not a park, but a treeless, grassless open space set off from the surrounding streets and intended for military training and other public ceremonies. Arcades around the plaza would mark the buildings flanking it as the commercial centre of the town.

This prescription seems authoritative, but it is puzzling if we read it as a rigid scheme to be applied to every settlement. Few Spanish colonial towns in North America followed it exactly. There was no need to, for the Laws of the Indies simply codified long-standing assumptions and familiar urban forms, some dating back to antiquity. The building blocks of the so-called Laws of the Indies towns could be found in New World Spanish towns like St Augustine, Florida (1565), laid out before 1573. They could be found in colonial towns built by the English in the thirteenth century to control Wales and parts of France, in the sixteenth century to conquer Northern Ireland, and in the early seventeenth century, at places like Jamestown, Virginia (1607), and Plymouth, Massachusetts (1620), to colonize North America.

The same planning techniques shaped New Orleans, founded by the French in 1718 to command the intersection of the Mississippi and the Caribbean basins [**30**]. Engineer Pierre Leblond de La Tour planned the town, which was laid out in 1721 by his assistant Adrien de Pauger. As in many Euro-American port cities, the main square, called

31

Common courthouse-square plans.

The names refer to towns that offer important early example of each plan-type.

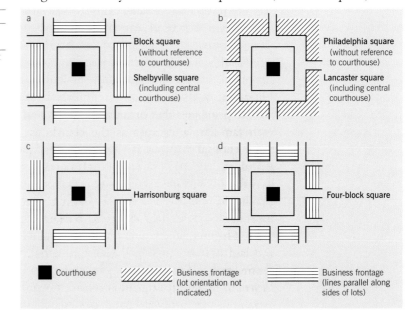

a Block square (without reference to courthouse)
Shelbyville square (including central courthouse)

b Philadelphia square (without reference to courthouse)
Lancaster square (including central courthouse)

c Harrisonburg square

d Four-block square

■ Courthouse

▨ Business frontage (lot orientation not indicated)

═ Business frontage (lines parallel along sides of lots)

Rock Springs Camp Meeting Ground, founded 1833, Lincoln County, NC.
Site plan. Camp meetings, spontaneous revival-oriented gatherings founded in the Second Great Awakening of the early 19th century, were institutionalized and regularly scheduled by the mid-19th century. The meeting ground typically takes a town-like form, with the brush arbour located in a central square, and the tents opening on to streets ranged concentrically around it.

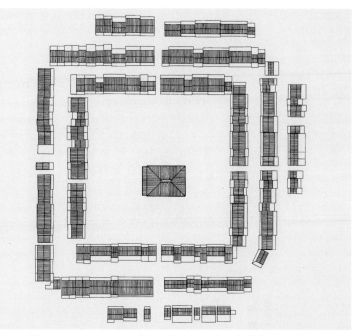

the Place d'Armes, was moved to the river-bank. The major instruments of power, the parish church, town hall, and jail, were aligned along the side of the square opposite the river, while two other sides were flanked with warehouses and officials' residences. The houses of ordinary citizens filled the back streets, but near the edges of the town there was little building of any kind. Although New Orleans was built in the middle of a swamp and was consequently never approachable by land, an axial avenue, Orleans Street (which led from the land side of the city toward the square, where it ran into the back of the parish church) was apparently inserted as a matter of habit. The city's swamp siting likewise freed it from serious threats from any direction but the river, so the encircling fortifications that were equally rote elements of the plan were only half-heartedly and flimsily constructed, and were never completed.

The principles that organized these colonial towns also structured such familiar landscapes as the courthouse squares of more than three thousand American county seats, particularly west of the Appalachians [31]. They appear also in unexpected settings, particularly those created by religious organizations. In June 1833 the Mormon prophet Joseph Smith sent a 'Plat of the City of Zion' to the new settlement at Independence, Missouri, to be used in laying out a new town there. The mile-square grid was to be aligned to the cardinal directions and laid out in half-acre lots. There would be three squares at the centre, two with twelve temples each, distributed according to the Mormon hierarchy of priesthoods, and one built up with communal storehouses. Southern county fairs and camp-meeting grounds also

33

Balls Creek Camp Meeting Ground, mid-19th century, Catawba County, NC.

Today 'brush arbour' where meetings are held is a permanent, open-sided wooden building (foreground), the wooden 'tents' (background) are privately owned, and the camp grounds are racially segregated by custom.

commonly followed the 'courthouse square' model, with communal activities in a central square surrounded by cabins. At the Rock Springs Camp Meeting (founded in 1832), Lincoln County, North Carolina, and the nearby Ball's Creek Camp Meeting (mid-nineteenth century), Catawba County, North Carolina, large central squares focus on the principal 'public' structures, the open-sided arbours, named after the improvised 'brush arbours' of the first camp meeting grounds. Privately owned, constantly rebuilt and upgraded wooden 'tents' (similarly named after temporary structures of the first camp grounds) are laid out concentrically in neat rows around them [**32**] [**33**].

To our eyes, the geographies of power at New Orleans or even the camp meetings are easily read. To what extent are our interpretative abilities valid cross-culturally? Are there universal physical signs of authority? The first Europeans assumed this. They assessed the social organization of indigenous people according to the resemblance of their landscapes to European patterns. In the same spirit, they assumed that Native Americans would understand European spatial patterns instinctively. For this reason, the *Laws of the Indies* suggested that the colonists should not 'allow the Indians to enter within the confines of the town until it is built and its defenses ready and the houses built so that when the Indians see them they will be struck with admiration and will understand that the Spaniards are there to settle permanently and not temporarily.'[5] Can we be so confident?

One of the earliest monumental structures in North America, now called Poverty Point (West Carroll Parish, Louisiana, c.1000 BCE), is superficially like New Orleans, with a waterside 'plaza' and axial paths leading to it [34]. The principal element of the site, which sits on a bluff above Bayou Macon, is a series of six concentric semi-circular ridges, about three feet high and about three-quarters of a mile across. These were built by piling up trash and covering it with earth, and they supported houses twelve to fourteen feet in diameter, sheltering a population that may have reached several thousand. The ridges are broken by four aisles leading to a central open space. Outside the ridges opposite the bayou is a large mound that may have been shaped like a bird, and several smaller mounds are scattered nearby.

Poverty Point embodies several common characteristics of Native American monumental architecture. These include a marked contrast between ambitious large-scale constructions, usually earthworks, and extremely modest buildings; a fondness for geometry, often very precisely plotted; the incorporation of animal imagery into architecture and material culture (at Poverty Point, a 'bird-shaped' mound is complemented by the scores of tiny carved owls found by excavators); scattered settlements sited near watercourses (but rarely right on the water) rather than continuous settlement covering the countryside; and the long-term significance of monuments and structures as sites of memory: they are enlarged, reworked, or reused, but rarely demolished.

Can we read Poverty Point as we did New Orleans? Although its builders were obviously well enough organized to marshal the labour power and materials to build on a grand scale, archaeologists are unable to describe how the site was used or who occupied what parts of the site. Were the earthworks really more important than the seemingly

34

Poverty Point archaeological site, c.1000 BCE, West Carroll Parish, La.
Reconstruction drawing of central district. The large mound at the rear (designated Mound A by archaeologists) may have been shaped like a bird.

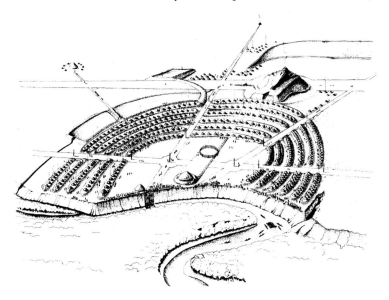

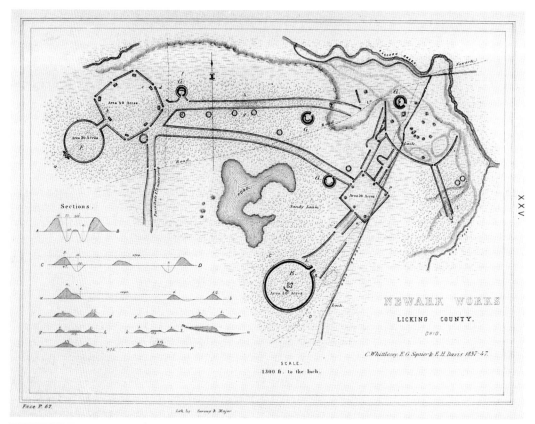

35

Newark Earthworks, *c.*200 CE, Licking County, OH.

Partly demolished in the 19th and 20th centuries. This survey drawing was made by the pioneering 19th-century scholars Ephraim G. Squier and Edwin H. Davis.

flimsy buildings that stood on them? Did the roads focus inward on the plaza or point outward towards the mounds? Or were they boundaries that divided the ridges into neighbourhoods? There are no answers to these questions: the forms convey no intrinsic information about social relationships.

Episodes of monumental building, each very different from the others and separated by centuries from them, recurred in the Mississippi River basin. In every case, we are confronted with the same problems of interpretation. A particularly spectacular architectural tradition was produced by the 'Hopewellian phenomenon' or 'synthesis' (to use the archaeologists' terms) which flourished *c.*100 BCE to 500 CE.[6] Among the most striking Hopewellian monuments are the 'ceremonial centres' of the Ohio Valley, such as that at Newark, Ohio, where a series of highly regular geometrical shapes are connected by what appear to be processional ways [**35**].

Beginning at the south end, the Great Circle, with its low central mound (possibly another bird effigy), was firmly enclosed with a ditch-and-bank wall higher than any others in the complex. It suggests a terminus, but whether a beginning or an end is impossible to say. A series of low, roughly parallel walls with periodic openings in them led from the single opening in the Great Circle to a low-walled square (the

Wright Earthworks), of which only a corner now survives. The complex turned a corner, then continued west to another terminus, a precisely laid out circle and octagon that were higher banked than the processional ways, but not so high as the Great Circle. Opposite a 'podium' on the south-western edge of the circle was a short processional way leading to the octagon. Small, low mounds at the open corners of the latter (some now flattened on top to serve as golf tees) acted as filters to vision, but did not prevent access. Other elements of the complex, which was surveyed in the early nineteenth century, have been demolished and are more difficult to interpret. They include a series of small single-opening circles that may have been constructed by members of the earlier Adena culture and reused by Hopewellian builders.

The architects of the Newark earthworks used some of the spatial techniques employed at Poverty Point over a thousand years earlier, and they seem to have added a dynamic or processional element to the mix, but once again it is difficult to say from the surviving architecture alone who used this complex or how, or to imagine the structure of the community beyond observing that it must have been a large and highly organized one. The scale of the earthworks testifies to that: the largest Hopewellian complex, at Portsmouth, Ohio, was 20 miles long. The Newark earthworks covered four square miles and totalled 7.5 miles long, a project that required the displacement of seven million cubic feet of earth. Individual elements are comparably scaled: the octagon is so large that it is difficult to see all the way across.

A half millennium after the Hopewellian synthesis disintegrated, a new monumental earth-building tradition of a very different sort appeared. The major site of this Mississippian culture was at Cahokia, Illinois, near present-day St Louis. Cahokia, which flourished for about three hundred years after 900 CE, was built as a series of mounds and platforms surrounding plazas. The largest of them, the so-called 'Monk's Mound' (named for a Christian church built on top in recent centuries) was over 1,000 by 700 feet in plan and about 100 feet high [36]. If Newark appears dynamic, Cahokia seems theatrical. The architecture suggests crowds gathered in the plaza to observe ceremonies performed atop the mounds, as they were on analogous Mesoamerican pyramids.

Although Cahokia ceased to be used around eight hundred years ago, Mississippian societies survived into the era of European contact. The Natchez, a group of about 3,500 people living in five villages along tributaries of the Mississippi River near the modern city named for them, were the last Mississippian mound builders. In the 1720s, just before they were dispersed in retaliation for an attempt to drive out the French, Antoine le Page du Pratz lived for a time in their major town, called the Grand Village. His published account, based on Natchez

Monk's Mound, c.1000 CE, Cahokia, Ill.

Monk's Mound was the central and highest mound in the principal enclosure of the Mississippian centre at Cahokia. Its name derives from a church built on its summit by French colonists.

PHOTO TIMOTHY HURSLEY, LITTLE ROCK, ARK.

37

Tattooed Serpent's funeral, 1725, Grand Village of the Natchez, vicinity of Natchez, Miss.

Tattooed Serpent was the brother of the Great Sun, the Natchez leader. The drawing depicts the winding funeral procession from Tattooed Serpent's house, at the lower left, through the plaza to the temple, set on its low mound. When the procession reached the temple, Tattooed Serpent's family members and retainers were strangled as sacrifices. This is shown at either side. The swan-like birds on the temple's ridge are meant to be eagles.

explanations and his own observations, illuminates our understanding of the Natchez architecture of authority and revises our reading of the theatrical nature of Mississippian architecture.

At the Grand Village, as at nearby Poverty Point, the contrast between impressive earthworks and humble architecture was notable. In the midst of a cluster of small houses built of poles set in trenches and plastered inside and out with mud were two low mounds about seventy-five feet square. The central mound was the residence of the head man, called the Sun or Great Sun. About 450 feet south of the Sun's Mound, across a plaza, was the Temple Mound, with a ramp extending into the plaza. Both the Sun's house and the temple were built of the same light construction as the houses of ordinary people, the only distinction being the eagles set on the ridge of the temple [37].

According to le Page du Pratz, the Grand Village's mounds were less places of performance than of seclusion, 'into which only princes and princesses should have a right to enter', and the Sun's house and the temple were concealed by screens in front of their doors.[7] The mounds served as a kind of grandstand from which Natchez dignitaries watched ceremonies that took place in the plaza, such as the elaborate ritual in which the Sun moved between his house and the temple and, even more dramatically, the funeral of the Great Sun's brother, Tattooed Serpent. Attendants carried the deceased's body from his house, accompanied by an entourage that included two wives, his aides, his servants, and admirers. This funeral party, each member attended by eight male relatives, led a longer procession that made

several circuits around the plaza before arriving at the temple. The mourners arranged themselves in a semi-circle in front of it, and their male attendants placed deerskin hoods over their heads, then strangled them. Tattooed Serpent and his wives were buried in a trench in the temple, his principal courtiers were interred in front of it, and his house was burned.

The Grand Village of the Natchez suggests the possibilities and the limits of formal interpretations of the architecture of authority. Without the written accounts, something of the processes of architectural and social change could be read in the archaeological evidence for the repeated reconstruction of the mounds, which were enlarged after the death of each Sun. The differentiation of mound and plaza is also evident. However, the particularity of the monuments and their use—those elements that made them unique at the same time even as they participated in the long tradition of Native American monumental building—are more difficult to see in the physical evidence. Only documentary sources convey this information.

Most tellingly, the account of Tattooed Serpent's funeral rebukes our tendency to read other people's architecture as evidence of values shared by all members of a society. The archaeological remains hint at the general order—at the stratification of Natchez society between a privileged élite and the despised commoners, or 'Stinkards'—but they cannot reveal the reception of the architecture's political message. Le Page du Pratz noted that one of the victims sacrificed at the Tattooed-Serpent's funeral was killed because she had shouted 'What! Is that the Tattooed-Serpent, that rare man? He is a Stinkard chief. I do not want to die for him'. Even among the élite crowd gathered on the Sun's mound there were sceptics. The French did not worry that their disparaging comments had been overhead by the Sun's wife, wrote le Page du Pratz, because 'this law did not please her enough for her to find fault with those who spoke ill of it'.[8] In short, the Grand Village of the Natchez speaks most eloquently of the ambiguities of the formal representations of political authority and their interpretation.

Metaphors

Visual imagery and metaphor have been as important, and as culture-specific, as spatial form in the architectural representation of American communities, yet there have been cross-cultural continuities as well. Domestic metaphors that celebrate the centrality of the family in most American societies were particularly favoured in both Euro-American and Native American architectures. Their very familiarity enabled communities to incorporate radical changes while retaining a sense of identity, as the story of the Iroquoian longhouse illustrates.

About 1500 years ago, peripatetic groups of north-eastern Woodland Indians began to settle in small communities by waterways and to

38

An Iroquoian house, *c.*900 CE.
This reconstruction drawing
was based on an example
excavated at the Eldorado
site, Ontario, Canada. The
bench around the perimeter,
the central fire, and the
partitioned storage area at
the far end of this small house
were characteristic features
of the classic longhouses of
later centuries.

build ovoid wooden houses. Typically, these dwellings incorporated
low benches around their perimeters, and one or more central hearths
[**38**]. As time passed, these ancestors of the northern Iroquoian peoples
of New York State and adjacent Quebec and Ontario gathered in larger
and larger towns, relied more and more on agriculture, and established
matrilocal, communal households. By the sixteenth century these
small Iroquoian houses had evolved into dwellings that were about 20
to 25 feet wide and 40 to 200 feet long and that were packed into
formidably palisaded towns that the Europeans called 'Castles'. These
'longhouses' were made of saplings inserted into the ground and bound
at the top into an arch 15 or 20 feet high, then covered with bark [**39**]. A
corridor, punctuated with hearths every 20 feet or so, ran the length of
the building. Along the sides, framed compartments with raised floors
and low ceilings housed nuclear families of five or six people.

The 'interior spatial geography and the experiential legacy of count-
less hours spent confined within them during the snowy winters of
Iroquoia', according to historian Daniel Richter, encouraged an ethic
of sharing and reciprocity that the people extended to their political
self conception. Some time between 1400 and 1600 CE, the Mohawk,
Oneida, Onondaga, Seneca, and Cayuga of upstate New York and
adjacent Quebec formed a political confederation.[9] The People of the
Longhouse, as they called themselves, imagined their confederation as
members of a common *ohwachira*, the kinship group that formed the
population of a longhouse. The Iroquois described their territory in

Elevation des Cabannes Sauvages

39

'Elevation des Cabannes Sauvages', c.1720.

This Iroquoian longhouse was illustrated on the margins of the French *Plan du Fort Frontenac ou Cataraouy*.

upstate New York and adjacent Canada as a longhouse, with the Five (later Six) Nations lined up in it. The Mohawk were named Keepers of the Eastern Door, the Seneca Keepers of the Western Door, and the centrally located Onondaga were Keepers of the Fire.

After European contact the longhouse was abandoned as a residence. By the eighteenth century most Iroquois lived in single-family dwellings, but longhouses continued to be built as ceremonial structures that reminded their users of Iroquois bonds. In 1743 traveller John Bartram lodged in an Onondaga council house that was built in the form of a traditional longhouse but used only for diplomatic business. Half a century later, in response to the social demoralization and military conquest of the Iroquois, the prophet Handsome Lake began to preach revitalization through a return to the old ways. The religion that was formalized after his death, a reinterpretation of traditional Iroquois beliefs overlaid with Christianity, is known as the 'Longhouse Religion'. Contemporary adherents worship in long rectangular buildings built of logs or timber frame, covered with gable roofs, and furnished on the inside with two rows of benches around an open central space [**40**]. The interior organization of these religious longhouses, with their bench-lined walls and elongated shape, recalls the domestic longhouses from which they take their name. The image of the longhouse and the memories of the society that used it have served the Iroquois as a stabilizing metaphor for nearly three centuries after the longhouse ceased to be the principal Iroquois dwelling, but the longhouse itself also changed during the intervening centuries. In fact, religious longhouses resembled the meeting-houses of the Quakers who proselytized among the Iroquois in the nineteenth century as much as they did traditional Iroquois dwellings. Like modern Iroquois longhouses, Quaker meeting-houses had separate entrances and separate seating for men and women on raised, inward-facing benches. Nevertheless, the domestic metaphor helped to navigate social and religious changes and cultural contact.

Citizenship

The longhouse first symbolized a political confederation and then collective loyalty to the old culture. The creators of the new United States government also strove consciously to symbolize a political community. In 1792 a competition was held for a capitol building at the new city of Washington. Entries were received from all over the United States. The judges, who included George Washington and Thomas Jefferson, permitted William Thornton, an unknown physician from the West Indian island of Tortola, to enter late, then awarded him the premium.

Thornton's winning design employed a straightforward domestic image: it looked like an English country house. After the judges had allowed him to revise his scheme by consulting the other competition entries, the initial conception began to evolve, even drift, through a tangle of alternative schemes further complicated by the rapid turnover of supervising architects, the most notable of whom were Benjamin Henry Latrobe and Charles Bulfinch.

During its initial construction in the early nineteenth century and its alteration in the succeeding decades, the United States Capitol took shape through bricolage, the ad hoc assembly of available odds and ends, which is one of the primary processes through which landscapes are infused with meaning and invention. In their imaginations, builders dismember old forms and reassemble the resulting spatial fragments, visual images, metaphors, and names. If they do their jobs well, the new forms evoke a similar response, as subsequent builders dismember and scatter them, and the process begins anew.

The United States Capitol was cobbled together out of ideas

40

Sour Springs Longhouse, 1870s, Six Nations Reserve, Canada.

This log building was built to house the rituals of the Iroquois Longhouse Religion. The Iroquois, like many other Native Americans, learned log building from European colonists in the 18th century.

borrowed from colonial state-houses, classical antiquity, prominent European baroque buildings, and neo-classical geometry. Like the prerevolutionary capitols that preceded it, the new Capitol housed the fundamental institutions of government—the Senate, the House of Representatives, and the Supreme Court—in a single structure [41]. The formal armature of two identical houses joined by a gathering place may have been derived specifically from the Virginia Capitol (1701–4; rebuilt and remodelled 1751).[10]

The intellectual foundations of the Capitol were thoroughly neo-classical. The new sense of intellectual command over the world that we encountered at Monticello had both its natural and its cultural sides. By *nature*, neo-classicists meant the founding principles of nature, such as the laws of physics and optics discovered by Isaac Newton, a neo-classical hero. These were often represented architecturally as regular geometrical forms, such as circles, spheres, cubes, cylinders, or pyramids. The cultural counterpart of this new sense of intellectual understanding of the natural world was the desire for direct knowledge of the classical past unmediated by traditional authorities such as Vitruvius or Palladio. Eighteenth-century archaeology had shown classical architecture to be an exciting and flexible tradition, far different from the rule-bound canon described by earlier authorities. Classicism seemed new, vigorous, and near, particularly to a people who wanted to think of themselves as heirs of the Romans, as Americans did.

In Benjamin Latrobe's revision of Thornton's design for the Capitol, the principal public rooms of the Capitol employed neo-classical geometries: they were domed, top-lit, semicircular spaces focused on

41 William Thornton, Stephen Hallet, Benjamin Henry Latrobe, Charles Bulfinch et al.

United States Capitol, Washington, DC, 1793–1916. This plan of the main (second) floor as it was in 1832–4 was drawn by Alexander Jackson Davis. The large semicircular room on the left was the House of Representatives' chamber, while the smaller semicircular chamber on the right accommodated the Senate. The Supreme Court was housed on the ground floor.

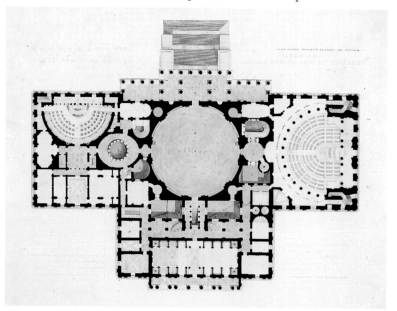

United States Capitol
Washington, DC, 1793–1916.
This daguerrotype of the
east front, taken c.1846,
shows Charles Bulfinch's
original wooden dome and
Benjamin Henry Latrobe's
domed and top-lit House and
Senate wings.

podiums or benches framed by arches. For their architect the symbolic qualities of these spaces were augmented by their practicality, for he believed that their shapes would focus sound as well as vision. The building was clothed in Roman classical architectural garb, enriched by three newly invented orders based on an idea of French neo-classical theorist Marc-Antoine Laugier and depicting several of the principal cash crops of the country: corn (maize), cotton, and tobacco.

Latrobe also envisaged the central rotunda, which he never had the opportunity to build, as a museum after the fashion of Jefferson's Indian Room at Monticello. Twenty-four niches would shelter statues of revolutionary heroes. This neo-classical didacticism was endorsed by his successor Charles Bulfinch, who did build the rotunda. He commissioned eight sculptured panels depicting the European discovery and conquest of North America for the rotunda, and crowned the space with a wooden exterior dome, higher than the one Latrobe had planned, to complete the first Capitol [**42**].

One of Latrobe's most significant though little-noticed contributions to the Capitol was to accommodate the bureaucratic as well as the ritual aspects of republican government. During his two terms as architect of the Capitol, he embedded the ceremonial spaces in a network of offices and conference rooms that would be required for the day-to-day operation of the government [**41**]. Still, like the Grand Village of the Natchez, the Capitol was an idealized and somewhat schematic representation of the new national government intended to depict political consensus. With its allusions to a mythic Roman republican past, to universal geometries, and to historical events, it gave the institutions of government an appearance of seamless wholeness

43 Thomas U. Walter

Design for new east front of the United States Capitol, 1855.

The original Capitol is bracketed but not obscured by the new wings and dome.

that belied national divisions. For example the iconography of the Capitol celebrated the economic products of the new nation rather than the social institutions, such as slavery, that created them. It sought inclusiveness by avoiding specificity.

This evasion was exposed when the Capitol was enlarged beginning in 1851. Philadelphia-born architect Thomas U. Walter added larger wings to the ends of the building to accommodate new House and Senate chambers. To match the scale of the new building, Bulfinch's wooden outer dome was replaced by an elaborately engineered 4500-ton cast-iron dome [**43**]. The 1850s were a decade of bitter debates over slavery and political power in the republic. As a result the Capitol's symbolism was carefully scrutinized. Thomas Crawford's statue *Freedom Triumphant in War and Peace*, which was to crown the new dome, originally wore a liberty cap, a traditional sign of revolution. Senator Jefferson Davis, later president of the Confederacy, complained that the liberty cap had been the head-gear of freed Roman slaves and consequently inappropriate to be associated with 'freeborn Americans'. Crawford substituted Roman military headgear decorated with feathers 'suggested by the costume of our Indian tribes'.[11] In Davis's view African-Americans were appropriately excluded from symbolic reference in the Capitol as they were from political participation in daily life. Similarly, the Capitol's builders consigned Native Americans to the status of mythical forebears rather than contemporary citizens. The controversy over the dome's crowning figure thus re-emphasized the Capitol's builders' strategy for representing political community allegorically, at the same time that it made clear who did *not* belong to the republican community.

Walter's Capitol is essentially the one that stands today, an image so familiar that we hardly even see it. When we do care to look, we discover a rambling, ungainly structure. This is exactly the point. Over the past two centuries, the builders of the United States Capitol have been more interested in building a mythology, the central task of an architecture of citizenship, than a coherent formal composition. The United States Capitol was created through acts of bricolage consolidated by classical visual language and the neo-classical didacticism that pervades its iconography.

In turn, the Capitol was the starting-point for later essays in the representation of citizenship, including, predictably, state capitols and county court-houses nationwide. Even those that appeared to depart most from the model, such as the skyscraper capitols and city halls of the twentieth century, most often retained the commitment to classical architecture and civic didacticism, and with them took on the difficult problems of inclusion and exclusion in political symbolism. The Nebraska State Capitol and World War I Memorial of 1922–32 is characteristic, both in its adherence to the tradition and in its substitution of a vision of continuous progress for the more static neo-classical conception of the virtuous and prosperous republic embodied in the United States Capitol [**44**].

The Nebraska Capitol was as self-consciously symbolic as the national capitol and, as the product of a single building campaign, was much more systematic in the effort. The work of the architect, Bertram Grosvenor Goodhue, was closely co-ordinated with that of sculptor Lee Lawrie, mosaicist Hildreth Meiere, and painter Augustus

44 Bertram Grosvenor Goodhue, with Lee Lawrie, Hildreth Meiere, Augustus Tack, and Hartley Burr Alexander

Nebraska State Capitol and World War I Memorial, 1922–32, Lincoln, Nebr.

Photograph c. 1934.

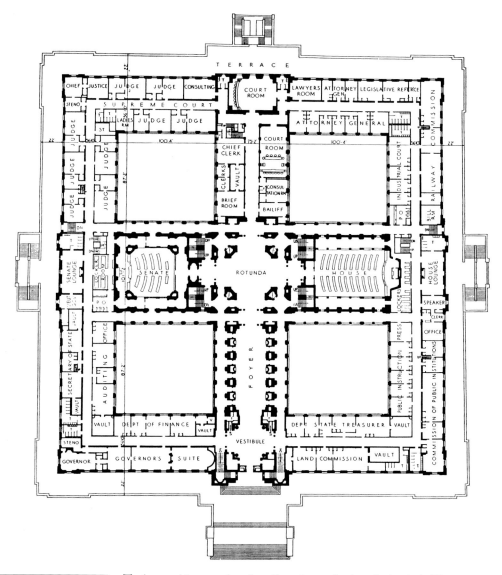

45

Nebraska State Capitol and
World War I Memorial.

Main- (second-) floor plan.

Tack, working under the direction of a 'symbologist', University of
Nebraska philosophy professor Hartley Burr Alexander.[12]

Both the skyscraper form and the steel-framed structure seemed
progressive to Goodhue, who wondered whether they might not have
'put, or so I think, all historical forms on the blink', cutting off access to
the traditional classical language of citizenship.

It seems to me that it does. Of course I grant you it's very difficult to know just
how to steer one's way through such a maze of difficulties. I don't claim to have
done it myself with any success and don't know of anyone who has, for the
moment you sail past the rock of dry-as-dust precedent you find yourself in
the whirlpool of originality which means art nouveau and a lot of other crazy
stuff.[13]

Goodhue resorted to a Byzantine variant of classical architecture, suggesting the power of classicism in American civic expression, even in the face of 'theoretical' objections. This classicism formed the matrix for an iconographic programme whose message was that this recently colonized state was now a full-fledged part of the modern world, standing at the vanguard of human history.

Goodhue conveyed the message architecturally by composing the building as a tower on a podium. As at the United States Capitol, the base contained halls for the state Senate and House of Representatives, connected by a rotunda, and accommodations for the state Supreme Court [45]. Equally important, the podium housed the rational, bureaucratic part of government. A century of growth in the size and complexity of public administration since the United States Capitol was built necessitated a ratio of offices to ceremonial public rooms much greater than in the Latrobe-Bulfinch building. Double-loaded corridors surrounded four central light courts, following the pattern of the 'modern' government office buildings of the 1830s and 1840s, such as the United States Treasury Building and the Post Office Department headquarters at Washington. Goodhue hoped that visitors would associate this plan with the urban grid, the rectangular land survey, and the flatness of the landscape. In contrast to the workaday administrative podium, the architect imagined the tower that rose from it as an aspiring, mystical landmark. The sense of emergence was reinforced by a characteristic device of Goodhue's, monumental figures that seemed to grow out of the building stone like crystals.

The decorators embellished the architectural armature with interlocking narratives that were also divided between the base and the tower. Alexander explained the building much as Goodhue had. The base represented 'the quarter of the Earth and the historic course of human experience', while the tower was 'a gnomon of the Heavens and symbol of the more abstract conceptions of life derived from historical experience. Unitedly they express that combination of action and thought which is the essence of all human life, social as well as individual.'[14]

The capitol's iconography transformed historical vignettes into a vision of the future. The base was encircled with a series of sculptural panels depicting government and law from ancient times through the present, as well as with a chronicle of human life in Nebraska. State history carried the viewer from the outside into the ground floor, where the imagery became progressively more allegorical, culminating in the central rotunda. Its dome was decorated with mosaic figures representing eight virtues necessary for a civilized society, such as temperance, courage, justice, and wisdom. High above the rotunda, Lawrie's *The Sower* crowned the tower, alluding to the agricultural history of the Plains, but sowing the seeds of noble living, wisdom, justice, power, and mercy. The result was a quasi-Hegelian narrative of transcendence. Citizenship was a religious quest. The stern and virtuous republican citizen of the United States Capitol had become the seeker after personal fulfillment: 'Political Society Exists for the Sake of Noble Living' read one inscription. History, the actual, was spiritualized and subsumed to the Oversoul, the possible.

The precociously New Age qualities of Nebraska's capitol were underscored by the treatment of the state's Indians. They appeared as part of the prehistory of the state, anachronisms superseded by the pioneer and the urbanite. Judging from this building, there were no Native Americans in twentieth-century Nebraska. Instead, they acted as a natural force, like the buffalo who appeared on the pedestals bracketing the stairs and whose flanks were inscribed with an Indian prayer. Mosaic thunderbirds, an indigenous symbol of the heavens and the life that the heavens give the earth, encircled the tower just below the gilded dome. In this manner, Native Americans and their symbols were subsumed to the political-personal mythology of the state and incorporated into the path to spiritual transcendence. In its imaginative construction of a state full of possibilities and promise the Nebraska State Capitol's symbolism of community once again raised troubling issues of inclusion and exclusion. Who was represented? Whose history counted? Who belonged to the community and in what capacity? To whom did Nebraska belong?

Ancestral Homelands

In its references to the topography of the Great Plains, to the indigenous inhabitants, and to the agricultural settlement of the state, the Nebraska State Capitol implied a primordial connection between land and people. In doing so, it drew on one of the most common ways of representing communities: the imaginative construction of an ancestral homeland. Ancestral homelands evoke special qualities—memories, experiences, knowledge—shared by a restricted group of people. Their purpose is both to include and to exclude.

The metaphor of the ancestral homeland extends far beyond the construction of state capitols and other official structures. The American landscape is blanketed with intersecting, often contradictory, ancestral homelands. They are 'invented traditions', in which the selective recall, exaggeration, and sometimes outright fabrication of traditional practices are used to define a distinctive, territorially based cultural identity for a nation or some fragment of one.[15] The authenticity of identity does not depend on the authenticity of the vehicle. In an ancestral homeland, no distinction is necessary between the documented and the undocumented, the historical and the mythical, for the metaphor works either way.

The Navajo ancestral homeland, for example, is tightly defined.

The Navajo emigrated into the Four Corners area of New Mexico, Arizona, Colorado, and Utah from the north a relatively short time before the Europeans arrived, but they consider the south-west to be their place of origin. In this place, which they call Dinetah and which is delimited by four sacred mountains, the Navajo first emerged to the surface of the earth from the lower world. Dinetah is composed of Holy People, who take the visible form of landscape features, animals, plants, the air, and heavenly bodies. Because the entire landscape encompasses distinctive individual personalities, it is said to be a sacred whole. The landscape serves as a mnemonic device whose features help people to remember detailed sacred stories, stories that are not to be shared with outsiders and in many cases cannot be shared with other Navajo either. And just as Nebraskans adopted the Plains Indians as their mythic forebears, so the Navajo claim the abandoned Anasazi pueblos as the homes of their ancestors.

We might also read the Navajo ancestral homeland as a kind of historic landscape that serving the same kind of testimonial function as Plymouth Rock or Mount Vernon, which likewise remind us of holy people and events. In fact the idea of a historic landmark—a place of special significance set in an otherwise neutral landscape—is one that contemporary Navajo can accommodate alongside their traditional view of the ancestral homeland as an unbroken, sacred whole. They commemorate recent historic sites such as Navajo Fortress in Canyon de Chelly, Arizona, where the Navajo were besieged by Kit Carson and his federal troops in 1864.

Nevertheless, the idea of the ancestral homeland as a neutral field studded with discontinuous historic sites is one that is more characteristic of European-American than of Native American culture. The first landmarks of a Euro-American ancestral homeland were mapped shortly after the founding of the republic. In Hingham, Massachusetts, townspeople decided in 1791 to preserve their seventeenth-century meeting-house as a monument to their ancestors. In rapidly growing Philadelphia the eighteenth-century State House, the 'Hall of Independence' where the Second Continental Congress and the Constitutional Convention met, was rescued from demolition in 1811 and converted to a shrine at the time of the Marquis de Lafayette's visit to the United States in 1824. Its long-vanished steeple was replaced and an approximation of the original panelling was installed in the room where the Declaration of Independence had first been read. A quarter of a century later, an eighteenth-century Dutch house at Newburgh, New York, that had briefly served as George Washington's military headquarters became a museum of the state of New York, while an organization of women led by South Carolinian Ann Pamela Cunningham succeeded in prying Mount Vernon, Washington's own house, from family hands in 1858 to make it a shrine.

In the words of the Historic Preservation Act of 1966, the founding document of contemporary preservation practice, 'the spirit and direction of the Nation are founded upon and reflected in its historic past'.[16] Yet the historic past is intangible and ephemeral. It may be no accident that the origins of history museums and historic preservation in the United States coincided with the growth of a consumer society. In keeping with the consumer's substitution of the tangible for the intangible, architecture is summoned to stand for 'the spirit and direction of the Nation'. This equation of sign and signified is characteristic of consumer culture, but in architecture, as in other aspects of material culture, it rests on confusing notions of authenticity. While the artefact is testimony to the authenticity of values, it need not be authentic itself. One nineteenth-century commentator proposed replacing the original wooden Mount Vernon with a stone replica for permanence. This differed only in technological sophistication from modern historic restoration practice, which often involves the complete replacement or reconstruction of the structure and interiors of a building, often with different, superior, even synthetic materials. The building remains 'historic' as long as its skin is intact or accurately reproduced—as long as it appears historic.

Among the most conspicuous ancestral homelands in the United States was that created by adherents of the so-called Colonial Revival, an architectural and cultural phenomenon that first appeared in the mid-nineteenth century and that has never disappeared from American architecture. Under the aegis of the Colonial Revival, historic preservation, architectural historical research, and historicist architectural design fed off one another to shape a landscape evocative of colonial times (by which Colonial Revivalists often meant anything dating before the Civil War). For example, antiquarians fought in 1863 to preserve John Hancock's eighteenth-century house adjacent to the Massachusetts State House in Boston. Although the house was demolished, architect John Hubbard Sturgis made a set of measured drawings of it that have come down to us as architectural historical documentation of a significant colonial Boston structure. In the late nineteenth century Sturgis's drawings were used by architects as raw material for the design of numerous new houses and public buildings, including the Massachusetts Building at the World's Columbian Exposition held in Chicago in 1893 [46].

Needless to say, no architectural movement—or more properly, architectural mood or attitude—that has lasted for nearly a hundred and fifty years should be oversimplified. As an evocation of a mythicized pre-industrial past used to unify a fragmenting industrial and commercial society, the Colonial Revival was a nation-building strategy that had many counterparts internationally. The English Queen Anne style, which romanticized post-medieval English vernacular architecture and which made inroads among those in the United States who stressed the English roots of American institutions, was most closely related to the Colonial Revival, and many American architects worked in both modes. The late-nineteenth-century folklife museums of Scandinavia, the Heian Jingu shrine of 1895 in Kyoto (a vastly overscaled model of an early Japanese palace), and the Heimatstil architecture of Germany all shared the nationalist aims and antiquarian strategies of the American Colonial Revival—all were elements of ancestral homelands in those nations.

As an outgrowth of picturesque architectural theory, the Colonial Revival in architecture, like the local-colour movement in literature, sought to embellish the spirit of regions by evoking the distinctive visual qualities of their oldest buildings. Between the late nineteenth and the mid-twentieth centuries, architects as diverse as Peabody and Stearns and J. Frederick Kelly in New England, George Howe and Charles Morse Stotz in Pennsylvania, or William Lawrence Bottomley and Thomas Tileston Waterman in Virginia designed Colonial Revival buildings closely attuned to their regions' architectural character. Their counterparts in other parts of the country, men such as Richard Koch in Louisiana, John Gaw Meem in New Mexico, or A. Page Brown in California, were equally adept at emulating the earliest French and Spanish architecture of their homes.

Nevertheless, during the half century after 1875 when the Colonial Revival was most influential, it was above all the ancestral homeland of those who defined themselves as Anglo-Saxon, Teutonic, Protestant, or simply white. The Colonial Revival was an origin myth told through landscape, as the Navajo origin myth was. It adopted the rhetoric of a

47 George I. Lovatt
St Rita of Cescia Roman
Catholic church,
1907, Philadelphia.

48
Bank of Canton (formerly
Chinese Telephone Exchange),
1909, San Francisco.
This small building, based on
a type of Buddhist religious
monument called a pagoda,
originally housed Cantonese-
speaking telephone operators.

revitalization movement, harkening back to a time when people were ostensibly more virtuous, more public-spirited, more homogeneous, and led simpler lives. Its aim was to counter the sectional division, political corruption, ethnic cacophony, and cultural erosion that Colonial Revivalists believed they saw around them. The curators of the period rooms (displays of early American furniture and decoration arranged in domestic settings) in the Metropolitan Museum of Art's new American Wing warned in 1925 that 'The tremendous changes in the character of our nation, and the influx of foreign ideas utterly at variance with those held by the men who gave us the republic, threaten, and unless checked, may shake its foundations'. They hoped that the American Wing would help 'revive those memories' of the founders' values and aid in 'the Americanization of many of our people', surely a curious aim for an art museum.[17] Similar reasoning led the founders of charitable institutions aimed at immigrants to choose colonial architectural styles for their buildings.

As the example of the Colonial Revival illustrates, ancestral homelands in the United States have commonly been associated with ethnic groups, and they have served to reinforce competing claims to dominance. At a time of heavy southern European immigration to the United States, for example, some American academics began to search for signs of ancient occupation of the continent by northern Europeans. In

1870, architect R. G. Hatfield announced that the Newport Tower, the ruin of a seventeenth-century windmill in Newport, Rhode Island, was in fact a Viking baptistry, inside which he had discovered a Viking burial. Two decades later Eben Horsford, a Harvard professor of chemistry, proclaimed Lief Eriksson the founder and first settler of a Viking settlement on the site of Cambridge, Massachusetts, that had left behind the remains of an elaborate canal system. Using the most recent techniques of place-name analysis, Horsford went on to demonstrate that the Indian place-names of New England were corruptions of Old Norse words. For men like Horsford, the idea that Italians might have a claim to America based on its 'discovery' by Christopher Columbus was intolerable. He built a replica Viking ship and took it to the World's Columbian Exposition in Chicago to protest against Columbus's claim. The Newport Tower and Viking Cambridge became landmarks in an ancestral 'Anglo-Saxon' homeland where, as in Dinetah, exclusion was as important a function of the ancestral homeland as inclusion.

While statements such as Halsey's and Tower's or actions such as Horsford's seem sinister because they were so often turned against immigrants, African-Americans, and others of the powerless, it is important to remember that, as an invented tradition, the Colonial Revival had counterparts among American minorities. They too created landscapes based on mythicized versions of their own pasts to claim the right to participate in American society. The overscaled early-twentieth-century Renaissance, Baroque, and Byzantine urban churches constructed for eastern and southern European Roman Catholics and Orthodox Christians, for example, linked lower-class immigrants to the classical high cultures of their home countries, in response to Colonial Revival appropriation of the Renaissance legacy [47].

When San Francisco's Chinatown was reconstructed after the 1906 earthquake and fire, pseudo-Chinese architectural decorations and street furniture created a fantasy Chinese city like none known in Asia [48]. These masonry buildings, occupied by people from south-eastern China, were embellished with false fronts evoking the élite classical architecture of northern China. Owing to legal restrictions on Chinese property ownership, most of Chinatown's buildings were owned, and usually designed, by Caucasians, but they were intended for Chinese tenants, who sometimes requested that pseudo-Chinese decorations be added to otherwise plain façades. For non-Chinese, this decoration marked the district as an exotic playland, which suited those Chinese merchants who catered to them. For residents, it served the purpose that invented traditions often do, of giving a cohesive public identity to people who were divided by social class, religion, dialect, or regional origin both in their native lands and in the United States.

Building sand-castles alongside a *casita* in El Barrio, New York, NY, *c.* 1988.

Casitas are community houses built by Puerto Ricans in New York City. They are usually nostalgic evocations of Caribbean folk houses. This *casita*, with its gable-end porch, recalls a kind of house created in the islands in the 17th century by the fusion of indigenous, African, and European house types. In the 19th century, it was carried to the Gulf Coast as the shotgun house. In the 20th century, it has appeared in the north-east as a common *casita* type.

The delineation of ancestral homelands remains an important function of American architecture. Puerto Ricans in the South Bronx use vacant lots as sites for small community houses called *casitas* [**49**]. They commonly take the form of *bohios*, traditional Caribbean rural workers' houses formed from a synthesis of European, Indian, and African architectural ideas. The choice of a building type rarely built in Puerto Rico any longer founds ethnic identity in a mythic homeland evoked in *casita* names such as Villa Puerto Rico, La Brisa del Caribe, and Añoranzas de Mi Patria (Yearnings for My Homeland).

In Washington, DC, in the 1970s, African-Americans painted Ndebele-style decoration on the Capitol Hill alley buildings of Frederick Douglass Court [**50**]. During segregation blacks had been relegated to the alleys of Capitol Hill, but they were being driven out by gentrification in the 1970s. The paintings were a response, a reclaiming of alley space, but the choice of decoration was telling. The Ndebele are a southern African group, not historically among the enslaved peoples brought to North America, but their distinctive graphic designs, so strange in an American urban setting, were called on to assert pan-African pride and identity in a hostile social environment.

Cultural Authority

Architectural definitions of community such as those embodied in imagined ethnic ancestral homelands stress boundaries, excluding some people altogether from the communities in question. Other built images of community are more inclusive, but emphasize ranking people within the community. When colonial Anglo-Americans attended church, for example, they took seats according to their social identities. In Quaker meeting-houses men were separated from women, adults from children, and sometimes whites from blacks. Among the Puritans and Anglicans the same distinctions were usually observed, and in addition communicants were seated according to their social rank in the community. In every congregation, a local élite governed the church and their dominance was acknowledged architecturally. Even though the Quakers had no formal clergy, for example, prominent members sat on raised benches facing the rest of the congregation. In the established (state-run) Anglican churches of eighteenth-century Virginia, the élite sat nearest to the altar or, later, in private galleries (balconies) secluded from the rest of the congregation. In fact, a domestic metaphor claimed the church as the domain of the élite. Anglican churches and Puritan meeting-houses closely resembled the houses of the colony's gentry in size, material, form, and architectural decoration [**51**] [**52**]. The liturgical fittings—the textiles,

50

Ndebele-style decoration, 1970s, Frederick Douglass Court, Washington.

These decorations were painted on alley buildings behind the Frederick Douglass House, a museum, to celebrate the African roots of black Washingtonians.

Westover, *c.*1750,
Charles City County, Va.
Although Westover is
traditionally thought to
have been the home of the
renowned diarist William
Byrd II, it was probably
built after his death by his
son, William Byrd III.

communion tables, communion silver—all replicated those that could
be found in the colony's finest mansions. To reinforce the connection,
the donors often engraved their own names or coats of arms on objects
that were, metaphorically, Christ's household furnishings. The similarity of the ritual environment of the church to the domestic environment of Virginia's grandees made the visual point that the existing
social order of the colony was divinely ordained: God was the greatest
gentleman in the neighbourhood. This metaphor had biblical underpinnings, alluded to by the seventeenth-century Massachusetts diarist
Samuel Sewall, who dreamed of heaven as a 'House not made with
hands, which God for many Thousands of years has been storing with
the richest furniture . . [a]. Magnificent Convenient Palace, everyway
fitted and furnished'.[18] The same metaphor inspired Utah's Latter-Day
Saints (Mormons), who fitted out their nineteenth-century temples
with parlours and other public rooms reminiscent of the most elegant
houses.[19]

The point was distinction. Sewall's heavenly home was dramatically different from the earthly homes of his yeoman neighbours. Virginia's Anglican churches were like gentry houses, but, equally important, they were unlike those of most Virginians. The difference was a function of money, of course, but it was also a function of appearance. In American architecture social hierarchy has often been worked out in a struggle for cultural authority, a struggle to identify certain aspects of culture as Culture, an élite homeland as exclusive in its own way as an ancestral homeland. The key battles were fought in the late nineteenth century.

Before the Civil War the landscape of culture (in the artistic, as opposed to the anthropological sense) was disparate and diffuse. Much of it lay in the commercial domain, in theatres, public gardens, circuses, and similar venues that made little distinction between what would now be called high and popular culture. At the same time, the notion of culture as a personal attainment, part of a middle-class process of self-creation akin to Jefferson's self-creation, gained ground. Among the so-called respectable working classes, culture, like evangelical religion, served as a vehicle for social advancement. Singing schools and other musical organizations, as well as the many athenaeums and occupation-specific libraries (mechanics' libraries, apprentices' libraries, mercantile libraries) founded by antebellum urbanites, left the mark of self-improvement on the built landscape. Other cultural organizations, such as mechanics' institutes and art museums, served as vehicles for promoting technical advances and public recognition for practitioners. In short, antebellum Americans saw culture as a part of the glittering urban life but also as something discrete and inherently worth cultivating. It was a commercial commodity but also a genteel accomplishment and, increasingly, something that transcended the commercial realm.

52 James Wren, designer and undertaker

Falls Church, 1767–70, Falls Church, Va.

The Anglican church was the state church of Virginia and other royal colonies. Each parish was controlled by local gentry, who modelled the buildings on houses like Westover—on their own residences, that is.

53 Furness and Hewitt

Pennsylvania Academy of Fine
Arts, 1872–6, Philadelphia.

This view was made around
1880, just after the
Pennsylvania Academy
moved into its new home.

54

Pennsylvania Academy of
Fine Arts.

First- and second-floor plans.

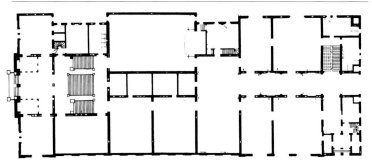

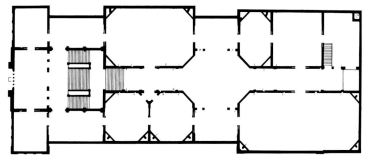

Above: Second floor. Below: First floor

The Pennsylvania Academy of Fine Arts, constructed in Philadelphia in 1872–6 to coincide with the Centennial celebrations, was a product of this pre-war mixture of motives [53]. The new building was the third home of an institution that had been founded in 1803 and remained an old-style trade school and a space for artists' self-promotion. Essentially, it was a large two-storey shed, with galleries on the upper floor and the art school on the ground floor, with the whole fronted by a striking head-house containing the stairs and some offices [54]. The head-house-and-shed format was reminiscent of a common railway-station plan, or of a commercial building with an elaborate show-room façade and a plain warehouse behind. The long vista down the main hall, with its iron-ribbed skylights, similarly evoked shopping arcades in a city that was home to the first American arcade [55].

The Academy was meant to embellish the city. It stood just two blocks north of an ambitious new city hall that began to rise in the same year. The two new buildings prompted the Reverend William Henry Furness, the dedication speaker and father of the Academy's principal designer, Frank Furness, to exclaim that the 'monotony of our streets is disappearing: the spirit of beauty is beginning to brood over our city'.[20] As an urban ornament, the Academy was called on to transcend mere commerce, which was not capable of generating emblems worthy of a great city. So Furness designed a building that was consciously 'artistic' and based closely on current French and English architectural theory. The head-house had a mansard roof and in the French manner was broken visually into a central pavilion with wings (as the new city hall was). Along the north side, where the studios projected beyond the second floor to accommodate skylights, the upper-storey brick wall was supported on a trussed iron beam. Following the precepts of Eugène-Emmanuel Viollet-le-Duc, who argued that a modern architecture should blend historical imagery with the frank and distinctive use of modern materials, Furness left the beam exposed on the exterior and worked it into the polychromed brick pattern. Inside, the architect similarly bridged the openings between galleries with exposed I-beams supported by columns that appeared to be Gothic piers made of machine parts, again following Viollet-le-Duc's precepts [56].

The Academy's colourful exterior was inspired by the writings of English critic John Ruskin, who was obsessed with the surface qualities of buildings. Ruskin advocated mixing materials of different natural colours to produce an effect of 'structural polychromy'. He also recommended compact ground-plans with strong horizontal cornices and simple skylines, as well as ornament founded in natural forms, all of which characterized Furness's design.

If it looked back to antebellum notions of culture as self-improvement (and traditions of 'metropolitan improvements' to the

56

Pennsylvania Academy
of Fine Arts.

Gallery interior, with
exposed I-beam and
mechanistic columns.

cityscape), the Pennsylvania Academy of Fine Arts also marked an early stirring of 'the sacralization of culture', to borrow historian Lawrence Levine's phrase. Certain arts of the common, mixed, diffuse cultural life of the nation were redefined in the late nineteenth century as Culture, 'spiritual . . . inviolate, exclusive, and eternal', something to be set aside, revered, and protected.[21] Sacralized culture was the domain of artists and experts, and could be observed by amateurs and audiences only from a respectful distance.

While the sacralization of culture owed something to antebellum aspirations toward self-improvement, the post-Civil War movement was more intense and more class-bound than anything earlier, as cultural institutions were singled out as arenas for élite self-assertion. Traditionally, European élites had several avenues for social action, including the endowment of religious institutions, a practice almost non-existent in the Protestant-dominated United States, and the patronage of secular charitable institutions. The latter had been popular among American philanthropists in the early nineteenth century, but by mid-century they appeared to have failed and were in disrepute as recipients of élite benefactions. Furthermore, the élite had little to gain by cultivating a constituency among the poor. Consequently, their attention was redirected after the Civil War towards cultural institutions that could memorialize families and keep their names before the public. At the same time they promoted élite disengagement from charitable relief in favour of forms of philanthropy that made poor and working-class Americans responsible for their own individual self-improvement.

57 Henry Hobson Richardson
Oliver Ames Memorial Library, 1877–9, North Easton, Mass. Exterior *c.*1880.

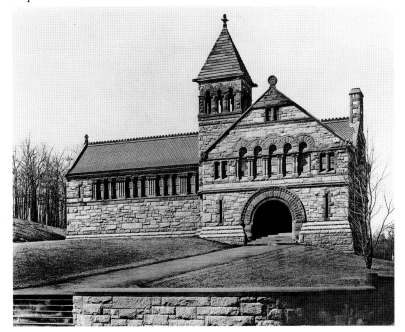

The Oliver Ames Memorial Library at North Easton, Massachusetts, one of a series of libraries designed by Henry Hobson Richardson, did all these things [**57**]. An off-centre entrance, marked by a huge arch and an adjacent stair tower, led into the reading-room. To the left was the book room, marked by its row of high windows. The late-nineteenth-century donor saw himself (almost always *himself*) as a paterfamilias. As historian Abigail Van Slyck has noted, 'Nineteenth-century philanthropy, like paternal love, imposed upon its recipients a debt of gratitude that they had not asked to incur and that, no matter how hard they tried, they could never adequately repay.'[22] In the Ames Library, the relationship was established through hierarchical domestic metaphors similar to those used in eighteenth-century churches. The lush interior focused on a fireplace fit for a Renaissance prince and decorated with a portrait medallion of Oliver Ames, claiming for the Ames family a pre-eminence in the cultural as in the economic life of North Easton. The books were kept in old-fashioned alcove stacks, an arrangement opposed by professional librarians but preferred by donors, from which they had to be delivered to readers by a male librarian, the donor's surrogate [**58**]. The librarian gave the book, the patron did not take it. In these settings, through these rituals, literary works that were previously diffused through public and private life, popular and commercial culture, were recast as something that could be given by a patron to neighbours who might not otherwise have access to them.

The Ames Library was part of a carefully shaped baronial landscape that may be unique in American architectural history, a Mecca of cultural authority. It began prosaically enough when Oliver Ames opened a shovel factory at North Easton in 1803. He and his sons Oliver and Oakes built up North Easton as a small, family-owned New England mill town like hundreds of others. Although Old Oliver, as he was called, died in 1863, his sons continued to prosper. They profited handsomely from defence-contracting in the Civil War, and they became major investors in the Union Pacific Railroad. Oakes was elected to Congress, where he was caught in the Credit Mobilier scandal of 1873 and died in disgrace shortly afterwards. Oliver died in 1877.

At this point, Oakes's and Oliver's sons Oakes Angier Ames and Frederick Lothrop Ames swung into action to repair the family name. They had always aspired to something lofty, and at mid-century had built elaborate houses for themselves near the Queset River—a Gothic villa for Oakes and an Italianate mansion for Frederick. They reworked the utilitarian mill-race as a picturesque watercourse. After the deaths of their fathers, they transformed North Easton into a memorial landscape. The two houses became the nucleus of a manorial array. A Gothic church was built to one side of them, with a family burial plot in the cemetery behind it. The disgraced Oakes was interred on a small knoll, with successive generations of Ameses laid out concentrically around him. The Oliver Ames Memorial Library was set on the other side of the houses, with the Richardson-designed Oakes Ames Memorial Hall constructed next to it in 1881 [**59**]. Frederick Law Olmsted was called in to landscape the site and the town square across

59 Henry Hobson Richardson, architect; Frederick Law Olmsted, landscape architect

Oakes Ames Memorial Hall, 1879–81, North Easton, Mass.

from it. Richardson was also hired to build a railroad station, a new gate lodge in 1881–2 for Frederick L. Ames's estate Langwater, on the edge of town, and a monument to Oakes and Oliver to be set next to the Union Pacific tracks in Wyoming [**60**] [**61**]. Almost as an afterthought, a monument to Old Oliver was erected in 1911 adjacent to the company offices.

The Memorial Hall, the gate lodge, and the monument bear a closer look. The hall's rusticated ground floor appeared to be an extension of the outcropping on which it was built, while its five arches were echoed in Olmsted's rustic grotto across the street. The brick upper storey implies that only a minimal human supplement was needed to turn a natural site into architecture. The same rusticated stonework was used at the Wyoming monument, a stepped pyramid inscribed in a sixty-foot cube. From a distance, it is difficult to distinguish the monument from the natural outcroppings that dot the mountain pass around it. The boulders that were used to construct the gate lodge appear to have been subjected to the same minimal human effort, as the rock that the nineteenth-century photographer included in the foreground of his portrait (and that remains in its original location) pointedly suggested.

These monuments naturalized the Ames family. Striking as they are, Richardson's works were only the finishing touches on a coordinated landscape, constructed over several decades, that also used up-to-date Gothic architecture and allusions to English picturesque landscapes to obscure the Ames family's rise from small manufacturers to industrial magnates and politicians behind a manorial imagery that suggested that they had been there forever.

There was nothing in these buildings of the rationalistic, or of

the mundane worlds of industry and commerce on which the donors' fortunes were built (and, in the case of North Easton, which could be found in the factories that stood directly across the street from the donated buildings). Architectural languages were chosen that deliberately set the donors' domain apart from that of the beneficiaries—Ames employees—and that set the sacred world of Culture apart from everyday life.

Community

The issues of inclusion and exclusion, the aspiration towards encompassing symbolism in the face of the ethnic and class divisions embodied in ancestral homelands and monuments to cultural authority, continue to puzzle public bodies and designers charged with creating architectural representations of American community. At the same time, it is now less possible for a few politicians, philanthropists, or designers to decide issues of public representation in private. They are likely to be challenged at every turn. This is a healthy development for democracy, although proponents of design often lament the increased difficulty of creating public art. As the case of the Grand Village of the Natchez suggests, however, the issue may be less one of a breakdown of consensus than of the greater visibility of dissent now than in the past.

In the 1980s the Greater Cincinnati Bicentennial Commission planned to honour the two-hundredth anniversary of the city's founding by clearing a water front industrial district to create a park. They chose sculptor Andrew Leicester to design the Cincinnati Gateway, a monumental entrance to the new park [**62**]. Leicester believed that his lighthearted work

**62 Andrew Leicester,
artist, Meyer, Scherer &
Rockcastle, architects**

Cincinnati Gateway,
1987–8, Cincinnati.

Close-up of entry showing
steamboat-stacks, Pigasus
and (in background) the Flood
Column, topped by Noah's
Ark, and marked to indicate
the high-water points of
Cincinnati's major floods.

provides an emblem for the city; a gathering place and a site from which to view the river. It involves the community in its development and seeks to interact with the visitor through its use of symbols. … It seeks to intrigue and in doing so to impart knowledge about the city. … Perhaps the most important objective of this project is to establish an interaction with the community and the individual visitor, for it is through this interaction that the work will acquire the special meaning and acceptance accorded to a true public place.[23]

The Cincinnati Gateway was a quintessential specimen of visual bricolage, and the designer's choice of his kit of parts was particularly interesting. A 480-foot-long mock-up of the Miami-Erie Canal lock that once stood near the site served as the Gateway's armature. Along the top ran a scale model of the Ohio River, while the walkway that passed underneath—the gateway proper—depicted the Cincinnati Arch, the geological formation on which the city sits.

The outside wall of the Gateway was studded with reminders of past inhabitants of the region. Stylized ceramic fossils and masks based on the artefacts of the Adena culture, mound-builders who preceded the Hopewellians in the region, were embedded in tilework 'strata'. The hand-rails on the Gateway's stairs were equally stylized representations of the Great Serpent Mound (c.1070 CE), a nearby Mississippian earthwork that may be the most famous American Indian mound. The historical and geological givens of the site were paired with reminders of the city's nineteenth-century economy. The course of the Miami-Erie Canal was mapped in tile inside the gate, while the structure was

63

Cincinnati Gateway.

Pigasus.

PHOTO ANDREW LEICESTER, MINNEAPOLIS, MINN.

crowned with four tall smokestacks, emblematic of the riverboat traffic that filled the Ohio River in the last century. In the course of his research, Leicester also learned that nineteenth-century Cincinnati was the largest packer of pork in the world, and had been known as 'Porkopolis'. So he topped the smokestacks with life-size bronze winged pigs, which he named 'Pigasus' [**63**].

Unlike the capitol buildings, the historic monuments, or the cultural institutions, the Cincinnati Gateway offered no lessons in citizenship or culture. Yet it was a government-sponsored project that aimed to encapsulate an entire community and its history. Leicester presented his intriguing fragments of the past, apparently without comment, as facts rather than metaphors. The undisguised *bricôlage* delighted many viewers, who accepted the Gateway as a layered urban image without an obvious narrative.

No image is that naïve. The Gateway was rife with implicit commentaries on community. It hinted at who belonged and who did not. As at the Nebraska Capitol, Native Americans were included, but while they were not as romanticized or as mysticized as in Goodhue's building they remained firmly a part of the past, coupled with the fossils. Moreover, the Indians were the only cultural group explicitly represented. Eliding historic contemporary ethnic and social divisions, Leicester's monument lumped together everyone who lived in Cincinnati since 1788 as an undifferentiated commonalty united by the city's economy. The racialized and gendered economic life of the nineteenth century were no more evident in Leicester's canals, hogs, and smokestacks than they had been in Benjamin Latrobe's corn, tobacco, and cotton capitals at the United States Capitol. And just as the slaves who grew the cotton and tobacco were excluded from reference in Crawford's statue, so the women who lived in Cincinnati were ignored in the focus on steamboats, slaughter-houses, and canals, all sites of male work. Nor was the city's cultural or political history mentioned. Even though Cincinnati, a border city and the home of Lane Theological Seminary, a prominent abolitionist-oriented institution, was in the forefront of the battle over slavery, this did not figure in Leicester's work. Instead, Cincinnati's nineteenth-century commercial and industrial economy was held forth as its urban identity.

As a result, this celebratory monument, which strove for visual delight and appealed openly to our sense of humour, aroused a storm of public reaction that focused directly on issues of representation, memory, and mythology. Most people approved the romantic allusion to steamboats, but many were bitterly opposed to Pigasus. Curiously for a monument that studiously ignored ethnicity, one critic described Pigasus as 'an ethnic slur'. For another, to recall the era of slaughter-houses, when the Ohio River was nicknamed 'Bloody River' after the profusion of pigs' blood and entrails floating in it, was to undermine

Cincinnati's 'progressive image'.[24] That critic accepted the premiss of cultural authority that a community's highest values transcended commerce and the gritty realities of making a living. The tension between the desire for common ground and enduring divisions within American communities continued to confront Leicester as it had the builders of the United States Capitol two hundred years earlier.

Communities

The ambiguities of community, authority, and citizenship are of more than symbolic interest. The formulations of inclusion and exclusion encompassed in civic representations have practical consequences in the landscapes of American daily life. At the most mundane level, they bear on the simple right to use public space, an urban issue that has been debated continuously since the early years of the republic. Antebellum city governments passed ordinances forbidding loitering, and they prohibited street vending, scavenging, and other kinds of marginal activities that often meant the difference between subsistence and the almshouse for poor Americans. Other laws prohibited reclining and smoking (which were believed to be quintessentially lower-class recreations) in public squares, as a way to restrict those spaces to genteel users. Landscape architect Frederick Law Olmsted wanted his late-nineteenth-century urban parks to be open to all city residents, but only if they adhered to prescribed standards of conduct. Sports and other active pastimes were prohibited, and Olmsted wrote of the need to train the lower classes in proper park use. The right of the poor to use the city streets is still a sore point for the privileged, who complain about street vending, begging, and the simple presence of the urban poor on the street. Modern ordinances outlaw sitting on sidewalks, 'aggressive' panhandling, and selling without an expensive licence, while individual property-owners fence off sheltered niches, scatter broken glass, install fraises along sittable ledges, and erect plastic stacks to vent steam (that might otherwise warm a person) high into the air. Those who can afford it retreat to gated communities and office parks where all the space is legally private, and anyone can be excluded.

In the face of these enduring divisions in the American community, some designers have imagined new communities that might be inclusive but undisturbed by social divisions. The most recent, who call themselves New Urbanists or neo-traditional town planners, envisage a more pluralistic urbanism than that of the gated communities and anti-panhandling ordinances. They have declared themselves in favour of the city over the country, of more density rather than less, of tightness over sprawl, of urban diversity over suburban homogeneity, although most of their work, at such developments as Seaside, Florida, and Laguna West, near Sacramento, California, has been suburban or exurban.

New Urbanists favour integrated pedestrian-scale neighbourhoods containing many of the public and commercial facilities that residents need over automobile-dependent suburbs. For eastern neo-traditionalists Andres Duany and Elizabeth Plater-Zyberk, the proper articulation of pedestrians and cars and easy traversibility are key, while West Coast planner Peter Calthorpe stresses 'a specific aesthetic of place—scaled to the human body, timed to a stride, patterned to ceremony, and bonded to nature'.[25]

While neo-traditional planners acknowledge diversity and advocate planning for mixed populations and mixed uses, their designs incorporate the same unresolved conflicts that have characterized representations of community throughout the past two centuries. The diversity incorporated in neo-traditional plans is ethnic and economic. Social class, the idea that differences among members of society may run deeper than skin colour or bank balance and affect the fundamental cultural values by which people choose to live, has been given little thought by these planners. However, developers and purchasers give them much thought, and they resist the incorporation of mixed-income housing when new-town plans become new towns.

By the same token, cities have long served as places to escape small-town claustrophobia, places where people can get lost or simply be anonymous, yet New Urbanists envisage a congenial face-to-face community of shared values based on a romanticized image of the pre-automobile town. When neo-traditionalists Duany and Plater-Zyberk travelled through the southern United States with their client Robert Davis, they saw 'a pattern of streets, parks, and squares, with houses and their porches close to the street, and strong community bonds', qualities that they attempted to incorporate into their plans for Davis's Florida new town, Seaside.[26]

The statement reveals an astonishing blindness to the particular racial history of the American South as well as to the social history of American cities, where social atomization and the privatization of public space have been the rule, but it also says something about the issues of authority and architectural form in the New Urbanism. Formally and socially, neo-traditionalism combines ideas derived from the picturesque suburbs of the nineteenth-century, the turn-of-the-century City Beautiful Movement, and the early-twentieth-century Regional Planning Association of America, an alliance of architects, planners, and urbanists who sought to apply English garden-city ideas to American automobile cities. Laguna West, planned in 1989 and still under construction, is a prototypical essay in new urbanist bricolage [64]. The 800-acre site, laid out on former farmland in the Central Valley, is divided into five neighbourhoods, each the responsibility of a different developer. A civic centre at the northern edge of Laguna West is connected by City Beautiful radial boulevards and a grassy

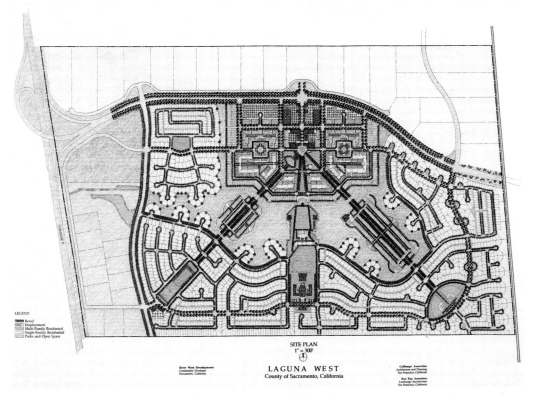

LEGEND
Retail
Employment
Multi-Family Residential
Single-Family Residential
Parks and Open Space

SITE PLAN
1" = 300'

River West Developments
Community Developer
Sacramento, California

LAGUNA WEST
County of Sacramento, California

Calthorpe Associates
Architecture and Planning
San Francisco, California

Ken Kay Associates
Landscape Architecture
San Francisco, California

64 Calthorpe Associates, Ken Kay Associates, Fehr & Peers Associates, Jack Mixon, and The Spink Company, project team

Laguna West, 1991– , Sacramento County, Calif.

Site plan.

axis to the residential neighbourhoods, where most lots stand on RPAA-type cul-de-sacs laid out in sweeping curves, the twentieth-century developer's interpretation of the curvilinear planning of nineteenth-century picturesque suburbs.

Laguna West's developers acknowledge these forebears in the streets of the public sector, which are named for Calvert Vaux (a planner of New York's Central Park), Lewis Mumford (intellectual leader of the RPAA), Parisian planner Georges Haussmann (an inspiration to the City Beautiful movement), and (inexplicably) Gothic Revival architect James Renwick. The selection of sources is telling, for all three New Urbanist inspirations relied heavily on cultural authority to shape cities. They and their allies among politicians and urban reformers believed in a city that promoted genteel values among people of all classes. Theirs was a managerial vision as much as it was an aesthetic one. By proper guidance, the establishment of wise regulations (such as the carefully drawn zoning codes that neo-traditionalist planners favour), Americans could be steered to form the proper kind of community.

The New Urbanism shares the vagueness about community, authority, inclusion, and the role of built form that has characterized American building since the beginning of the republic. Although it acknowledges social heterogeneity, the success or failure of New

65

Laguna West.

Single-family house.

Urbanist towns demands a homogeneity of values that has never been achieved in American history. The socio-economic divisions that New Urbanists regret protect Seaside and Laguna West from their own *naïveté*, for their location, cost, and developer policies defuse the threat that they will ever be called upon to house a genuinely diverse, genuinely urban population, or that such people will ever be attracted to them.

Finally, the New Urbanism returns us to issues of the relationship between built form and communal structure that opened the chapter. Like their predecessors, New Urbanists have great faith in the role of physical form in creating a new community. The City Beautiful planner Daniel Burnham wrote that 'The jumble of buildings that surround us in our new cities contributes nothing valuable to life;... Let the public authorities, therefore, set an example of simplicity and uniformity, not necessarily producing monotony, but on the contrary resulting in beautiful designs entirely harmonious with one another.'[27] In the same mood neo-traditionalists Alex Krieger and William Lennertz offer ultra-conservative aesthetic philosopher Roger Scruton's comment that 'The classical idiom [employed at several of Duany and Plater-Zyberk's new towns]. does not so much impose unity, as make diversity agreeable.'[28] They imply that visual uniformity will encourage uniformity of social values, or at least disguise its absence.

In practice, neo-traditionalist towns tend to incorporate nostalgic architectural imagery. The planners sometimes disavow these, arguing that they provide only the site plans and the zoning codes, but the neo-traditionalist architecture harmonizes with their own vision of small-town life [65]. And neo-traditionalists have faith that spatial devices—pedestrian scale, mixed use, greenery, front porches—and other physical amenities can create community. It is a faith honoured by time if not by success.

Nature

3

Since Adam's sin, people have required the discipline of a divinely ordained civil government and a state-supported church to obey God's laws, according to the Christian politico-religious doctrine of civility. To be in a state of nature, undisciplined by church and state, was to be alienated from God, not fully human. Both children and indigenous people (often called 'naturals') were near-animals who needed to be raised up to humanity by being civilized. Nature—the undisciplined landscape—required similar order and discipline, for the proponents of civility emphasized the biblical injunction to subdue the land, which they interpreted to mean that they were to clear and cultivate it.

For the first European colonists, adherents of the doctrine of civility, nature was an enemy. They made no distinction between the land and its people. God was an urbanite, a partisan of civil society: the natural, the forest, the Indians' home, was the domain of Satan. As the Pilgrims gazed at Cape Cod in 1620, they understood that they had 'no friends to welcome them nor inns to entertain or refresh their weather-beaten bodies; no houses or much less towns to repair to, to seek for succour. . . . Besides, what could they see but a hideous and desolate wilderness, full of wild beasts and wild men—and what multitudes there might be of them they knew not.'[1] Architecture was an ally against nature. To defend against the vast and howling wilderness, Massachusetts deputy governor Samuel Symonds sent orders for a house to be built for him before his arrival. Fresh air and pleasing views were of no interest to Symonds. 'For windowes let them not be over large in any room,' he wrote, '& as few as conveniently may be; let all have current shutting draw windoes [interior shutters].'[2]

Architecture could civilize the naturals as well as taming the wilderness, and to that end French, English, and Spanish colonial officials all built European-style houses for indigenous leaders. In 1618, the Virginia Company official George Thorpe built 'a fayre house according to the English manner' for the Virginia werowance (chieftain) Opechancanough, who 'formerly lived only in a cottage, or rather a denne or hog-stye, made only with a few poles or stickes, and covered with mats after their wild manner'. According to Thorpe, Opechancanough seemed sincere in his 'joy, especially in his locke and key, which hee so admired, as locking and unlocking his doore an hundred times a day; hee thought no device in the world comparable to it'.[3] When the happy householder led an uprising that almost eradicated the colony in 1622, the English felt betrayed, so closely did they associate architecture with civility.

The unwavering hostility evident in most early European-American statements about nature and the naturals masked a long-standing Judaeo-Christian ambivalence towards the land. The story of the Fall treated the natural world as a manifestation of divinity, rather than its antithesis. Before Adam sinned, Adam and Eve lived in a garden, a paradisal image in many of the world's cultures. Eden was a point of effortless contact with the divine. It was only after the Fall that people were condemned to labour, and forced to work their gardens. In short, the metaphors of divinity, nature, and culture were fluid. Nature could be God's vessel or Satan's; it could be the master or the servant of humanity; it could be spoiled or improved by human activity. Even in the earliest years of the European invasion of North America, occasional accounts of awestruck encounters with a natural paradise relieved the rhetoric of conquest and mastery.

Beneath such formulations of natural-human (or nature-culture) relationships lies a sense of nature as a unitary, active agent, whether as friend or enemy.[4] The monotheistic male God is paired with an unacknowledged female one, Nature, who possesses all the characteristic stereotypes of the feminine in the western tradition. This personification of the natural world as something distinct from the human was incomprehensible to members of many other cultures, as William Cronon has pointed out, and alien even to many European-American folk builders.

Perhaps the closest to the Judaeo-Christian sense of Nature as an intelligent being was the Asian(-American) belief in an earth animated by a constant energy called *chi*, which could help or harm people

66

Ukrainian folk house, early 20th century, Alberta, Canada. Plan, showing holy wall.

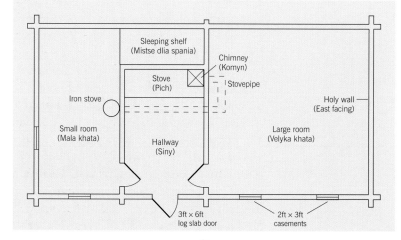

Sleeping shelf (Mistse dlia spania)

Chimney (Komyn)

Stove (Pich)

Stovepipe

Iron stove

Holy wall — (East facing)

Small room (Mala khata)

Large room (Velyka khata)

Hallway (Siny)

3ft × 6ft log slab door

2ft × 3ft casements

67
Blackfeet tipi circle, 1896,
location unknown.

depending on the strength and direction of its movement. Chinese geomancy, or *feng shui*, taught that topographical features such as water and mountains were keys to analysing the flow of *chi* through the landscape. With the aid of geomantic experts builders sought certain kinds of sites, such as those backed by hills and fronted by water, and constructed south-facing structures (since the most powerful and dangerous *chi* flowed from the north) planned to channel *chi* through them in the most auspicious manner. With its intricate interpenetration of ocean, bay, and Coast Range mountains, the San Francisco Bay Area closely fits geomantic prescriptions for an ideal site, although no one has yet demonstrated the use of geomantic ideas in designing any specific Chinese-American building. Nevertheless, paths of movement and the placement of mirrors in such locations as entries and exterior window-heads in Chinese-majority districts of contemporary American cities reveal a continuing concern for geomantic principles.

The difference from European Nature is that *chi* is not a personality that interacts intelligently with humans. Instead, it is a cosmic force that must be accommodated. A similar sense of a cosmic order shaped many European folk traditions brought to North America. For example, the Ukrainians who came to the Great Plains of the United States and Canada beginning in the 1890s built three-part houses with a larger and a smaller room separated by a narrow central space that served as an entry and contained a built-in cooking and heating stove [**66**]. These derived from a major European folk-housing tradition that linked the central and eastern parts of the continent from Scandinavia to the Balkans, and that differed from the houses western Europeans brought to North America in the early years of European

INTERIOR OF THE UNITARIAN CHURCH, BALTIMORE.

68 Maximilian Godefroy

Unitarian Church,
1817–18, Baltimore.
Interior, c.1830.

colonization. Ukrainian versions of these houses were built facing south, with the largest room on the east. That is, the house was oriented, and the east-end wall of the main room, corresponding to the chancel of a Christian church, was covered with icons, religious calendars, and other images.

Elements of both views—of the world as animated by life and of the world as cosmically structured space—can be found in Native American architectures. American Indians distinguish no separate entity called 'nature'. Life and divinity flow through animate and inanimate objects alike, making it difficult to differentiate people from their environments. Humans are one part of an intricate system of spiritual and material provision and debt contracted among all living beings, none of whom is absolutely superior to others. Some Native Americans believe that many life forms are capable of transforming themselves from one kind of being to another, making it even more difficult to think of nature as a unitary entity separate from humanity. This idea was shared by people as widely separated as the Micmac of Maine, who believed that old moose might enter the water and become whales, and the Northwest Coast tribes, whose art and architecture were filled with images of transformations of one creature to another.

The seamless integration of people and their world is evident in many kinds of Native American dwellings, which tended to be adapted to the structure of the cosmos more than to the specifics of site or environment in the modern sense. The Plains Indians' circular tipis (this Dakota Siouan word means *to dwell*), and the circular encampment in which they were erected, echoed the sacred circle of the horizon [67]. Conversely, the tribe's territory was represented as a large tipi, with the directions representing the lodge poles that supported the covering. The sun entered the world at the east, the direction that the tipi's door and the camp circle's opening both faced. The house fixed nomadic wanderers in an absolute space.

Neo-classical and Romantic Nature

Since the eighteenth century ideas of universal structure and of an animating life force, derived from European intellectual sources rather than from folk traditions, have coloured the Judaeo-Christian nature-human dichotomy in distinctive ways. Neo-classical ideas, imported to the United States through publications, visits to Europe, and the work of European-trained immigrant architects and intellectuals, promoted a view of nature—by which neo-classicists meant the invisible ordering rules of the visible world—as the place where God was accessible in the most unmediated ways to humanity. In élite architecture built in the early years of the republic, the austere beauty of pure geometrical forms such as spheres, cylinders, and cubes alluded to the divine order of the natural world. French émigré Maximilian Godefroy's Unitarian Church (1817), Baltimore, is a simple example. The exterior of the church is a cube embellished by a portico and a cornice. Inside, a cubical nave is framed by four semicircular arches that support a hemispherical dome on pendentives [68]. Such a rationalist composition seems particularly appropriate for a Protestant denomination with intellectual roots in the Enlightenment.

69 Louis I. Kahn

Salk Institute for Biological Studies, 1959–65, La Jolla, Calif.

The stark geometry of Kahn's stair towers reveals a debt to neo-classicism shared with many other modernists of the 1950s and 1960s.

70

Salk Institute for Biological Studies.

In the courtyard, geometry is tempered by the picturesque. Ranks of buildings separated by a water channel continue the natural ravine that runs down to the Pacific Ocean, while the office boxes mix materials in a way that recalls late Victorian design.

A fascination with science and technology resuscitated the neo-classical interest in universal structures for early-twentieth-century designers. The shapes of machine parts and their paths of motion, dictated by the laws of physics, served the same purpose of making the invisible structure of the physical world visible to the human eye as the placid purity of geometrical solids did for neoclassical architects. Explicit machine idolatry was relatively short-lived, but the aesthetic appeal of elemental geometries and mechanistic imagery was not. At the Salk Institute for Biological Studies (1959-65) in La Jolla, California, Louis I. Kahn constructed a series of rectilinear boxes attached to both sides of parallel spines that form the laboratories. The prisms that lined the perimeter and housed stairs and elevators were as austere as any neoclassicist could want [**69**]. The courtyard was more complex [**70**]. Here, the boxes stood on legs that formed a kind of arcaded piazza. In contrast to the placeless purity of neo-classical geometry, these boxes, which housed the scientists' offices, were partially clad with unpainted teak panels whose colour and texture resembled the shingles popularly associated with California architecture. The office façades were angled to offer views of the Pacific Ocean. A narrow axial water channel, borrowed from the Islamic garden tradition, alluded to the truism that California's climate is Mediterranean and emphasized the orientation of the central space, a highly artificial extension of a natural ravine that runs down towards the coast. In other words, Kahn's geometries were inflected by another, more pervasive conception of nature, derived from the romantic traditions of the early nineteenth century, one that calls on the builder to respond to the peculiarities of site and to draw on the riches of architectural history to evoke viewer response.

Where neo-classical nature, a product of the Enlightenment tradition, was rationalist, based on structures manifested in universal geometries, romantic nature was suffused with immanent divinity, made visible through the accidents and specificities of the physical world, particularly the idiosyncrasies of place, site, and region. We discover nature's indwelling spirit through our feelings rather than through rational investigation. For the romantics, we act *naturally* when we behave in keeping with our inherent sense of ourselves, or *artificially* when we act in a false and misguided manner. From this point of view, children and indigenous peoples approach the divine most closely, their natural tendencies unspoiled by civilization. The dichotomy between the natural and the artificial spun off endless corollary oppositions, between the city and the country, the primitive and the refined, the garden and the wilderness. This was the nature of Huckleberry Finn, who was driven to 'light out for the territory ahead of the rest, because Aunt Sally she's going to adopt me and sivilize me, and I can't stand it'.[5]

Although the romantics understood nature as a manifestation of God, they inherited the traditional Christian ambivalence towards it. Nature might be a benign, nurturing force or a savage, destructive one. The dichotomy was acknowledged in the aesthetics of the *picturesque* and the *sublime*. These terms derived from eighteenth-century theories that divided aesthetic pleasure into the beautiful, which is universal and based on classical rules of line and proportion; the sublime, stimulated by the great, terrifying, overwhelming, or deeply moving; and the picturesque, produced by variety and contrast. The picturesque encompassed topographical irregularities as well as the characteristic cultural forms that evoked the diversity of human history and geography. In search of the picturesque, architects and landscape architects cultivated the *genius loci*, the peculiar character of a place from which good design took its cue, and drew on the visual richness of architectural history to stir viewers' emotions. The picturesque implied human action, in contrast to the sublime, which implied human helplessness in the face of nature's power. A garden can be picturesque; a wilderness is sublime.

Eighteenth- and nineteenth-century Europeans and Americans were fascinated by the strangeness of North American topography, its living things, and its people. Europeans often interpreted the new republic's culture and politics as products of the *genius loci*. Americans took it for granted that their landscape was superior in scope, novelty, freshness, and fertility to the tame and tired European landscape.

Mount Auburn Cemetery, opened 1829, Cambridge, Mass.

View from Consecration Dell, 1860. Consecration Dell was named after the cemetery dedication ceremonies that were held there. Although Mount Auburn and its cousins are now packed with monuments, the founders of rural cemeteries envisaged them as settings for isolated graves, as this mid-19th-century lithograph illustrates.

Nineteenth-century Americans, in particular, liked to think of their nation as a second Eden and of themselves as a new race of innocents with another chance to inhabit paradise. Invocation of the land (which included its plants and animals, but also its indigenous people and its 'naturalized' European colonists) was a patriotic affirmation.

Country Life

The entwined concepts of nature and culture have been the more powerful in the American landscape because they provide a common, largely unexamined, metaphorical language full of often contradictory meanings. Among some Americans, the idea that nature must be subdued or even vanquished for human good remains strong, while others are equally certain that nature is a delicate spirit in imminent danger of extinction. In architectural history, however, there is no doubt that the romantic strain—of the natural as a vehicle for restoring the alienated soul to God, to spirit, to itself—has dominated the so-called designed landscape since the early nineteenth century. Yet even within this tradition there is a fundamental contradiction. Americans are often urged to benefit from the immanence of divinity in nature unspoiled by humanity, but they find these qualities in picturesque landscapes shaped by human agency.

This paradox was evident in the rural cemeteries that introduced picturesque landscaping to the American urban public. Rural cemeteries responded to a change in middling Americans' attitudes towards death. Where earlier harder-nosed generations had seen death as inevitable and, for the saved, a welcome release for the soul, genteel Americans in the early republic grew uneasy about the fate of their loved ones' remains in the public graveyards of cities and religious congregations. They responded by creating new, privately owned burying grounds at the urban edges, where they could own plots (which was not permitted in the older graveyards) and be assured that their families could remain intact and secure even in death. These new proprietary cemeteries tended to be miniature cities, with gridded plans and street-type plantings. In the late 1820s a group of physicians and horticulturists in Boston took the next step by organizing Mount Auburn Cemetery (opened 1829), which combined the new privatized cemetery with an experimental garden. The site they chose was a popular picnic ground outside Cambridge, a rolling tract that lent itself to picturesque landscaping, with ponds, lakes, and private plots laid out along winding paths named for trees and flowers [71] [72]. Here the dead could return naturally to the earth and the living could mourn in contact with all the ghostly and topographical spirits of the place. Yet the *genius loci* required cultivation: the terrain was necessarily, and without apology, 'improved by human care', as one contemporary writer noted, and surrounded with fences and gates to set it aside as a

Prang & Mayer's, Lith.Boston.

VIEW FROM CONSECRATION DELL.

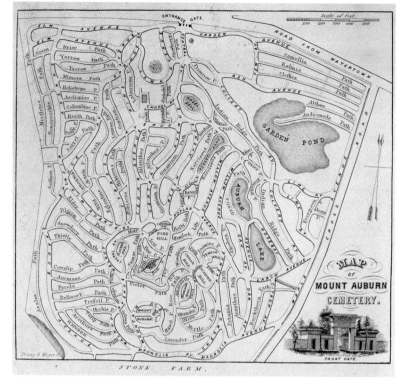

sacred landscape (as well as to protect it from grave-robbers working for medical schools). 'It is *unnatural* to leave it to itself; and the traces of art are never unwelcome, except when it defeats the purpose, and refuses to follow the suggestions of nature.'[6]

Andrew Jackson Downing (1815–52), a key figure in the popularization of the picturesque aesthetic in America, was caught up in the same paradox. Downing published a magazine and several books of advice on landscape and domestic architecture and furnishings. He was a synthesizer who, he told Swedish novelist Frederika Bremer, had come along at the right time. Downing enunciated a rationale that tied together a striking, varied, easily understood collection of prototypical architectural and landscape designs (most contributed by professional architects) with aesthetic theories derived from English sources, particularly from garden-writer John Claudius Loudon's books and magazines. It was Downing's talent to make this motley collection of images appear to be more coherent than they were, and he published them in wittily written and above all cheap books that introduced these ideas to a wide popular audience, and that remained in print long after his death.

Downing urged American gardeners to renounce fashionable exotic plants and landscape plans borrowed from books like his own and instead to take their inspiration from the land forms and plant materials of their own regions. True art in landscape gardening, he wrote, 'selects from natural materials that abound in any country, its best sylvan features, and by giving them a better opportunity than they could otherwise obtain, brings about a higher beauty of development and a more perfect expression than nature itself offers'.[7]

The art of gardening had a social purpose. Like most of his contemporaries, Downing assumed that the family was the central unit of society, but that urbanism, capitalism, and industrialism had weakened it. Downing did not oppose any of these, but he wanted to offset their harmful side-effects. His solution was family life in a natural setting. Moral values and psychic energy could be restored in a country house, by which he meant a suburban house relatively far from the city. It should be surrounded by a fairly large amount of land and be actively cultivated, but not for profit. Downing's country house was a post-Fall Eden whose benefits were accessible only to those who submitted to its discipline by entering actively into its peculiar rhythms and rules. Nature works for us when we work nature. Downing was scornful of city people 'who expect to pass their time in wandering over daisy spangled meadows, and by the side of meandering streams. . . . They have an *extravagant* notion of the purity and simplicity of country life. All its intercourse, as well as all its pleasures, are to be so charmingly pure, pastoral, and poetical!'[8]

If the home's therapeutic task in urban commercial society was acted out in the city family's submission to the discipline of the land, it should also be made visible in the country-house landscape. Downing urged that the house be tied to its site by its colour and its shape. Builders should paint their houses neutral tints that minimized contrast with their settings. In addition, the mass of the house should harmonize with the surroundings. Downing described the curving roof profile of his Lake or River Villa as 'a repetition of the grand hollow or mountain curve formed by the sides of almost all great hills rising from the water's edge', and a connecting link harmonizing the perpendicular and horizontal lines of the house and the land.[9]

To be indigenous in this sense, to meld into the land, was truer than to stand out from it as the alienated city did. But the naturalness was deeply cultural. Downing invited us to read his designs in gendered terms. While he expected the exterior of a house to be a portrait of the male head of the household, the landscape, particularly the garden, should be female space, in keeping with the widespread metaphor of Nature as a fecund woman. Many of his houses dramatized the refinement of male energy by surrounding the house with a sheltering veranda and setting it in a softening, essentially passive, gardened landscape that dramatized feminine qualities and served as a particular touchstone for the rejuvenation of the female head of household [23]. 'Everything which relates to the garden, the lawn, the pleasure-grounds,' Downing wrote, 'should claim [women's] immediate interest.

73 Olmsted and Vaux

Central Park, 1856–83, New York.

Overpasses separated the 'natural' terrain of the Park, above, from mundane urban traffic, below.

... Every lady may not be "born to love pigs and chickens" (although that is a good thing to be born to); but, depend upon it, she has been cut off by her mother nature with less than a shilling's patrimony, if she does not love trees, flowers, gardens, and nature, as if they were all part of herself.'[10]

Downing also believed that city people would benefit from rural landscapes in their midst. He pointed to the recreational popularity of rural cemeteries to demonstrate a need for large urban parks of a new kind. Early-nineteenth-century American cities already had plenty of parks, including public squares such as Philadelphia's Washington Square or New Orleans's Place d'Armes (now called Jackson Square), which received their first ornamental landscaping during this period; commercial beer-gardens, which often doubled as horticultural gardens; and ad hoc gathering places such as New Orleans's orange-tree-embellished levee, Brooklyn Heights in Brooklyn, and the rural cemeteries. They were valued as promoters of public health (as the 'lungs of the city'), botanical instruction, social rituals such as promenading, and simple informal recreation.

Downing dismissed these public places as 'little door-yards of space' and called for something on a larger scale and with different purposes.[11] New York's Central Park (1856–83), planned by competition-winners Frederick Law Olmsted and Calvert Vaux, Downing's former partner, met Downing's demand. Olmsted and Vaux landscaped the Park, a long narrow rectangle, in a manner designed to create 'contrasting and varying passages in scenery' (a good, succinct definition of the picturesque) and to suggest a great range of rural landscapes, while taking maximum advantage of the natural topography.

Although Central Park retained elements of earlier urban parks, it was intended, as earlier urban parks and squares were not, as an artificial countryside that could restore alienated urbanites to contact with immanent divinity, as Downing's country houses did for the well-off. Where Downing argued the necessity to work one's garden, Olmsted and Vaux believed that rejuvenation required passive contemplation. Active sports or social activities distracted people's attention from nature.

As in the rural cemetery and the country house, Central Park was riddled with the contradictions inherent in the nature-culture dichotomy. The Park's nature was a human product, the result of radical alteration of an existing landscape. It was protected by cultural devices to keep the artificial out, including separation of circulation to segregate vehicular traffic through the Park from pedestrian traffic [73]. In addition, a park that was intended to restore people to nature was based on an aesthetic of property, or control over nature. The landscaping of eighteenth-century British country houses, the ultimate source of nineteenth-century American picturesque landscapes, asserted the landholder's 'natural' dominion over apparently infinite space. Similarly, Olmsted and Vaux's insistence on excluding active

74 Olmsted, Vaux and Company

General Plan of Riverside, Illinois, 1869.

Central Park's picturesque forms have been tamed to suit the demands of Real-estate sales.

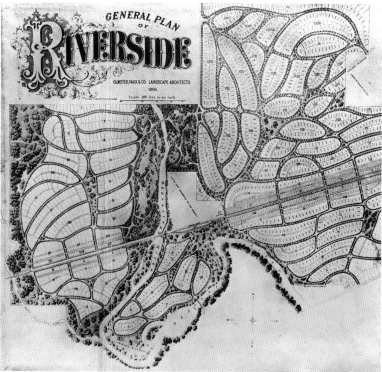

75 Reginald D. Johnson and Wilson, Merrill, and Alexander, associated architects; Clarence S. Stein, consulting architect

Baldwin Hills Village (now The Village Green), 1940–1, Los Angeles.

The modernist 'row houses' lining a tree-filled village green speak of a nostalgia for village life that has characterized American urbanism since the early 19th century. The village green at Baldwin Hills Village and the 'garden courts' that open off it are descendants of the small greens incorporated into the plan of Riverside.

uses of Central Park deflected its possible alteration. Nature, ordinarily something that grows and changes, should remain as it was designed to be.

From the day the Park opened, this aesthetic of passivity and control has been a source of conflict, offering a rationale for excluding buildings, playing fields, zoos, and large gatherings. Beginning with the Metropolitan Museum of Art, under way before the Park was finished, all these things eventually found their way into Central Park at the demand of one or another of its constituencies. The conflict over proper use of the Park has recently been inflected with overtones of ancestral homelands and cultural authority in casting the argument against change in historic preservation terms: Central Park is 'an Olmsted park', the work of a great artist that must be protected from philistine intrusions by the unappreciative. Since Olmsted and Vaux's view of the Park accorded with the interests of the adjacent upper-class residential neighbourhoods that have fringed the east and west sides of Central Park for the past century, historic preservation had the additional benefit of preserving the Park as their genteel front yard.

Central Park was an early step towards the urbanization of nature. For Riverside, Illinois (1869), a new suburb nine miles west of Chicago, Olmsted, Vaux and Company furnished the developer, E. E. Childs, with a plan that featured familiar picturesque landscaping devices but rejected the isolation of the country house or the passivity of their own Central Park [74]. In contrast to Downing, who ridiculed the 'cockneyism' of those who wanted urban comforts in the country, Olmsted and Vaux accepted 'the strong tendency of people to flock together in great towns'. They offered 'not a sacrifice of urban conveniences, but their combination with the special charms and substantial advantages of rural conditions of life' on a site conceived as a village. Streets curved, but not so much as to impede real-estate sales, creating an effect that was 'informal, but, in a moderate way, positively picturesque', and periodically diverged to form small open spaces that were intended to function as village greens, giving a sociable quality to the plan that was augmented with a park and a promenading ground. 'The grand fact that they are Christians, loving one another, and not Pagans, fearing one another [is to be recognized in] the completeness, and choiceness and beauty of the means they possess of coming together, of being together, and especially of recreating together on

76

Baldwin Hills Village.
Plan of garage court and
flanking garden courts.
The village green is at the
bottom of the plan.

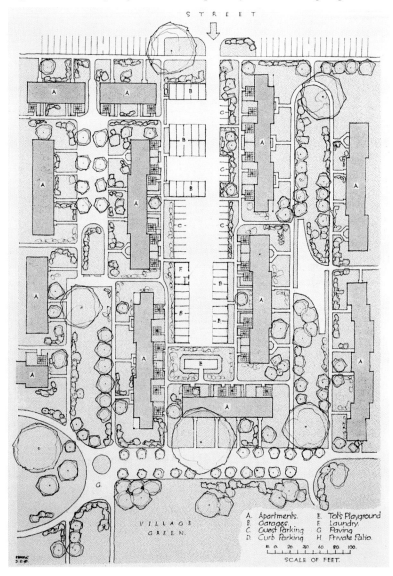

common ground', Olmsted wrote.[12]

Sociable nature also characterized the work of the architects, planners, and social thinkers who comprised the Regional Planning Association of America, the sponsors of a series of highly visible housing schemes between the 1920s and the 1940s. Like their nineteenth-century forebears, the RPAA sought to create a modern, benevolent capitalist city, with nature as a critical element, but their personal tastes leaned towards romantic, anti-modern anti-urbanism. In an introduction to Clarence Stein's *Toward New Towns for America* (1957), a valedictory summary of the RPAA's achievements written by one of its most active planners, Lewis Mumford recalled that the group's avocations included square dancing and performing Appalachian folk ballads, under the leadership of environmental planner Benton MacKaye. Inspired by the common stereotype of the upland South as a primitive land untouched by time or urban civilization—a white ancestral homeland—MacKaye had created a regional plan that would use modern technology to protect the traditional ways of life of 'that primeval area'.[13]

It is not surprising that the RPAA's notion of a city wasn't very urban. At first they were influenced by the English garden city movement, which proposed limiting the sizes of cities and using open space to buffer them and break up their masses. They hoped to build an American garden city but the closest they came was the never-completed Radburn, New Jersey (1928–33), an outlying suburb of New York City and their best-known effort.

Radburn was uncharacteristic. Most RPAA projects were located in or at the edges of cities and resembled Riverside in their subordination of nature to sociability. Baldwin Hills Village, Los Angeles (1940–1), the last RPAA undertaking, was built on an eighty-acre super-block in the path of, but just beyond, the city's development. A central Village Green served as a spine that radiated fingerlike 'garden courts' [**75**] [**76**]. Two-storey apartment buildings that Stein called row houses faced the courts.

Baldwin Hills Village incorporated an unstable mixture of nature and culture. Stein presented the scheme as a haven from the city, and particularly from the automobile. He likened Americans' attachment to their cars to a European peasant's need to keep cattle in the house. In comparing the automobile, the quintessential sign of twentieth-century urbanism, to the savage, the rustic, the unurbane, Stein harkened back to the old notion of the alienated quality of the un-natural and the uncultivated. Still, he acknowledged that Los Angeles was an automobile city and sought a way to incorporate the convenience of cars while minimizing their hazards. The solution was to separate the garden courts by garage courts based on the cul-de-sacs pioneered at Radburn. The houses faced the garden courts, while the

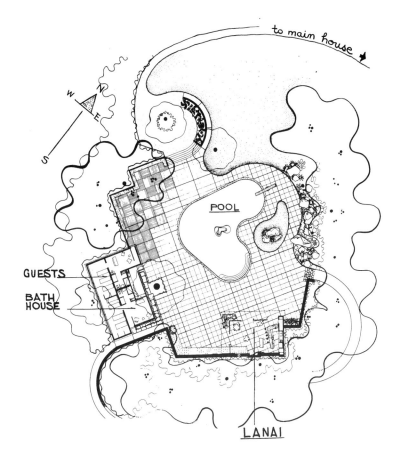

garage courts provided automobile access at the perimeter of the site, convenient to each apartment but away from the open spaces and pedestrian pathways.

Baldwin Hills Village's planners assumed the benefits of nature and even incorporated a hint of the sublime into the site. The primary function of the green 'is visual,' Stein wrote, 'or perhaps I should say spiritual. The calm, long, orderly lines of the row houses and contrasting sweep of the brown hills behind—low hills though they are, they seem to tower above the domestic space of the homes—give the feeling of spreading spaciousness'.[14]

Stein hoped that the natural environment would produce a 'natural' community, even though he acknowledged that the Village Green was underused. Children remained close to home in the garden courts and adults showed a regrettable preference for spending time in the small fenced-in patios behind each ground-floor unit rather than in the open communal spaces. The anti-social implications of romantic nature accepted by planners and tenants alike compromised the efforts of those who claimed to be the city's partisans. Urbanizing nature undermined the foundations of urban life.

Despite their state's reputation since the early twentieth century as a nature-obsessed place, Californians have been quite energetic in domesticating the natural. For Thomas D. Church, the senior member of a school of California modernist landscape architects, the challenge of California was to create landscapes that could succeed within the constraints of the state's semi-arid climate and its rugged terrain. Church liked to say that 'gardens are for people', by which he meant that, rather than submitting to the discipline of the country as Downing argued, nature should be shaped to the economy and domestic habits of mid-century Californians. This entailed no obligation to imitate, or even to respect, natural terrain or plantings; the spirit of the place was social and economic, not topographical. Church strove to create well-defined spaces of limited extent through the use of paving, raised planting beds, and screening walls. The curvilinear pool at his hilltop Donnell Garden (1948–9) was vaguely organic in shape, but made no pretence to naturalistic imagery [**77**]. Rather than strive for the picturesque effect of extensive vistas and the illusion of unlimited control, a border of shrubbery separated the pool area from the distant landscape. One opening framed a glimpse of the countryside as a picture, after the fashion of a Japanese gardening technique called *shakkei*, or borrowed scenery, which drafted distant landscapes into the service of undisguisedly constricted gardens [**78**].

78

Donnell Garden.
View towards distant
landscape.

Church's Donnell Garden suggests how far the metaphor of the *genius loci* had drifted in modernist design from its original meaning in picturesque theory: Downing's cockneyism had triumphed in the country. The landscape was closely controlled; the California modernists made no claim to naturalism.

Strict subordination of nature constitutes the dominant popular vernacular attitude toward the natural, as well. Houses painted white or other light colours, distinguished from the surrounding landscape in colour and shape, convey the image of preference [**79**]. Carefully tended lawns are prized even in dry places like Phoenix, Salt Lake City, or Los Angeles, where they require constant infusions of water. Foundation plantings and flower borders are protected by picket or chain-link fences. Since Olmsted and Vaux, nature at home and in the city has been an amenity rather than the radical challenge to urban life that Downing enunciated. As the 'natural' recedes from the twentieth-century city, those seeking 'untamed' nature are forced to find it in the large national parks established within easy automobile-striking distance of most large cities over the past hundred years. The consequent surge in the parks' popularity has revived, nineteenth-century debates over nature and culture, active and passive recreation, sociability and solitude.

Place

By the twentieth century the clichés of the *genius loci* and the constellation of nature-culture metaphors had become part of the instinctive vocabulary of American architecture but their meanings had become so diffuse that they could be used in support of quite disparate architectures. The idea of the *genius loci*, for example, splintered into very different attitudes towards place. Drenched as it is in the rhetoric of Nature, the truism that a building needs to be tied to place is rendered ambiguous.

80 Fay Jones and Associates

Thorncrown Chapel, 1980,
Eureka Springs, Ark.

Fay Jones and Associates came close to a literal application of Downing's precept that the building should blend visually with its site in their mountainside Thorncrown Chapel (1980) [**80**]. The chapel rephrases the aisled, masonry, compression structure of a medieval church as a light wooden structure built of two-by-fours layered over one another in some places and joined end to end with metal fittings in others, resulting in a frame that works in tension. The old myth that Gothic vaulting was an imitation of the forest comes to mind and the association is strengthened by the immaculately clean, nearly invisible glazed walls that make the roof timbering appear to be part of the natural canopy of trees that envelops the chapel. The enclosing glass and the name allude to a particular medieval building, the Sainte-Chapelle in Paris, built as a reliquary to house the crown of thorns. The Thorncrown Chapel, although owned by fundamentalists, is a reliquary of pantheistic Nature in the romantic tradition. The surrounding forest acts both as the object of devotion and and as a substitute for the decoration furnished at the Sainte-Chapelle by its renowned stained glass. An off-axis steel cross that stands outside the glass at the chancel end helps to hold the visitor's attention outside the building, an effect only slightly marred by the tape-recorded funeral-parlour organ music that fills the space and emphasizes its enclosure.

Typically, twentieth-century architects have construed the relationship of architecture and nature much more loosely than at the Thorncrown Chapel. San Francisco's Palace of Fine Arts (1915), a classical rotunda fronting a plain curving exhibition hall for works of art, was meant to evoke California [**81**]. The architect, Bernard Maybeck, was anxious that his work should be correctly understood, so published his own interpretation of it. Maybeck assumed that a building should convey a feeling appropriate to its contents: the tone of an art museum should be 'a modified sadness or sentiment in a minor key'. The solution was to create a rotunda and colonnade that resembled a

PHOTO TIMOTHY HURSLEY, LITTLE ROCK, ARK.

81 Bernard Maybeck

Palace of the Fine Arts, 1915,
San Francisco.

Like many exposition buildings, Maybeck's Palace was constructed in plaster for the Panama-Pacific International Exhibition. It was reconstructed in concrete in 1962.

82 Frank Lloyd Wright

Fallingwater (Liliane S. and Edgar J. Kauffman, Sr, Residence), 1935–6, Bear Run, Pa.

Viewed from the approach, Wright's famous house appears much different— more urbane and more European in appearance— than in the more familiar view taken from a difficult-to-reach spot in the stream below the house.

Roman ruin, then surround it with a modern landscape inspired by California's topography. Clear Lake, a hundred miles north-east of San Francisco, was a model for the small pond with islands that, to Maybeck's mind, provided a foreground with just the right note of melancholy for his building.[15]

Maybeck's interpretation derived from a version of picturesque theory called associationalism. Associationalists urged designers to manipulate mental connections, or associations, between times, places, events, or moods and the visual forms characteristic of them to elicit emotional responses to architecture. In this manner, Maybeck sought to evoke the essence of California without drawing on a localized historicism. He wished instead to create a union of place and architecture through borrowing the qualities of nature.

Over the course of a long career, Maybeck's (and Church's) contemporary Frank Lloyd Wright embraced all the many variants of the natural metaphor in complex ways and folded them all into his umbrella word *organic*. *Organic* meant natural in its simplest sense of growing, but it also encompassed the romantic opposition of the natural and the human, meaning the artificial, the rational, and the mechanical. The organic was something unforced, faithful to the inherent qualities of things. *Organic* could refer to sites and building materials, but also to people and societies that were uncorrupted and faithful to immanent natural impulses. In this sense, human works could be organic rather than artificial: 'The old architecture, always dead for me as far as its grammar went, began literally to disappear. As if by magic, new effects came to life, as though by themselves, and I could draw inspiration from Nature herself. I was beholden to no man for the look of anything. Textbook for me? "The book of creation" '.[16]

Fallingwater (1935–6), Wright's vacation retreat for a family of Pittsburgh department-store owners, was organic in all these senses [**82**]. From the approach drive, the low, horizontal, banded building resembled one of Wright's Prairie houses redesigned by a 1920s European modernist. In the nineteenth-century tradition to which Wright clung, a variety of architectural devices blurred the line between the outside and the inside, the natural domain and the human. A trellis covered the entrance walk, echoed by another in the living-room ceiling. The living-room trellis opened that room to the sky, while stairs under it led down to Bear Run. In addition, Wright shielded the interior spaces with deeply projecting balconies analogous to the enveloping porches of a Victorian house, and at the same time enclosed the house with glass walls set in thin, unobtrusive metal casements. A native boulder was left in place near the living-room hearth, and the fireplaces throughout the house were made to appear as though they had been carved out of living rock. The total effect, as the plan suggests, is one of a cave from which to look out on the surrounding woods, although Wright said that he strove to create not caves but 'broad shelter[s] in the open' [**83**]. At first glance, then, Wright seems to have sought a union of house and site far more extreme than any Downing dreamed.

At second glance, no nineteenth-century picturesque designer would have understood Wright's decision to place Fallingwater directly over the site's most striking feature, a small waterfall on Bear Run. The architect trumped conventional natural beauty with his own work, whose visual appeal derived, as in so many of his buildings, from an idiosyncratic structure. Four concrete piers lifted the house above the stream and anchored it into the rock of the hillside. The balconies

83

Fallingwater.
Main-level plan. As usual, the servant-staffed kitchen is excluded from the openness of the family parts of the house.

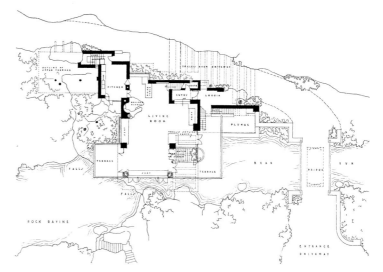

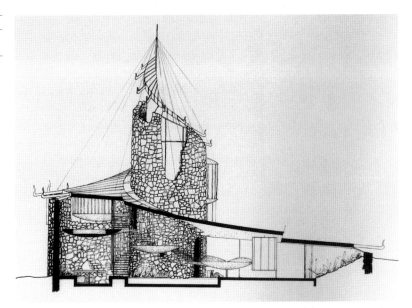

84 Bruce Goff

Bavinger House, 1950–5,
Norman, Okla.
Section.

85 Henry I. Greber

J. C. Nichols Memorial Fountain,
1950, Kansas City, Mo.
Greber depicts Plains Indians
as wood sprites, in a fountain
honouring the founder of a
pioneering shopping-centre
and housing development
[**157**]. (Kansas City seems to
enjoy imagining its
businessmen as heroic figures:
a monument to another local
merchant takes the form of a
cowboy on a bucking bronco.)

and their rails projected on a series of concrete trays. The disparity between the stone verticals and the concrete cantilevers might be read as
either a contest or a partnership between the natural forces of gravity
and the human ingenuity that defied them. The contrast would have
been even more striking had the concrete been gold-leafed and the
window muntins been painted a brighter red as Wright wished.

In Wright's special terminology, both Fallingwater and its site were
organic; the difficult relationship between nature and culture was unresolved. In this context, it is worth noting that the famous view of
Fallingwater, the one that celebrates Wright's dominance of the site
most explicitly, can be seen only after clambering down a wooded bank
to balance precariously on a rock in mid-stream.

The Primitive

At the Bavinger House (1950–5) in Norman, Oklahoma, Bruce Goff
strove to depict the organic literally [**84**]. The plan is a logarithmic
spiral whose continuous wall rises from a height of six feet at the
outside to fifty feet at the centre. The roof was suspended by cables
from a central mast but not connected directly to the walls. Originally
the open interior was a water-garden fitted with pools, plantings, and
a waterfall, within which living areas were defined by suspended
platforms.

Goff, who briefly worked for Wright, strove for a picturesque image
of nature intensified, rejecting anything that resembled conventional
architecture or the product of human skills. The rough rock and
irregular openings of the walls were designed to be made by the owners
and their friends, and to look as though they had been. The redeeming
value of cheap unskilled handwork, unspoiled by training or sophist-

86 Antoine Predock
Centennial Complex,
American Heritage Center
and Art Museum, 1986–93,
University of Wyoming,
Laramie, Wyo.

Rows of pueblo-like blocks
lead to the building's tipi-
like cone.

ication, is a central tenet of an anti-artificial moralism that pervades much American architecture. Yet the naturalism of the Bavinger House was a transparent metaphor: the spiral plan, structure, and pools and plantings were unmistakable products of human ingenuity, as carefully engineered as Fallingwater. Furthermore, the house was as controlling as it was controlled. Its idiosyncratic plan and structure limited domestic life, while the Oklahoma climate made the interior with its pools almost unliveable, and they were eventually filled.

For all its deliberately individualistic imagery, the Bavinger House belonged to the mainstream of a primitivist tradition. Unlike the comfortable and accommodating picturesque, primitivism appears at first glance to be an uncompromising rejection of culture. It holds that whatever is human-made is artificial, refined, corrupt, but also effete, while whatever is wild and unmarked by humanity is pure, natural, innocent, and powerful. The primitive is a corollary of the sublime. An architecture that strips away all the debilitating effects of civilization risks exposing us to the consequences of our own unadulterated, uncivilized natures: Norman legend claims (wrongly) that the Bavinger House had driven the family's sons insane.[17] Primitivism, as much as any other version of the natural metaphor, is an exploration of the nature of humanity, its failures and its needs.

Primitivism was born of Enlightenment anthropology and the popular-culture figure of the noble savage uncorrupted by institutions, whom Europeans believed they had met in eighteenth-century Polynesia. Jean-Jacques Rousseau's *The Social Contract* (1762) made the noble savage intellectually respectable through its speculations about the nature of humanity before civil life—in a 'state of nature'.[18] In the United States it was easy for whites to see Native Americans as noble savages, a stereotype that was overlaid on, but did not replace, the hostile assessments of earlier generations. In the abstract, the Indian became a kind of wood-sprite, a natural force or a naturalized version of the elves and fairies of European mythology, as in Kansas City's J. C. Nichols Memorial Fountain (1950), where an Indian in a Plains war-bonnet battled an alligator, a creature not normally found on the Great Plains [85]. The pair coexisted in mythological space as allegories of the distinctive American landscape.

The American Heritage Center and Art Museum (1986–93) at the University of Wyoming draws on the same assumptions, though more subtly. The main structure, a concrete cone sitting on its haunches, resembles a Plains Indian tipi. The reference is reinforced by an interior timber frame that resembles lodge poles, the smoke hole at the top, and the exterior skin which appears like the rolled-back covering of a tent [86]. Local people call the cone The Tipi, but the architect, Antoine Predock, describes it as a mountain aligned with others in the landscape. There is no contradiction; as we have seen, the association of

The carefully posed Grass
Dancers are meant to be a
portrait of the unchanged
primitive but the photograph
instead documents cultural
change. The Grass Dance was
a response to the
disappearance of the buffalo
and old ways of life in the face
of white settlement, and the
dancers stand in front of a
European-type log house that
19th-century viewers would
have equated with the men
standing in front of it.

buildings with land-forms is a common Native American metaphor.
Stretching out from the tipi-mountain, which houses archives, is a
long flat art museum whose galleries project as a series of brick-
coloured cubes. Predock has likened these to a village at the foot of the
mountain, and their colour and shape calls to mind an abstracted Rio
Grande pueblo, or a butte.[19] In short, Native Americans are once more
drafted into service as *genii loci*, naturalized by being associated with
land-forms. The cubes also resemble the towers at the rear of Kahn's
Salk Institute [**69**]. The association with Kahn's building triply legitimizes Predock's design by triangulating it between the land, a canoni-
cal monument of high modernist design, and a classic modernist myth
of indigenous building, which held that the elemental geometries of
'architecture without architects' were products of a natural aesthetic
unspoiled by overly sophisticated, effete professional education. Folk
builders tapped intuitively into the powerful living visual forms that
great architecture requires. This is the essence of the primitivist
metaphor, and Predock uses it to turn historical cultural symbols into
universal formal images.

Such explicit allusions to Native American buildings have been
more common in popular architecture than in high-style design. The
still-prevalent assumption that American Indians are uncorrupted and
directly attuned with nature was responsible for the late-nineteenth-
century beginnings of anthropological and folkloristic study of indigenous people and their architecture, and it fired the imaginations of hosts
of artists, including George Catlin, Frederick Remington, and
Edward Curtis, all of whom produced heavily romanticized images of
Native American life [**87**]. By extension, all people who reside far from
metropolitan centres or in some other sense lived a 'primitive' life were

pure, strong, and admirable; so was their architecture. Log houses—
and folk architecture in general—have become pervasive emblems of
the primitive.

Log construction is an ancient, intricate, highly sophisticated
technology that was widely used in both Europe and North America
for large and substantial buildings. It requires the iron tools of civilization, and the majority of log structures were much more carefully
crafted than the crude round-log buildings of popular imagination. In
defiance of these inconvenient facts, log construction is the architectural sign of wilderness and the simple life, employed in prefabricated
rural houses, summer camps, and even the huge log resort hotels built
in national parks since the end of the nineteenth century.

At the same time, their imaginative connection to the land and
to the farmers who worked it made log houses, like Indians, seem
characteristically American. Since the primitive and the unspoiled was
by definition the upright and the moral, the log house became the
quintessential home of the sturdy yeoman. Nineteenth-century architectural handbook writers such as Charles P. Dwyer and John Bullock
promoted log building as a form of cheap construction appropriate for
the average homebuilder.

As an aboriginal form, the log house was the quintessential
birthplace. Beginning with the 'Log Cabin Campaign' of 1840, even
the wealthiest presidential candidates thought it expedient to claim
to have been born in one, while villages, schools, and other institutions often preserved log houses as their most ancient relics, even

when they were not.

The originary and moral implications of primitivism found reinforcement in European primitivist theories that understood the earliest or crudest forms of classicism as the purest. A log 'American House' published in Alexander Jackson Davis's *Rural Residences* of 1837 fused the American and European strains in turning the logs upright in the manner of classical columns. Davis's log house alluded to the French neo-classical theorist Marc-Antoine Laugier's renowned primitive hut, the origin of architecture, and to the Vitruvian theory of the origins of classicism, available to Americans in a host of native and imported architectural handbooks.

Although the primitive is rooted in the sublime, then, its architectural expressions have been derived from the picturesque, as the example of log building, symbol of primitive purity and of American cultural values, demonstrates. El Alisal (1897–1910), built by its owner Charles F. Lummis in the Arroyo Seco, Highland Park, Los Angeles, epitomizes this American fusion of primitive and picturesque naturalism [**88**]. Lummis was a student of western life in a primitivist mode. Among the first to look closely at the south-western Indians, especially the Pueblos, he founded the Southwest Museum in Los Angeles. He was also interested in the history of Spanish-Mexican California and helped found the Landmarks Club, first restorers of the California missions. Lummis wrote scholarly books on all these topics, but he was also a popularizer who edited *Land of Sunshine* magazine and published *The Home of Ramona* (1886), which gave credence to the belief that the Estudillo House, a Mexican vernacular building in San Diego, had been the home of the entirely fictional title character of Helen Hunt Jackson's best-selling novel.

Lummis's house synthesized his interests architecturally. The long, narrow, L-shaped, rustic structure, formed of stones pulled from the Arroyo Seco by Lummis and his crew of Indian labourers from Isleta Pueblo, New Mexico, was surrounded by a garden composed only of native plants. Visually, El Alisal cobbled together images of 'primitive' indigenous New Mexico and 'primitive' Spanish-Mexican California. The guest houses resembled pueblos, while the main house sported an espadaña (bell gable) modelled on the Mission San Gabriel outside Los Angeles. The main room, El Museo, was another Jeffersonian Indian Room, filled with Navajo blankets, Indian pots, and regional crafts. The stony terrain, the Indians of the south-west, and the Spanish-Mexican colonists were all rolled together into one synoptic image of primitive, picturesque, natural California.

The Simple Life

As Lummis was completing El Alisal, architects Charles and Henry Greene built houses in Pasadena, a few miles up the Arroyo Seco, that have been called 'ultimate bungalows'. The name and the idea of the bungalow originated in south Asia, but as it was transplanted from country to country in the late nineteenth century the bungalow was so radically transformed that little but the name remained to recall its origins. In turn-of-the-century American popular culture, small wooden bungalows were associated particularly closely with California.

The bungalow had a double appeal in a rapidly growing but relatively underdeveloped state. Bungalow advocate Henry H. Saylor jokingly defined a bungalow as 'a house that looks as if it had been built for less money than it actually cost'.[20] It was simple in outline and decoration, efficient in layout and equipment, relatively cheap, and peculiarly suited to a simple, informal, servantless domestic life. As a result, the bungalow became the building block of lower-middle-class California urban and suburban neighbourhoods and served also as farm housing in rural districts of the state.

Bungalows were more than cheap shelter: they represented, in Saylor's view, a life-style more than a house type. Their 'natural', informal, unpretentious appearance reinforced the popular image of California as a healthy place where one could live a 'bully' life, in direct contact with nature, and virtually without working. As a popular song put it, California was

> the home of the orange blossom,
> …the land of fruit and honey,
> Where it does not take much money,
> To own a little Bungalow.[21]

In short, bungalows fused metaphors of nature as a restorative force and nature as primitive moralism with intimations of effortless life into a recognizable image that could be bought and sold.

Such images appealed to immigrants of all social classes to the Golden State. In 'Dear Okie' country singer Doye O'Dell evoked the power of California's pastoral reputation in attracting Okies and Arkies, migrants from the Dust Bowl states of Oklahoma and Arkansas, to the state's Central Valley in the 1930s. Rather than employment 'Rakin' up gold/playin' fiddle in the follies', however, they found only backbreaking agricultural labour awaiting them.[22] Bungalows and the bungalow style of living were for farm managers and owners; dust-bowl migrants lived in government-sponsored Farm Security Administration housing if they were lucky, in owner-provided shacks, tents, or their own vehicles if they were not. 'Now he'll be lucky if he finds a place to live,' sang O'Dell. 'But there's orange juice fountains flowing for those kids of his.'

For those at the top of the social scale California was truly a playland, a respite from the formality and the hectic pace of eastern industrial cities. These were the clients of the Greenes' ultimate bungalows.

89 Greene and Greene

Gamble House, 1908,
Pasadena, Calif.

Rear.

The mansion-sized Gamble House (1908), a winter residence for Cincinnati soap manufacturer David B. Gamble, can be called a bungalow only in the sense that it embodies an overscaled interpretation of bungalow imagery and lifeways [**89**]. Like the ubiquitous humble bungalows of Los Angeles, it was a shingle-covered frame house unembellished with the formal architectural elements and building materials preferred by the wealthy in other regions of the country (and occasionally in California). The Greenes employed standard images of domesticity, including deep sheltering eaves and cantilevered sleeping porches that extended the interior living space beyond the walls.

At the Gamble House, nature served as a metaphor for region and site. The stained-glass panels around the entrance and in the ground-floor rooms depict the live oaks and golden hills that turn-of-the-century Californians associated with their state. A rear terrace extends the living space out into the grounds, a strategy the California modernists later used. Clinker bricks, deformed by the heat of the brick kiln into twisted, quasi-organic shapes and mixed with roughly shaped stones, enclose the terrace and form the foundation of the house, fusing building and site.

The Gamble House garden works another variant on the picturesque theme of 'nature improved'. Here it is improved in ways that incorporate elements borrowed from Japanese Zen gardens. At the

90

Gamble House.

The quasi-Japanese character of the joinery in the entrance hall and living-room is most evident in the truss that defines the inglenook. It recalls the *karahafu* eaves and 'frog-crotch' brackets of 17th-century Japanese timber building.

same time, the timber framing, particularly the interior decorative joinery, evokes Japanese carpentry traditions [**90**]. To Americans in the early twentieth century, and particularly to Californians, Japan was a highly aestheticized culture, held close to nature by its indigenous religion, Shinto. The unspoiled, quasi-primitive values of the Japanese were evident in their simple, caring craftwork, which stood in stark opposition to the shoddy products of industrial civilization. The Japanese-style joinery of the Gamble House was thus in keeping with the relative informality of the house: honest joinery was appropriate to the natural wood and simple living spaces. Yet simplicity was created at great cost and through great exertion, for show. Many of the joints are in fact held together by concealed wood-screws.

The Gamble House synthesizes most variations of the natural metaphor, and illustrates its great power and organizing role in the American built landscape. It illustrates as well the way that the naturalism so ardently promoted as a way of life by its advocates can easily be transformed into a commodity for sale. With enough money, the Gambles demonstrated, one could buy the simple life unavailable to those who truly worked the land.

Act Naturally

Picturesque naturalism, primitivism, and the search for the simple life all treated the human-nature relationship morally and psychologically.

From these perspectives, they examined what nature could do for people and what civilization had done to them. A third strain of naturalist thought has focused on the physical—what is now called the *ecological* or *environmental*—consequences of human building in the natural world. In recent decades architectural environmentalism has been allied with lay people and scientists concerned with calculating the broader economic, biological, and psychic costs of human actions to the land. Yet concern for architecture's environmental qualities—its role as a physical mediator between people and nature and its effects on the natural world—dates back at least to the nineteenth century.

Comfort, health, and economics have dominated environmental experimentation in architecture until recently. Mid-nineteenth-century domestic advisers offered their readers the latest medical findings about the effects of heating and ventilation on human health. Simply put, people needed access to adequate 'good' air and needed even more to escape or ventilate the 'bad' air that their own bodies produced. The encircling porches of nineteenth-century houses thus acquired a hygienic rationale, and gradually the interior of the house was opened up to nature's healthful breezes as well. By the turn of the century, open-air dining-rooms and sleeping porches (such as those at the Gamble House) allowed middle-class householders to live daily life exposed to the elements, something vernacular builders had anticipated in the common practice of painting, plastering, or otherwise decorating front porches like interior rooms [91].

The Depression, coupled with a recurrent quest among architects and social reformers to create affordable single-family houses for larger numbers of Americans, raised the question of energy-conservative design for economic reasons long before it appeared that energy supplies might be exhausted. Chicago architects William and George Fred Keck, intrigued by information on optimal solar orientations published by the Royal Institute of British Architects in 1931–2, began to experiment with orientation and the use of large panes of window glass for heat gain. Later, they designed more ambitious passive-solar devices, including external aluminium blinds housed in pockets to control the heat and light in rooms, deep eaves to screen out the high-angle summer sun but not the low-angle winter sun, and even a roof-top pool to cut heat gain through reflection and evaporation [92]. With the introduction of Thermopane glass in 1935, George Fred Keck began to design houses as long south-facing strings, with corridors and service spaces providing insulation along the north side.

After World War II, Massachusetts architect Eleanor Raymond designed a passive-solar house as part of a series of experiments in new, cheaper house-building technologies funded by her patron, Amelia Peabody. Raymond built a 'sun-heated house' for Peabody at Dover, Massachusetts, in 1948 [93]. As in the Kecks' houses, Raymond's con-

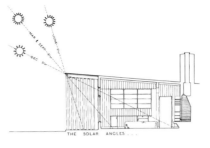

tained a long south-facing string of rooms under an enormous shed-roof. The entire upper south façade was the solar collector, glazed with ten-foot-high double sheets of glass backed by a thin black-painted metal sheet. Fans in an air space behind the glass blew the heat into pockets between the first-floor rooms. These 'heat bins' contained metal drums filled with a sodium compound that stored heat for up to eight days and distributed it to the living spaces as needed.

Although Raymond's system was weak and had to be replaced by conventional heating within four years, the houses of the 1930s and 1940s are the direct predecessors of the passive-solar technologies (and even, in Raymond's case, the photovoltaic cells) of later decades. A group of California state office buildings constructed during the Jerry Brown administration as experiments in energy conservation employed many of the concepts of the Keck-Raymond era in more sophisticated form. In the best-known of these structures, the Bateson Building (1978) in Sacramento, the Office of the State Architect was charged with saving 75 per cent of energy costs [**94**]. To accomplish this, the architects took lessons from the 1930s. Every side of the Kahnian concrete-and-wood-panel exterior differs according to its exposure. The southern windows are shaded with deep trellises and decks, while the eastern and western façades are fitted with retractable

93 Eleanor Raymond
Sun-heated house, 1948,
Dover, Mass.
What appear to be second-
storey windows are the
solar collectors of the single-
storey dwelling.

canvas shades, and the northern elevation is glazed with flush clear panes.

The interior of the Bateson Building is organized around a four-storey courtyard that serves as a thermal buffer and air-circulation space [**95**]. The sawtooth monitors are fitted with louvres on their south faces to control heat gain but unshaded on the north to admit light. Four tall fan-ventilated canvas tubes prevent thermal stratification by circulating the air in the courtyard. The most important energy-conservative devices are invisible. A rock bed under the building acts as a thermal mass. Night air circulated over the rocks cools them and they in turn cool the internal air of the building during the day. One of the architects, Peter Calthorpe, described the Bateson Building as a living organism that would respond almost sentiently to changes in environmental conditions. It did not, for many of the passive-solar devices have never worked as intended.

The technically sophisticated Bateson Building has a social as well as an environmental agenda. The scale and exterior appearance of the building are intended to make it a friendly neighbour in a largely residential district. Clearly visible paths of interior circulation guide visitors to their destinations. In addition, the architects originally imagined that the workers would be organized in groups of twelve to

94

Office of the State Architect,
Bateson Building, 1978,
Sacramento, Calif.

South façade.

twenty-four people, who would control the lights, ventilation, and other environmental amenities in their own areas. Natural ventilation and lighting were placed in the service of a 'natural' community of workers and neighbours.

Calthorpe's image of the building as a sentient being responding to its congenial human community, a kind of artificial Nature nurturing its human occupants, is telling. It propels the Bateson Building from the technical domain of building science back into the metaphorical realm of nature and culture. Environmental commentators have rarely resisted the temptation to inject a moral dimension into their consideration of the interaction of people and nature. For the designers of the Bateson Building it was important to conserve energy, not merely to save tax dollars but also because humans have an ethical responsibility to minimize their impact on the natural world.

The corollary of guilt about what humans have done to nature is the fear of nature's vengeance. In mid-nineteenth-century New Orleans, for example, physicians explained the city's frequent yellow-fever epidemics as the product of the confluence of great heat, the 'putrefying vegetal matter' of the primeval swamps on which the city was built, and the respiration of the human population. Although their analyses were framed in the language of science, they derived from the discourse of nature, from a fear that epidemics might be Nature's way of avenging our insults. Urbanites paid a price for their own existence, they believed. New Orleans physician Edward H. Barton produced an elaborate map showing the places in the city where yellow fever were most prevalent. These were the sites of excavations to construct levees and drainage canals necessary to make the site usable. When people bruised Nature's body, Nature struck back.

To put it another way, Nature's body is our body: whatever we do to her, we do to ourselves. Recent green (ecological) designers carry this line of imagery a step farther. Greens see contemporary environmental problems as products of consumer society that has lost this sense of the oneness of Nature's body and our own. Nature has been reduced to a commodity that we consume, or use up, frivolously—we waste it. The builders of the Integral Urban House, a Berkeley ecological experiment of the 1970s, claimed that the 'typical home now largely wastes the solar income it daily receives', then went on to describe the toll this extravagant house exacted from the far-flung ecosystems that sustained it and from the local community to which it bequeathed its wastes. They concluded that the average home was 'a total parasite', so 'it is not surprising that the occupants experienced themselves as victims or, at best, ineffectual ciphers in a large, impersonal centralized system'.[23] In the course of one paragraph, the saga of the typical house was transformed from one of wasteful human consumption of nature to one in which people and nature were equally victimized by an abstract economic system.

For green designers, acknowledgement of human alienation from nature reveals a remedy, for if people consume nature in the alienated, modern economic sense, they also consume it in a physiological sense. They ingest, transform, and excrete nature as part of the process of life. In relating the story of a composting privy at the Green Gulch commune in Marin County, California, ecological designers Sim Van der Ryn, an architect of the Bateson Building, and Stuart Cowan observed that when commune members helped the architects to design the privy, the 'involvement necessarily connected them with their own biological processes'.[24] This imagery is quite explicit in the National Audubon Society Headquarters, New York, a 1990–1 retrofitting project of the Croxton Collaborative. The building was renovated using materials salvaged from the remodelling, and contains elaborate systems for feeding off itself by recycling and reusing its waste products. Consumer waste was transformed to natural waste feeding growth.

In short, a long-standing empirical concern for the biological and physiological costs of human building and an equally long-standing fear of the moral consequences of environmental degradation have become in green design a tale of the self embedded problematically in its surroundings. By commodifying and wasting the blessings of Mother Nature, we become alienated from her. In our alienation, we are alienated in turn from our own true natures, a claim that the romantics might have endorsed.

This is ultimately a theological parable. The Judaeo-Christian

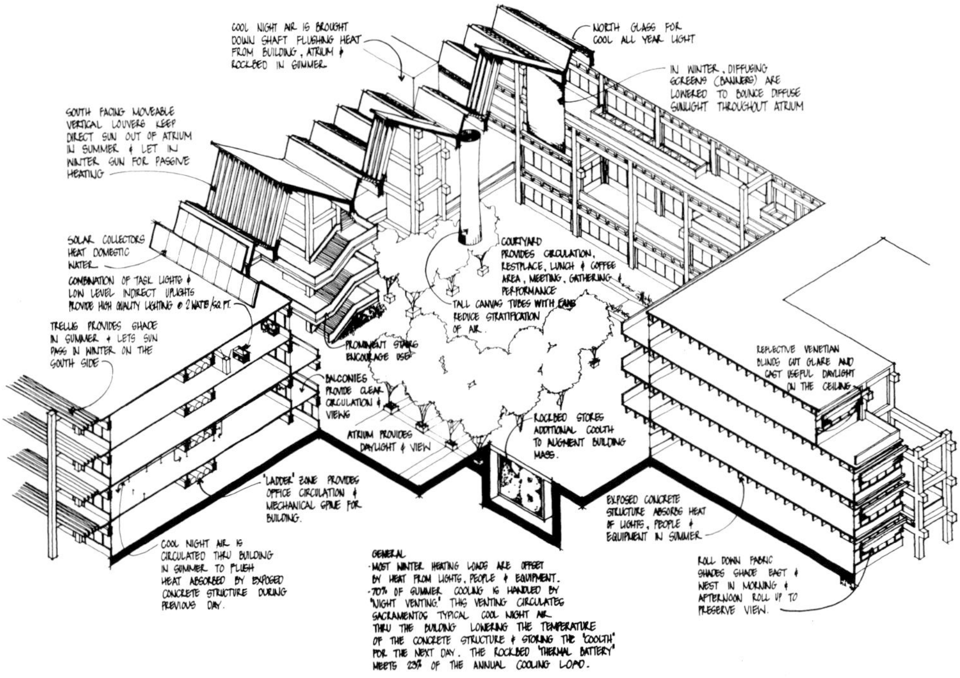

COOL NIGHT AIR IS BROUGHT DOWN SHAFT FLUSHING HEAT FROM BUILDING, ATRIUM & ROCKBED IN SUMMER
NORTH GLASS FOR COOL ALL YEAR LIGHT
IN WINTER, DIFFUSING SCREENS (BANNERS) ARE LOWERED TO BOUNCE DIFFUSE SUNLIGHT THROUGHOUT ATRIUM
SOUTH FACING MOVEABLE VERTICAL LOUVERS KEEP DIRECT SUN OUT OF ATRIUM IN SUMMER & LET IN WINTER SUN FOR PASSIVE HEATING
SOLAR COLLECTORS HEAT DOMESTIC WATER
COMBINATION OF TASK LIGHTS & LOW LEVEL INDIRECT UPLIGHTS PROVIDE HIGH QUALITY LIGHTING @ 2 WATTS/SQ FT.
COURTYARD PROVIDES CIRCULATION, RESTPLACE, LUNCH & COFFEE AREA, MEETING, GATHERING & PERFORMANCE
TALL CANVAS TUBES WITH FANS REDUCE STRATIFICATION OF AIR.
TRELLIS PROVIDES SHADE IN SUMMER & LETS SUN PASS IN WINTER ON THE SOUTH SIDE
PROMINENT STAIRS ENCOURAGE USE
BALCONIES PROVIDE CLEAR CIRCULATION & VIEWS
REFLECTIVE VENETIAN BLINDS CUT GLARE AND CAST USEFUL DAYLIGHT ON THE CEILING
ATRIUM PROVIDES DAYLIGHT & VIEW
ROCKBED STORES ADDITIONAL COOLTH TO AUGMENT BUILDING MASS.
'LADDER' ZONE PROVIDES OFFICE CIRCULATION & MECHANICAL SPINE FOR BUILDING.
EXPOSED CONCRETE STRUCTURE ABSORBS HEAT OF LIGHTS, PEOPLE & EQUIPMENT IN SUMMER
COOL NIGHT AIR IS CIRCULATED THRU BUILDING IN SUMMER TO FLUSH HEAT ABSORBED BY EXPOSED CONCRETE STRUCTURE DURING PREVIOUS DAY.
GENERAL
·MOST WINTER HEATING LOADS ARE OFFSET BY HEAT FROM LIGHTS, PEOPLE & EQUIPMENT.
·70% OF SUMMER COOLING IS HANDLED BY 'NIGHT VENTING.' THIS VENTING CIRCULATES SACRAMENTOS TYPICAL COOL NIGHT AIR THRU THE BUILDING LOWERING THE TEMPERATURE OF THE CONCRETE STRUCTURE & STORING THE 'COOLTH' FOR THE NEXT DAY. THE ROCKBED 'THERMAL BATTERY' MEETS 23% OF THE ANNUAL COOLING LOAD.
ROLL DOWN FABRIC SHADES SHADE EAST & WEST IN MORNING & AFTERNOON ROLL UP TO PRESERVE VIEW.

95

Bateson Building.

Isometric section.

ambivalence about nature and culture imported by the first European colonists re-emerges in green metaphors of environmental sin and retribution: environmental problems are a sign of guilt. Like the old Puritan deity, Nature is an avenging god, poised to strike back at those who flout her rules. The contemporary world suffers not merely from scientifically describable environmental problems, but also from a crisis of a sort unique in the history of the world, one that is fundamentally a crisis of values and that encompasses all aspects of society, economy, and technology. As a result, contemporary life is not 'sustainable', it cannot achieve a state of long-term balance. To make the right decision, to convert to ecological design, 'brings us back home'.[25] By renouncing the false gods of wasteful consumption, we can be reconciled to nature, through which waste is consumed and reborn.

In short, couched though it may be in the accoutrements of environmental and biological science and backed up by computer models, the movement towards a green architecture is a moralistic one. Hence the social aims of the Bateson Building. Following green theorist David Orr, Van der Ryn and Cowan note that mere 'technological sustainability' is insufficient: what is required is 'ecological sustainability'.[26] Ecological sustainability offers more than clean air and healthy bodies, it is a setting conducive to the 'fuller creative evolution of society and the individual'.[27]

It is difficult to imagine what such a society might look like, socially or architecturally, for the image of a sustainable society eventually dissolves into a collection of metaphors and mundane landscapes. It would be the Garden of Eden. Or it would be the resourceful hippie-frontier society of Ernest Callenbach's *Ecotopia* novels, or the macho West of Edward Abbey's Hayduke sagas. None of these fictions addresses real issues of social diversity, environmental justice (the fair distribution of inevitable environmental hazards), or differences of political values. As built—at Michael Corbett's Village Homes (1972–5) at Davis, California, or in the many projects of Calthorpe Associates—the new green communities resemble upper-middle-class commuter suburbs and resort towns more than they do moral utopias.

Technology

4

Technology extends our physical capacities in ways that we could not manage unaided. It drafts the facts of the natural world to human use. The word *technology* was coined to signify this fusion of science and art. To put it another way, the cultural realm of technology complements that of nature. Historical accident emphasizes the connection: the word was invented in 1828 by Harvard professor Jacob Bigelow, the principal founder of Mount Auburn Cemetery. Like nature, technology prompts self-reflection, calling our attention once again to the puzzling relationships of people and their environments. Technology also serves as a tool for incorporating our surroundings into personal and social identities: it is an instrument of the spiritual colonization of the physical world. In that sense, technology is part of the human-material symbiosis that we have labelled *consumption*.

For these reasons, technology must be understood as a social, and not simply a technical, issue. It is customary among architectural historians to treat technology almost as a force of nature, as a series of self-directed 'inventions' or 'developments' that have inexorably redirected architecture's trajectory. The development of the steel frame (along with the elevator, the electric light, and the telephone) led to the creation of the tall office building. The invention of the automobile was responsible for dispersed urban settlement and the destruction of urban centres. Historians of technology, on the other hand, point out that technological innovation follows demand rather than creating it. Intensified downtown land use and the subsequent dispersal of the city began decades before the steel frame or the automobile were available. Technology is to human society as the stick was to the proverbial monkey: it provides a convenient physical solution to a socially defined problem.

Work

The evolution of structural systems makes this point clearly. A principal theme in the history of construction has been the desire to extend human physical capacities and economic resources by making less labour do more work. This has been as true of the smallest structure as the largest, of the most commonplace structural system as

Detail of 119

the most innovative or idiosyncratic.

Consider the example of timber framing, the dominant structural system throughout the history of American architecture. Behind the similarity of material and the use of a skeletal structure lay a variety of differences that arose from what might be called structural logic, or the way the frame was imagined to work as a system. Eastern woodland Indian construction, as well as the rare traditional houses built by enslaved Africans, and a wide variety of simple European-American building technologies such as the palisade wall, French-American *pôteaux en terre* (posts-in-ground), Hispanic *jacal*, and the Newfoundland tilt, relied on the tensile and compressive strength of individual members, stabilized by the earth, for their structural integrity. The builders of Native Hawaiian buildings, Wichita grass houses, and Missouri River (Omaha, Hidatsa, Mandan, and Pawnee) earth lodges also relied on these qualities of the structure, but assembled them into simple unjoined post-and-beam frames reinforced by their lashed fastenings [96]. Even the massive plank-enclosed houses of the Northwest Coast Indians were stabilized primarily by the earth and the dead weight of the main frame.

96

Hidatsa twelve-post earth lodge.

Reconstruction drawing.

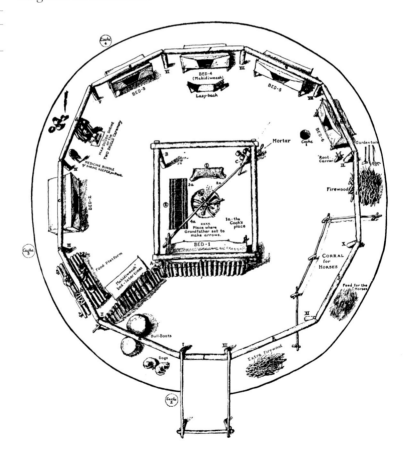

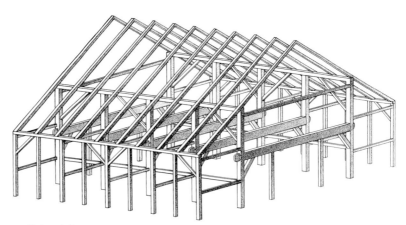

Joined frames, in which carved joints locked the parts together into a mutually supporting unit, were equally varied. Dutch, Chinese, and Northwest Coast Indian builders organized their frames into bents, quasi-independent post-and-beam units that ran across the building, creating a tunnel of space inside them [**97**]. Anglo-American traditional carpenters, on the other hand, imagined their frames as three-dimensional boxes in which each major timber was knitted to its neighbours by complex joints serving to brace it from several directions at once [**98**] [**99**].

Every part of the three-dimensional box frame was specialized. It had to be hand-crafted to fit a unique location in the frame. Carpenters' marks—Roman numerals or other signs—that aided in prefitting the wooden frames on the ground before they were erected testified to the non-interchangeability of the timbers. Not surprisingly, carpenters strove to minimize guesswork and unnecessary effort in this laborious process. Rules of thumb, simple ratios, or fixed dimensions eliminated calculations and reduced the possibility for error. Another technique was to simplify or eliminate parts. In the traditional timber frame, for example, the wall covering was attached to light vertical members, called studs, that were connected to horizontal beams at the top and bottom by mortise-and-tenon joints. In a two-storey house four joints were required, at the floor and ceiling of each level [**98**, *right end*]. The earliest Anglo-American carpenters often used studs that ran the full height of the building. A light horizontal member called a clamp or bearer was pegged to the studs' inner faces, eliminating two joints at each stud as well as the intermediate beam, or girt, into which they were tenoned [**98**, *left end*]. As an additional benefit, the second-floor joists that would otherwise have been tenoned into the girt were simply laid on the bearer, doing away with a third set of joints.

In early European America craftworkers were scarce and expensive but materials were readily available to the point that their abundance impeded development in the first years. As one Virginia colonist observed, at first 'wasting of Woods [was] an ease and a benefit to

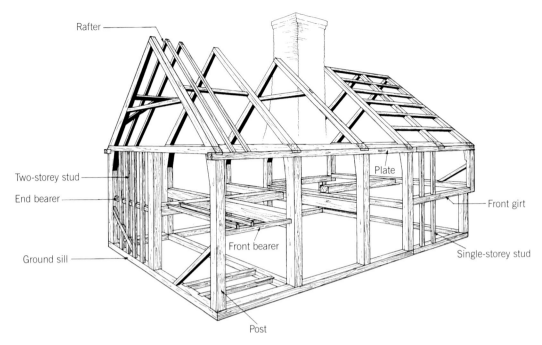

Rafter

Two-storey stud

End bearer

Ground sill

Front bearer

Post

Plate

Front girt

Single-storey stud

Gedney House, c.1665,
Salem, Mass.

The Gedney House illustrates
many of the techniques of
traditional Anglo-American
framing. The three left
structural bays were the
original portion of the house,
with the addition (c.1700) at
the right.

the Planter'.[1] This imbalance between manpower and materials re-inforced an age-old labour-conservative craft ethos. Early European-American builders were always ready to use materials profligately so as to skimp on labour. When water-powered sawmills permitted the mechanical production of building timbers, New England carpenters pushed the clamp idea a step farther, eliminating the studs altogether.[2] They nailed or pegged thick vertical planks to the exterior of the building, which braced the frame, enclosed the interior, and provided a foundation for finished surfaces all at once.

Plank framing was continually reinvented with the westward movement of European colonization. As box framing, single-wall framing, plantation construction, or balloon framing, it was used as far west as California and Hawaii, and as late as the early twentieth century. As a final step in the simplification of wooden construction, the frame itself was replaced by simple two-by-four boards nailed to the top and bottom of the planks, which now provided all the structural support.

In the seventeenth-century Chesapeake colonies tobacco, a very profitable crop at first, absorbed such vast amounts of meticulous attention during its growing season that planters preferred to invest in field hands rather than architecture. The result was a landscape comprised almost exclusively of flimsy earthfast structures. These rotted and disappeared so rapidly that only two of these buildings, Cedar Park (1702) and Sotterley (early eighteenth century), both in Maryland, survive, encased in more substantial shells.

Earthfast construction was a quick-and-dirty technique. A frame that stood in hand-excavated holes rather than on a levelled foundation was difficult to assemble with precision and it racked and sagged as its supporting members decayed. Builders made compensatory adjustments to the traditional system, jettisoning its complex joints and specialized parts. The distinctive timber framing tradition of the eighteenth- and nineteenth-century South was a legacy of these ad hoc adjustments. The timbers of the Southern frame were sawn to two standard sizes and shapes, one for structural members and one for infill, rather than hewn to individualized specifications [**100**]. Simple two-way tenoned or lapped joints were substituted for the complex multi-directional joints of the older frame, making the parts virtually interchangeable. The assembly was imagined as two long parallel walls held together at the top by floor joists notched like Lincoln logs and dropped on to them. In pursuit of a traditional goal, labour conservation, a traditional structural system had been completely reinvented.

Traditional Anglo-American framing was the ancestor of the better-known balloon frame. The historian Sigfried Giedion credited one man, George Washington Snow, with inventing that industrialized framing system, in Chicago in 1832 [**101**]. No such simple attribution is possible, however. The sawn standardized parts, simplified joints (now eliminated altogether in favour of nailed joinery), and two-storey studs and bearers (now called ledgers) link it to traditional carpentry, and particularly to the Chesapeake framing system, which had been carried west by emigrants from the upper South. Even the name balloon framing ties it to the older labour-conservative tradition. The term had first been used to designate plank or box framing, and was only later applied to light-studded structures.[3]

This new balloon framing *was* different from its traditional sources in one important way. When each nail had been made by hand, there was little advantage to nailing over joinery. After about 1790, nails could be cut rapidly and mechanically from sheets of iron. Forty years later, the invention of a machine to form heads on cut nails gave nailing the edge over joinery in speed and labour costs. The invention of fast steam-powered circular saws augmented balloon framing's advantages after 1840. Ordinary building was shifted to an entirely different, industrial footing.

Industrialization meant more than the simple use of powered machines and their products. It redefined the scale and organization of labour. In an industry, many people were involved in a single concentrated enterprise. Work that had been scattered over many *sites* was brought together at one, where powered machines could perform rapid large-scale work. On the other hand, the skills and tasks that had been performed by a single *worker* were broken down into small repetitious movements suitable for machines (which were capable of great speed

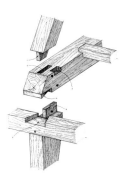

99

Fairbanks House, *c.*1637, Dedham, Mass.

This framing detail shows the four-way joint connecting (from top to bottom) the principal-rafter foot, tie beam, plate, and post.

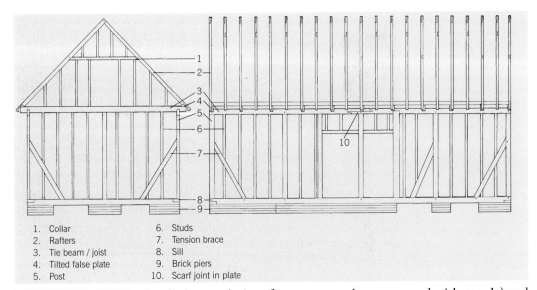

1. Collar
2. Rafters
3. Tie beam / joist
4. Tilted false plate
5. Post
6. Studs
7. Tension brace
8. Sill
9. Brick piers
10. Scarf joint in plate

100

Rich Neck Plantation Granary, early 19th century, Surry County, Va.

Chesapeake (southern) framing can be distinguished from earlier types of Anglo-American framing by the use of simple joints and light, standardized timbers.

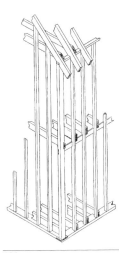

101

Balloon frame.

Like the Chesapeake frame, the balloon frame uses light, standardized timbers; however, they are nailed together rather than joined.

but little complexity of movement, when compared with people) and distributed among many workers, each assigned one small part of the whole process. This meant that the individual carpenter or building worker who devoted a variety of subtle skills to creating a unique building on one site gave way to the off-site machinist, whose equally subtle skills created a machine that could make many parts for many buildings at once. In short, building skills were not eliminated so much as centralized. Nail factories and sawmills were augmented by related industrial enterprises such as sash-and-blind factories, which made mouldings, mantels, window sashes, newels, and balusters; foundries, which created cast-iron façades, ornaments, and structural elements; sheet-metal fabrication shops; and the plants that created the many patent fixtures and wall and floor coverings installed in buildings of all sizes in nineteenth- and twentieth-century America.

This relocation of building skills narrowed the range of architectural form and appearance. Where these had once been determined independently (and sometimes idiosyncratically) on site, many choices were now reduced to the selection from a predetermined catalogue. Economies of scale facilitated by the industrialization of building made popular architecture available to a broader spectrum of the population, at the cost of variation in the detail and texture of the landscape and of the reduction in building workers' control over the conditions and economic value of their labour.

Just as the speed and power of machines extended the capacities of individual workers, it also extended their geographical range. Skilled labour no longer needed to reside in the same place as the construction project. Industrialized building materials helped to erase inequalities in the distribution of architectural forms. Labour could be exported in this manner from locales with more materials, more capital for

Quonset hut, *c.*1945, Z-Bar Ranch, near Strong City, Kan. Their lightness, ease of assembly and disassembly, and inexpensive materials made Quonset huts, originally manufactured for military use during World War II, readily adaptable for agricultural, commercial, and residential use after the war. This one is a farm equipment shed.

investing in equipment, or more skilled workers, to developing regions with fewer of any of these resources.

Prefabrication was the most comprehensive application of mechanization to building. To produce mass housing through industrial means—'Houses Like Fords' was the memorable twentieth-century slogan—was a recurrent dream of architects, developers, and industrialists. However, prefabrication tended to be most successful in specialized settings where building labour was at a premium. In the mid-nineteenth century both East Coast and European manufacturers exported prefabricated houses and warehouses to Gold Rush California. By the turn of the century the timber-rich Pacific Northwest, upper Midwest, and south-east were the headquarters of corporations that sold prefabricated mail-order houses, farm buildings, and commercial structures. Although they had some success with ordinary home-owners across the country, most of their customers could be found in the rapidly developing interior of the country and among start-up industries seeking to house a work force quickly. During World War II the Seabees, the construction arm of the United States Navy, created a kind of prefabricated all-purpose building that could be manufactured in the United States and shipped to war zones as needed [**102**]. These Quonset huts, named after the Quonset Point Naval Air Station, Rhode Island, where they were developed in 1941, were made of preformed wooden ribs sheathed with corrugated sheet steel and fitted with pressed-wood interior linings. The standardized parts in a limited number of sizes could be assembled into eighty-six different internal configurations. About 170,000 Quonset huts had been built by 1946. Many were brought back to the United States after the war, where they were used as cheap housing and as industrial and commercial buildings.

Ventilation

The complex history of vernacular timber framing demonstrates that it is not enough simply to talk about the 'effects' of technology on architecture. Architecture was embedded in the industrialization and technological development of the United States in ways that cannot be reduced to simple cause-and-effect relationships. This was even more evident in the history of environmental controls. Because comfort is socially defined, architecture's role in providing it has changed. Until the beginning of the twentieth century the relationship between people and their surroundings was defined by ventilation. The classic theories of disease rested on assumptions about the nature and function of air, an elusive element whose perceptible qualities were clues to its healthfulness. Domestic advice givers taught their readers that people needed access to 'fresh' 'elastic' air and needed to escape or ventilate the 'burned', 'vitiated', 'expired' air that their heating systems and their own bodies produced [**103**].

These medical theories most conspicuously shaped public institutions of confinement, whose inmates needed healthy air brought to them. Authors of nineteenth-century hospital, asylum, and prison literature were obsessed with air. They advised care-givers to burn the clothes of epidemic victims because bad air could penetrate porous surfaces. They recommended metal 'blacksmith beds' for use in institutions because wooden bedsteads were similarly liable to contamination [**104**]. The ideal hospital of the nineteenth century was summed up in the so-called Nightingale ward (endorsed but not invented by Florence Nightingale), an 'edifice built up out of pure air'.[4] A Nightingale ward was very narrow, to allow the penetration of breezes, and it was very long, isolating each bed as 'a territory to itself'.[5] It was also a high room, with windows that occupied at least a third of the wall area and extended close to the ceiling and floor to avoid trapping bad air in the ward.

United States Army physician John S. Billings followed these principles when he was called on to fulfill the bequest of Baltimore businessman Johns Hopkins, who left a large sum of money to build a

103 Andrew Jackson Downing

Room without ventilation.
In the mid-19th century, pattern books like Downing's *The Architecture of Country Houses* (1850) contained information about furnishings, health, heating, and ventilation as well as aesthetic advice.

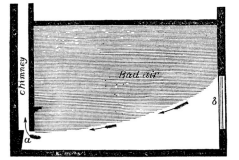

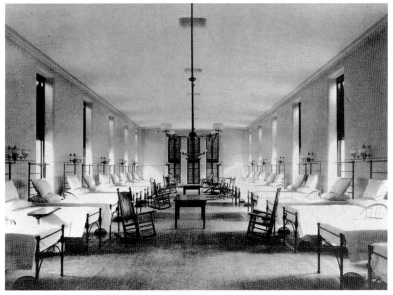

400–bed hospital based on the most up-to-date medical principles and available free of charge to people of any age, sex, race, or economic standing. Billings's plan for the Johns Hopkins Hospital (1876–85), concocted with the aid of architect John R. Niernsee, dramatically emphasized the layers of space around patients. Each Nightingale-type ward occupied a separate pavilion, a tall one-storey building set on a raised basement through which air was drawn into the ward by way of an outlet under each bed [104] [105] [106]. Vents in the ceiling and an 'aspirating chimney' drew foul air out through the roof space. Each patient was surrounded by a cocoon of moving air—at least in theory, for one study suggested that in systems of this sort the air moved in the intended direction only a little over half of the time, and stagnated or moved in the wrong direction otherwise.

The Nightingale system applied a veneer of science to the passive ventilating techniques long used in vernacular buildings. At the Johns Hopkins Hospital, an isolating ward for the very ill employed interior partitions and individual ventilating systems that crystallized the atmospheric cocoon of the common wards as individual cells whose environment could be adjusted to each patient's needs [105]. This arrangement linked the hospital to the celled spaces of penitentiaries and insane asylums, which could be fine-tuned to the specific social or mental failings of the inmate as the isolating ward could be fine-tuned to the physiological frailties of the individual patient. The isolating ward also tied the hospital to the celled spaces of nineteenth-century hotels and offices, where each guest or worker commanded a particular 'territory'.

The ranks of chimneys on the Johns Hopkins isolating ward dramatized a sense of independent selfhood that characterized the

105

Johns Hopkins Hospital.
Each patient in the isolating
ward had a room with its own
ventilating system.

emergent nineteenth-century middle class. They bespoke the sense of the individual as someone who could be picked out of the mass, someone with a distinct destiny or interest that could be controlled or at least influenced by architecture. These new middle-class Americans, who numbered among themselves the physicians and asylum keepers, prized a code of self-discipline and personal demeanour, called 'gentility', that defined distinctive individual personalities worthy of public respect. A respectable person imagined himself as the occupant of a discrete envelope of social and physical space within which he or she was entitled to remain undisturbed in return for respecting the integrity of others' boundaries. The late-nineteenth-century hospital served as an emblem of a good environment for, viewed through the lens of middle-class self-perception, the belief that bad air suffocated or poisoned its inhabitants by invading their bodies was as much a social as a medical judgement, one that found a kind of failure of personal integrity in the patients, clients, or inmates entrusted to their care.

Gender, Sex, and Filth

The conventions of gentility, with their heightened emphasis on the body and personal space, powerfully affected the evolving standards

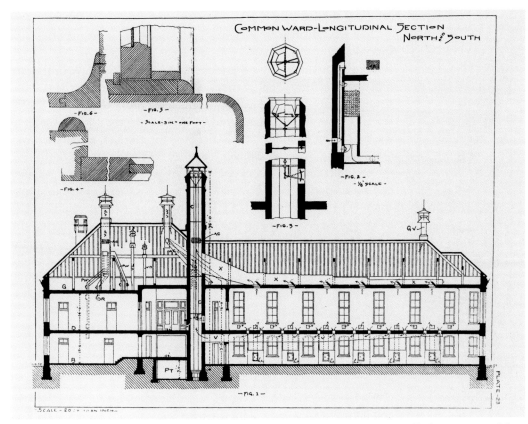

COMMON WARD-LONGITUDINAL SECTION
NORTH & SOUTH

-FIG.6-

-FIG.5-
-SCALE-3IN.-ONE FOOT-

-FIG.4-

-FIG.2-
-⅛ SCALE-

-FIG.3-

G V

-FIG.1-

PLATE-23

SCALE - 20 FT TO AN INCH-

106

Johns Hopkins Hospital
Section of a common ward.

of comfort that architectural technologies were called on to meet. Now buildings were expected not only to provide healthy air, but to insulate their occupants from one another. The use of environmental controls in Frank Lloyd Wright's famous administration building (1903–4) for the Larkin Company can be understood only in this context. The Larkin Company was a firm of Chicago soap manufacturers that moved to Buffalo after the fire of 1873, and subsequently expanded its business through mail-order premium sales. At the turn of the century Larkin executives decided to build a new headquarters that would follow the standard business practice of fronting a generic manufacturing complex with a relatively small, architecturally distinctive office building that doubled as a kind of corporate logo.

Wright's administration building was at once a head office, a factory that processed the five thousand letters the company received from its customers each day during the first decade of the twentieth century, and an enormous filing cabinet that stored them. It was organized as a high-walled, tightly enclosed, inward-looking building similar to the houses Wright was building during the same decade. An open interior court was surrounded by galleries and lit from the top, from a light well between the main building and its annex, and from triple windows set high in the walls above banks of built-in storage

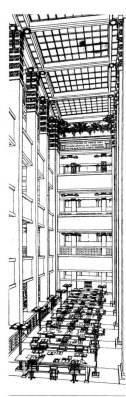

107 Frank Lloyd Wright

Larkin Company
Administration Building,
1903–4 (demolished 1950),
Buffalo.

Note the banks of built-in filing
cabinets in the partitions lining
the central court, the plants
trailing over the upper balcony,
and the Biblical epigraph.

cabinets [107].

The resemblance to Wright's houses was no accident, or even a simple matter of personal style or formal preference, for the Larkin Building was shaped by a domestic model of working life. In the late nineteenth century large commercial enterprises like the Larkin Company employed increasingly female clerical work forces drawn from the middle and lower-middle classes. Yet the Larkin Building was located in an industrial district near the railroad, a zone that was off limits to respectable women. To offset the disadvantages of the site, the architect and the client sought to establish an image of gentility and protection, a *homelike world*, a turn-of-the-century phrase that connoted the extension of domestic moral values into the world at large. Public employment was opened up to women by making the work-place resemble a household, their putative domain. Wright explicitly acknowledged this intention: he aimed to create 'a family gathering under conditions ideal for the body and mind', a 'family home' that would stimulate the company's employees to work hard for the profit of its owners.[6]

The Larkin Building was much more than a home: it was a self-contained genteel neighbourhood that included an employee lounge, a branch of the city library, a YWCA, a classroom, a cafeteria, and a conservatory. Inside, the women worked in open spaces under the watchful eyes of male managers, surrounded by organ music, plants, and uplifting architectural inscriptions, some drawn from the Sermon on the Mount and others grouped into cryptic triadic exhortations such as 'cheerfulness—patience—contentment' and 'adversity—refinement—sympathy'.

Environmental technology made the character-moulding isolation of the Larkin Administration Building possible. The structure was sealed off and supplied with air taken in through the roof, drawn to the basement through corner towers, passed over coils and water sprays to wash it, then sent back up through an intricate network of riser ducts to the working areas. Wright's explanation of the system evoked the nineteenth century's obsession with air: his mechanism served 'to keep the interior space clear of the poisonous gases in the smoke from the New York Central trains that puffed along beside' the building.[7] The allusion was deceptive. Since the construction of the Johns Hopkins Hospital, the germ theory of disease had come to dominate medical thinking. This attributed most illnesses to micro-organisms living in dirt, rather than to the innate properties of air. Wright sought not to ventilate the air in the nineteenth-century sense, but to clean and cool it. His system was concerned with the workers' skin rather than their lungs. It created a different kind of separation from that in the hospitals of a generation earlier. In the tightly packed space of the office, conditioned air wrapped individual bodies in a genteel envelope that protected them from the contaminating touch of their neighbours.

As a domestic architect (even in his public commissions), Wright shared his contemporaries' obsession with cleanliness. If the ventilated space of the hospital was the social metaphor of late-nineteenth-century houses, the sterile laboratory served the same purpose in the twentieth century. Builders rethought bathrooms and kitchens as sanitary places defined by hard white surfaces which revealed the dirt that carried germs and by high-technology fittings. Paradoxically, actual laboratories presented a very different aspect from the visual sterility that domestic designers sought.

John Galen Howard's Hearst Memorial Mining Building (1902–7) at the University of California, Berkeley, a memorial to a former United States Senator who had made his fortune in North Dakota mines, contained laboratories, offices, and classrooms fronted by a pavilion that formed the memorial proper [108]. This conservative, pleasant-looking building, funded by the honoree's widow, Phoebe Apperson Hearst, was shaped by a much darker social vision than Wright's antiseptic gentility. On the arcaded south façade, a red-tile roof supported on heavy timber brackets alluded to the California missions, claiming the historical and cultural past as a matrix against which the state's economic and technological progress could be measured. Straining corbel figures, representing 'the primal elements' on the west and 'the eternal forces' on the east supported the eaves brackets. Howard wrote revealingly of these figures that 'the profession

108 John Galen Howard, architect; Dean S. B. Christy, consultant

Hearst Memorial Mining Building, 1902–7, University of California, Berkeley.

of mining has to do with the very body and bones of the earth; its process is a ruthless assault upon the bowels of the world, a contest with the crudest and most rudimentary forces. There is about it something essentially elementary, something primordial.'[8]

Howard's iconography depicted the act of mining in terms of the clash between human bodies and Nature's body, revealing his familiarity with a widely disseminated late-nineteenth-century popular literature on gender and sexuality. This literature assumed that men were governed by a 'spermatic economy', meaning that their energies were limited and needed to be concentrated in one field of endeavour or another.[9] Socially productive activities such as the economic exploitation of the earth's resources required every bit of energy that men could summon, as the expressions on Howard's primal figures suggest. Yet men were naturally inclined to seek sexual pleasure, which diverted their energies from socially productive channels. Those who were able to subdue their own natures might conquer the earth and assimilate nature's energies to their own, expanding their powers exponentially. Curiously, the authors of popular treatises often used mining, particularly California gold mining and its all-male mining camps, as metaphors for the healthy direction of energies toward productive action.

Because the earth was female, mining was often described as a superior version of giving birth, or more accurately of delivering a baby. However, femaleness added other dimensions to Howard's iconography more in keeping with his words. According to accepted wisdom, women's sexuality threatened to rob men of their vital energies and to subvert the discipline that social order required. Fear of the disorder liable to ensue from women's natures if they were allowed to run unchecked prompted late-nineteenth-century surgeons to remove women's sexual organs to tame their temperaments (a practice still current when the Hearst Mining Building was constructed). In Howard's description of miners tearing the riches from the body of Mother Earth, we hear echoes of this hostile, Jack-the-Ripper-like gynaecology. The hard work of mining constituted a violent struggle with the earth that miners must win by any means for the good of society.

Just what was it that the miners were after in the earth's bowels? After all, women do not actually give birth from their bowels, nor are their sexual organs located there. The bowels are the excrement-filled organs that extract the last bits of nutrient from food. In the early twentieth century the ideal of efficiency, widely touted as both an economic and a technological goal, was extended to the human body. Regularity, control, and self-discipline were urged on refined Americans in their bodily functions as in their work. Women, in particular, were often encouraged to learn to control their excretory

functions as a step toward achieving gentility. The Hearst Mining Building, on the other hand, energetically celebrated its wastes. Furnaces in the bowels of the building digested ores whose toxic remnants were excreted—or ejaculated—promiscuously through the ranks of chimneys that bristled from the roof [**109**]. Metaphors of gender, of sexuality and elimination, of technology and nature, of technology and the body, are so densely entwined in the Hearst Mining Building that they are nearly impossible to untangle, but if Wright's building protected its female occupants from the consequences of their own bodily processes, Howard's revelled in its wastes even as it celebrated the conquest of Nature's female grossness.

Bodily metaphors remained powerful a half century later in Louis I. Kahn's Richards Medical Research Laboratory (1957–64) at the University of Pennsylvania, a biological and medical research facility clad in a skin-and-skeleton-like brick-and-concrete sheathing [**110**]. The environment is controlled by a system that also resembles the body's: the brain, in the central blocks, is separated from the excretory system contained in the attached towers. This separation of functions, which recalls the classic western mind-body dichotomy, follows a common Kahn organizational strategy that the architect described as a division of servant and served spaces, which is a social metaphor. The conspicuous ventilating towers speak of danger more than of celebration: this architectural body protects the bodies of the people who work there from the consequences of what they do inside. The excretory systems dwarf, and are more visually compelling than, the thinking spaces.

The Richards Laboratory intimates a kind of technological hubris. The dramatic exhaust towers suggest the riskiness of what is done there and by implication magnify the stature of the research and the

scientists who, it seems, work at the edges of human capacities. Its imagery allies the Richards Laboratory with the great works of nineteenth- and twentieth-century civil engineering that seemed similarly daring.

The Technological Sublime

David Nye, a historian of technology, has traced the American fascination with spectacular technology to the eighteenth-century aesthetic category of the sublime. On a continent where the natural landscape seemed so sublime, so vast and terrifying, it seemed appropriate, if a little daunting, to try to meet Nature on the same scale, with vast structures to subdue the earth and powerful machines to annihilate distance and time. To Ralph Waldo Emerson, these structures and machines were 'realized will . . . the double of man'.[10] The most 'empirical' or rational structures were often among the most ambitious of these efforts of the human spirit to colonize the natural world.

The renowned suspension-bridge builder John A. Roebling was certainly driven by a sense of the technological sublime. Roebling, who established a factory to make wire rope at Saxonburg, Pennsylvania, in 1841, began to construct suspension bridges a few years later. His ambition was not simply to build useful or even particularly long spans (although he did both), but to design distinctive ones that would celebrate human power over nature. Roebling sought to create 'a pleasing effect, and at the same time . . . strong and reassuring proportions which inspire confidence' through a visual balance among the tower, deck structure, cables, suspenders, and stays of his bridges.[11] That is, he devised a personal *visual* style, based on stays radiating from the towers, to set his bridges off from those of other engineers. At his East River (Brooklyn) Bridge (1869–83), Roebling experimented with varying patterns of stays and reinforced the deck beyond what was necessary to achieve the desired appearance [111]. He also cloaked its towers in quasi-Gothic garb because 'medieval architecture is distinguished for its remarkable lightness and great strength at the same time'.[12]

Roebling's aesthetic sensibilities inspired suspension-bridge engineers for seventy years after his death. Othmar Ammann, the designer of the George Washington Bridge (1927–31), New York, learned from his teacher, Gustav Lindenthal, that 'a great bridge in a great city, should be a work of art to which science lends its aid' [112].[13] On the example of the Brooklyn Bridge, Ammann and the project architect Cass Gilbert wanted to sheath the towers of his bridge with stone (veneered over reinforced concrete) to give them an appropriate dignity, but the cladding was omitted for budgetary reasons. Ammann also made the George Washington Bridge's deck much thinner than

THE GREAT EAST RIVER SUSPENSION BRIDGE.

CONNECTING THE CITIES OF NEW YORK AND BROOKLYN.   VIEW FROM BROOKLYN, LOOKING WEST.

111 John A. Roebling, chief engineer; completed by Washington Roebling and Emily Roebling

The Great East River Suspension Bridge, 1869–83, Brooklyn, NY, to New York NY. Currier and Ives print, *c.*1883.

was customary to make it appear more elegant.

The great suspension bridges of the nineteenth and early twentieth centuries fed a national sense of self. Roebling predicted that the Brooklyn Bridge's gothic towers would 'be ranked as national monuments [that would] forever testify to the energy, enterprise, and wealth of the community'.[14] Bridges and similar engineering feats were monuments of economic nationalism, proof of the American system's growing strength. The Brooklyn Bridge was described as the last link of a cross-country highway, despite the fact that it connected two islands, neither of which boasted a bridge to the mainland.[15] At the same time each bridge was a local victory, the mark of the special position of each particular place in the larger system, so each locality cherished the distinctive appearance of its bridge, whether it was a suspension structure by Roebling or his rival Charles Ellet or a unique span, such as Colonel James B. Eads's cantilevered steel bridge for St Louis (1867–74). Most of all, striking engineering achievements were another medium for examining the dichotomies between nature and culture. For Thomas Ewbank, the Commissioner of Patents, humanity's work would be finished when 'the planet is wholly changed from its natural wilderness . . . into a fit theatre for cultivated intelligences'. In this spirit, one dedicatory orator declared the Brooklyn Bridge 'a trophy of triumph over an obstacle of Nature'.[16]

As at the Richards Laboratory, human power had its risks. Travel at great speeds risked disastrous loss of control of the power at one's fingertips, as in the steamboat explosion that took the life of Andrew

Jackson Downing in 1852 or the space-shuttle Challenger explosion of the 1980s. To build heroically entailed exposure to hazardous terrains, extreme working conditions deep inside bridge caissons or atop the steel frames of skyscrapers, the risk of accidents, and an impulse to self-destruction. If technology was the extension of ourselves, the question often arose, were we over-stepping our proper boundaries? The fear of over-extending human capacity for artifice was the complement of the fear of trespassing on Nature's domain: both invited retribution from forces beyond human control. Green architects Sim Van der Ryn and Stuart Cowan caught the mood in warning that 'Thinking too big can make our human limitations a liability rather than an asset'.[17]

Van der Ryn and Cowan wrote as though engineers and technologists had forgotten this, but these anxieties underlay even admiring accounts of nineteenth- and twentieth-century technology. That was the meaning of the technological sublime. The undertone of fear, the possibility that a bridge might fall or a dam might break, made it the more admirable when it did not. Each new success reset the standards. Robert Stephenson, engineer of the widely admired Britannia Bridge in north Wales, wrote to John Roebling that 'If your [Niagara River] bridge succeeds, mine is a magnificent blunder.'[18]

112 Othmar Ammann, chief engineer; Leon S. Moissieff and Allston Dana, engineers; Cass Gilbert, consulting architect

George Washington Bridge, 1927–31, New York, NY, to Fort Lee, NJ.

113 Lacey V. Murrow, chief engineer; Leon S. Moissieff, consultant

Tacoma Narrows Bridge, 1939–40, Tacoma, Wash.

Collapse of the bridge in a wind storm, 1940.

The quest for lightness in the suspension bridges of the 1920s to 1930s can be understood in the same light. Deflection theory, first articulated in 1888 but introduced to American bridge design by engineer Leon S. Moissieff only in 1909, justified the effort, but the stimulus was a less rational desire to test boundaries. By substituting plate girders for the customary trusses as deck stiffeners, unprecedented attenuation could be achieved at the cost of a potentially disastrous flexibility. In November 1940, a bridge designed according to this theory, the newly opened, elegantly insubstantial Tacoma Narrows Bridge in Washington blew down in a wind storm [**113**].

Producers and Consumers

Great bridges, along with dams, railroad lines, and industrial works, were prominent landmarks in an optimistic landscape. Machines and technologies of all sorts became metaphors, catalysts, even drivers, of social change, their symbolic significance increasing with every passing decade. By the twentieth century mechanistic imagery was regularly equated with modernity, although, as the famous houses built for Los Angeles health guru Philip Lovell demonstrated, modernity might be interpreted in any number of ways. Lovell wrote a newspaper column on physical culture through which he advocated a healthy outdoor life of a familiar sort. Like many of his contemporaries, he also sought to achieve bodily efficiency and inner cleanliness through diet. In 1926 he commissioned Austrian immigrant architect Rudolph M. Schindler to design a house for Newport Beach, California, that would realize his ideas [114]. As a machine for human well-being, Schindler's design was remarkably old-fashioned. The two-storey shoebox stood on a small lot at the edge of the sand like thousands of other more ordinary beach houses in the United States. The end towards the ocean was glazed like a Victorian conservatory. Sleeping porches (now enclosed) opened off the upper-level bedrooms and, in response to the restricted lot, the house was raised above the street to provide a patch of open space (complete with barbecue pit) under it.

Of course this was no ordinary beach house visually. It was dramatically lifted by five massive concrete frames, creating a unique image. The beach house's spaces seemed to be defined by the accidental juxtaposition of the concrete frames and a series of intersecting horizontals. Where a nineteenth-century architect might have sought individuality through reference to the *genius loci*, or peculiarities of the site, Schindler emphasized the architect's heroic individualism but used a visual language, derived from early-twentieth-century European avant-garde design, that treated buildings as visible fragments of a universal gridded space. Schindler's Lovell House could have been dropped anywhere. Nature at this beach house was equally abstracted. It was not an adversary to be conquered, conciliated or improved, simply air, sun, and water, another technology available for building the new individual.

A year after Lovell's beach house was completed, he hired another Austrian newcomer, Richard J. Neutra, to design a house in the Hollywood Hills [115]. In its scale and siting, and even in its massing, the Lovell 'Health' House (1927–9) was a villa. Neutra was more solicitous of the *genius loci* of his site, setting the main wing dramatically at right angles to the steep hillside and using it, with its connected garage wing, as a dramatic background for a terraced amphitheatrical garden studded with Lovell's exercise equipment. The house was steel framed on a regular grid and coated with a kind of sprayed-on concrete called gunite. Although the finished building was not mechanically symmetrical or regular, its modular structure established a uniform ordering matrix.

The difference from Schindler's beach house could not have been greater. The Health House, which looked as though it *might have been* made of mass-produced parts, stood at a turning point in the architectural appropriation of technology in the United States. Where

Schindler produced a house by and for heroic individuals, Neutra designed one for members of a new society, but evoked several nineteenth- and early twentieth-century predecessors. Like Frank Furness's exposed iron beams at the Pennsylvania Academy of Fine Arts, Neutra's gunite and metalwork served as picturesque signs of modernity, characteristic expressions of the present. In the tradition of Greene and Green's nearby Gamble House, with its elegant carpentry, the Health House celebrated making, validating labour and labourers. Neutra's technological imagery intimated the new, just, rational mass society that industrial processes and industrial social organization might produce. In its opulence, Neutra's house also looked forward to the corporate and domestic settings that used highly finished, elegantly presented industrial products as contemporary equivalents of the luxury materials of the past. In the 1950s and 1960s self-conscious aesthetes like Ludwig Mies van der Rohe and his sometime disciple Philip Johnson jettisoned Neutra's social(ist) subtext and reclaimed the benefits of industrialism for a socio-economic élite [**116**].

Even as the 1950s modernists backed away from the social promise of industrialism in favour of its aesthetic pleasures, other architects began to question the aesthetic value of industrial products. Los Angeles architect Pierre Koenig complained that 'Industry has not learned the difference between what is beautiful in its simplicity and what is ugly although equally simple'.[19] Frank Gehry's chain-link-covered parking garage at Santa Monica Place (1979–81), a shopping mall, celebrates the crudeness that offended Koenig [**117**]. Chain-link, a mundane industrial product, is neither elegant nor socially promising, but it is certainly ubiquitous, a mass-produced building material consonant with the mass-produced goods sold in the shopping mall. Gehry's building really does use off-the-rack materials but in a way that sets the act of consumption off against the creative

114 Rudolph M. Schindler
Lovell Beach House, 1926,
Newport Beach, Calif.

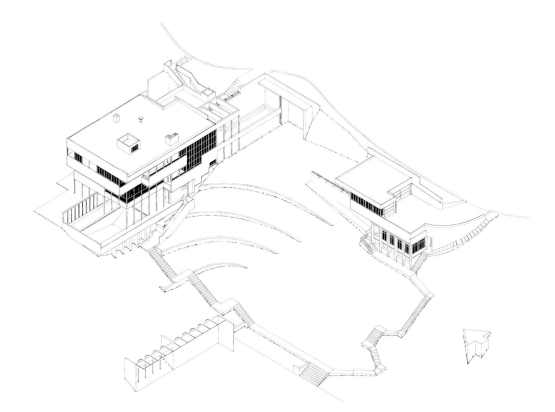

will of the architect: the producer is nowhere to be found.

Despite the differences in their attitudes toward particular industrialized materials, Angelenos such as Schindler, Neutra, Koenig, and Gehry shared a sense that, whatever its failings, industry was architecture's future. They shared as well an essentially technocratic vision of the way the future would be brought about. Twentieth-century architects inherited a nineteenth-century faith in the claims of expert knowledge to control building one that was mediated by Marxism and the popular scientism of the turn of the century. Koenig, for example, participated in the Case Study House programme, a series of twenty designs commissioned (thirteen built) by publisher John Entenza for *Arts + Architecture* magazine between 1945 and 1962, that were intended to 'lead the house out of the bondage of handcraftism into industry'.[20] Entenza's strategy was to create prototypical 'good' designs based at first on ordinary building products, but after 1950 on the improbable promotion of steel framing for domestic architecture. Architect Craig Ellwood, who contributed three such designs, bragged that the Case Study programme had 'helped to stifle' the craftsman.[21]

Whether they preferred a 1920s version of a socialist state or a 1950s version of corporate capitalism, ambitious twentieth-century architects allied their expertise to centralized and hierarchical organizations. Even architects who employ irrational visual imagery, as Gehry has done in recent years, assert their prerogatives as artist-architects in alliance with powerful corporations. As a result, technological imagery in twentieth-century American high architecture has offered a predominantly top-down social vision, with building production and design closely controlled from above.

The great suspension bridges of the nineteenth century were even more the products of expertise, but they had been interpreted as expressions of collective human will, signs of the greatness of an entire society. The twentieth century emphasized a thread that had always been present, one that set off the active producer from the passive consumer of technology's benefits. In retrospect, Schindler's one-off beach house, idiosyncratic even within his work, seems the more prescient of the two Lovell houses. Like Gehry's parking garage, Schindler's house celebrated the aesthetic heroism of the architect and the bully vigour of the consumer but had nothing to say about the lowly builder.

Consuming Architecture

In their circumscribed but exclusive realm, consumerist high architects developed skills like those that designers in the less prestigious popular arena had already mastered. During the Depression, a self-proclaimed new breed of visual public relations experts called 'industrial designers' began to offer the public technologically based 'modernistic' images in architecture, landscape, and portable objects. Most industrial designers had originally been trained as mechanical engineers, advertising copy writers, or stage designers. Like the civil engineers of the nineteenth

116 Philip C. Johnson
'Glass' House, 1949, New Canaan, Conn.

117 Rouse Corporation, developer; Frank Gehry, architect

Santa Monica Place, 1979–81, Santa Monica, Calif.

Parking garage enclosed with chain-link fencing.

century, they understood that the metaphorical qualities of technology required a careful eye to visual presentation to draw them out. Near the end of his life, pioneering industrial designer Raymond Loewy defended his profession against charges that they simply dressed up the work of engineers. 'What you call sheathing,' he observed, 'is really the self-expression of the machine . . . there is as much working backward *from* an optimal form *to* mechanics [in the design process] as there is *from* the machinery *to* what you call sheathing.'[22]

Industrial design combined sophisticated advertising techniques developed after World War I, when advertisers learned the importance of image, with the prestige of empirical scientific research. They began to pitch products as compensations for personal social defects rather than as remedies for specific problems. Industrial designers presented their work as a kind of research that augmented 'new' with 'and improved'. Evolutionary charts traced formal changes from the recent past to the present and into the future [**118**]. The object was not simply to sell this year's model, but to instill in consumers a trust in the expertise of corporate research and development. The subtext was that industry could improve lives as well as cars or toasters. Industrial designer Norman Bel Geddes predicted that the immediate future ('the coming era') would be characterized by the interweaving of four kinds of design: art, engineering to make machines work better,

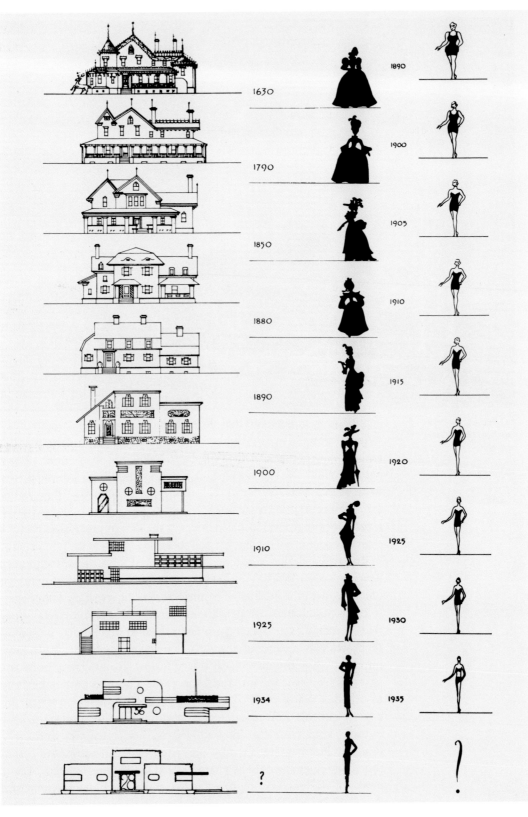

1630

1790

1850

1880

1890

1900

1910

1925

1934

?

1890

1900

1905

1910

1915

1920

1925

1930

1935

'Evolutionary Chart of Design',
1930.

This is a portion of a larger
chart that also includes
vehicles and household
objects and that compares the
streamlining and improvement
of houses, costume, and body
image.

product design to make everyday objects cheap, durable, convenient, and pleasant, and the design of social structure.[23] The visual and verbal formulations of industrial design equated the three forms of object design with the design of social structure. Material goods could resolve social and individual dilemmas. Loewy said it explicitly: 'I believe that one should design for the advantage of the largest mass of people, first and always. That takes care of ideologies and sociologies.'[24]

Design literature between the wars oscillated between describing what was, or almost was, and what might be. To understand consumerist architecture, it is critical to appreciate the ways popular modernists like Loewy and Bel Geddes as well as Neutra and other high modernists conflated contemporary design and production with future society. Corporate science and technology, packaged by industrial design, was on the verge of creating a new society, a technological utopia. The difficulty of distinguishing present from future made the latter seem achingly close.

A long-lived American utopian tradition had been rejuvenated in 1888 with the publication of Edward Bellamy's enormously popular *Looking Backward, 2000–1888*. Most turn-of-the-century utopias were worked out in publications rather than in actual communities as their predecessors such as those of the Shakers, the Harmonists, and the Oneidans had been, but they retained the significant assumptions of earlier communal societies: that utopia could be achieved instantly with sufficient will, that it took the form of a restructured family, and that a properly designed physical landscape was critical to its success. For example, Charlotte Perkins Gilman's *Herland* (1915), one of over two hundred utopian novels published in the quarter-century leading up to World War I, adhered to tradition in its depiction of a utopian society based on a restructured family. In Herland's manless society, women rejected categorization as mothers, wives, and servants.

Herland was told from the point of view of three men who happened upon this female utopia following the crash of their private airplane. The detail was significant, for by the beginning of the twentieth century utopian theory had become entangled with visionary technological futures. Popular novels and periodicals were filled with predictions, some idyllic, others nightmarish, but most forecasting a densely urbanized future that looked very much like the present but that was dominated by intensified scale, speed, and movement [119]. 'We enter a new era,' Bel Geddes proclaimed. 'We live and work under pressure with a tremendous expenditure of energy. We feel that our time is more urgent, complex, and discordant than life ever was before . . . . To-day, speed is the cry of our era, and greater speed one of the goals of to-morrow.'[25] If nineteenth-century engineers sought to dominate the landscape through technology, these twentieth-century visionaries dreamed of eradicating it, of having the

Cities of Tomorrow

The city of tomorrow, engineers say, will tend first to vastness; gigantic buildings connected by wide, suspended roadways on which traffic will speed at unheard of rates. This is the city the artist has pictured here. Traffic handled in huge underground tunnels, aerial ways, and in the air itself. Helicopter planes, capable of maneuvering about between buildings and roof-top airports, will take the place of the ground taxi. Each building will be virtually a city in itself, completely self-sustaining, receiving its supplies from great merchandise ways far below the ground. Dwellers and workers in these buildings may go weeks without setting foot on the ground, or the ground-level. In this city smoke will be eliminated, noise will be conquered, and impurity will be eliminated from the air. Many persons will live in the healthy atmosphere of the building tops, while others will commute to far distant residential towns, or country homes.

Copyright Amazing Stories, 1939.

'Cities of Tomorrow', 1939.
This image appeared on the
back cover of the August 1939
issue of *Amazing Stories*.
According to the caption,
tomorrow's city would be
characterized by vastness, by
traffic that would move 'at
unheard of rates', and by
salubrity: 'smoke will be
eliminated, noise will be
conquered, and impurity
eliminated from the air. Many
persons will live in the healthy
atmosphere of the building
tops, while others will
commute to far distant
residential towns, or country
homes.' The description and
the rendering betray close
acquaintance with the exhibits
presented at the New York
World's Fair in the same year.

power to transcend the ordinary facts of the world. Speed annihilated space by collapsing time.

The visionary cities of science-fiction magazines were translated, in advertising and design, into a commodified dynamic imagery. Streamlining, a curvilinear visual format ostensibly derived from the theory of hydrodynamics, packaged the power and speed of the coming era into manageable, saleable bits [**120**]. It fused dynamism, or literal movement, with progress, or cultural movement. The comprehensive vision of a technological future was reduced to a world in which social problems would be solved by durable goods.

While futurism was a useful corporate tool, its appeal carried it quickly beyond corporate hands. The tantalizing fusion of production and consumption in technological utopianism appealed to many Americans for reasons of their own. Individual thinkers, fantasists, artists, and ordinary people were drawn as powerfully to it as corporations and architects. Technocratic images ricocheted around American culture: the future and the present, corporations and individuals, high architecture and popular culture, the respectable and the cranks all mixed in ways that could not be neatly categorized.

Richard Buckminster Fuller, a member of an old New England family that had produced several illustrious Puritan ministers as well as the transcendentalist writer Margaret Fuller (whose grave is adjacent to his in Mount Auburn Cemetery), embodied nearly all of these qualities. His 4–D Utility Unit (1927) was a serious attempt to deliver cheap housing by mass production, a desire shared by many corporations and individual designers in the interwar period [**121**]. The living unit, enclosed with glass and casein and fitted with inflated rubber floors, would be suspended by cables from a central aluminium utility 'mast' that contained two bathrooms, the kitchen, sewage disposal tanks, an electric generator, and an air compressor for the floors. Fuller wanted his living units to be fitted with all sorts of personal appliances, including a vacuum electric hair-clipper, a vacuum toothbrush, a self-activating laundry that would wash and dry clothes in three minutes, and an automatic climate-control system that eliminated the necessity for sheets, blankets, or even clothes. His was an engineer's equivalent of the self-sufficient ecological house of later decades: it contained its own utilities and it could be placed anywhere, alone or stacked on masts to form an apartment house.

Fuller believed that his design could be mass-produced

immediately and he refused to allow a demonstration model to be built at Chicago's 1933–4 Century of Progress exhibition. Instead, he demanded $100 million to begin full-scale industrial production. Yet Fuller allowed a publicist to rechristen the 4-D Utility Unit, a thoroughly technocratic title, the 'Dymaxion House'. This neologism, intended to suggest dynamism and efficiency, propelled the work into the domains of popular culture, science fiction, and advertising, where Fuller's own '4-D' label, along with his proposed delivery system, had already done much to place it. The 4-D Utility Unit would be installed by a zeppelin, which would drop a bomb into the countryside, then set the base of the mast into the resulting crater [**122**].

In short, Fuller was unable to decide whether he was interested in production or consumption, in the present or the future. His Dymaxion House was an uneasy mixture of all of them, a technocratic solution to housing that would also be a consumer good that could be cheaply replaced when it wore out. Like most proponents of consumerist futurism, Fuller assumed that technology would solve social problems but he did not question the fundamental values of contemporary society. His houses were designed for the nuclear family as it existed in the 1920s and for gender roles as they then existed. The Dymaxion House was a bit of a boy's toy, complete with a nude female figure to demonstrate climate control.

The mixture of the present and the future in technocratic utopianism may have been a sign of personal confusion in someone like Fuller, but at the level of the corporation and the economy it created a

121 R. Buckminster Fuller

4–D Utility Unit (Dymaxion House), 1927.

The engineer poses with the second version of his creation.

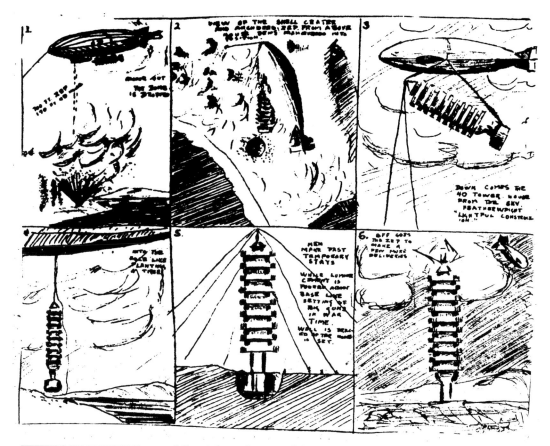

The text within the illustration panels reads:

1. THE 11 ZEP / AS HE LAY / ...
2. VIEW OF THE SHELL CRATER / AND MEMBERS ZEP. FROM ABOVE / ... / ...
3. DOWN COMES THE / 40 TOWER HOUSE / FROM THE SKY / "FEATHERWEIGHT / "LIGHTFUL CONSTRUCT- / ION."
4. INTO THE / ... LIKE / PLANTING / TREE
5. MEN MAKE FAST / TEMPORARY / STAYS / WHILE LOADING / CEMENT IS / POURED AROUND / BASE LINE / SETTING OF / ... SUNK / IN WAR / TIME / WALL IS READ- / ... UP THE ... / IS SET.
6. OFF GOES / THE ZEP TO / MAKE A / FEW MORE / DELIVERIES

122 R. Buckminster Fuller

'Zeppelin Delivery of 4–D Houses', 1927.

Zeppelins would plant the houses, which could be grouped on stacks, in craters excavated by bombs.

usefully rich ambiguity. The home of the future, the world of the future, would be only a little different from the world of today. The elements of the future were already in hand. This was the message of George Fred Keck's House of Tomorrow, commissioned by Century Homes Ltd for exhibition at the Century of Progress exhibition [**123**] [**124**]. This twelve-sided house was made to appear as different as possible from the familiar residences of the 1930s, and even had a hangar for a private airplane. Yet its purpose was 'to demonstrate mechanical equipment and new building materials that are now on the market'.[26] The central utility stack (probably inspired by Fuller's) was built first and fibre-concrete slab floors and ceilings were hung from it, fixed in place by a steel frame. In 1933 the exterior was sheathed with a patent covering called phenoloid board, but it was reclad with copper the next year. And the austere high-tech exterior was counterbalanced by an interior grounded in contemporary upper-middle-class comfort, even including a grand piano [**125**].

The House of Tomorrow, along with its companion Crystal House (built by Keck at his own expense during the 1934 season of the Century of Progress as a personal gesture of futurist faith) and the many more conventional-looking houses of tomorrow constructed at

123 George Fred Keck
House of Tomorrow, 1933,
Century of Progress Exhibition,
Chicago. Moved to Michigan
City, Mich.
The long garage door at the
lower right was meant to
accommodate a personal
airplane.

the expositions of the 1930s, offered powerful images of a future like the present, a present that was very like the future. They mixed intriguing images of industrial progress with reassuringly familiar domestic settings. Who could tell where today left off and tomorrow began? In the motto of the New York World's Fair of 1939, industry was 'Building the World of Tomorrow with the Tools of Today'.

The New York fair, at first entitled 'The Fair of the Future', was the work of businessmen who wanted to 'stress the vastly increased opportunity and the developed mechanical means which this twentieth century has brought to the masses for better living and accompanying human happiness'.[27] Urban theorist Lewis Mumford endorsed the effort, calling on the organizers to demonstrate 'the future of the whole civilization' through architecture, stressing 'this planned environment, this planned industry, this planned civilization'.[28]

To make their point the fair's organizing committee hired the leading industrial designers of the day, including Loewy, Bel Geddes, and Henry Dreyfuss, to create the buildings and the exhibits. Their decision, as usual, was to delineate a future driven by contemporary technology and cloaked in reassuring visual garb. At General Motors' renowned Futurama exhibit, visitors were told that 'by the spring of 1939 [engineers and inventors]. had cracked nearly every frontier of progress'.[29] More explicitly than other technocratic futurists, the designers of the New York World's Fair stressed public and private communal life, stimulated perhaps by the exhibition's secondary purpose of commemorating the sesquicentennial of the United States Constitution.

Industrial designer Gilbert Rohde created four dioramas for the Community Interests exhibit that traced progress in daily life from 1789 to 1939. The last showed Mrs Modern ordering everything for her

124

House of Tomorrow.

Plans. Despite its radical appearance, the House of Tomorrow incorporated the customary spatial divisions of middle-class domestic life, and even included a 'conservatory' reminiscent of nineteenth-century houses.

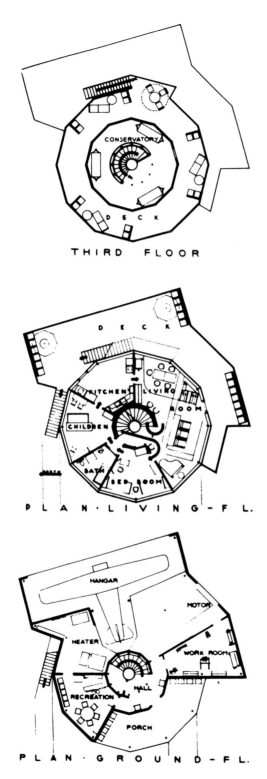

THIRD FLOOR

PLAN·LIVING·FL.

PLAN·GROUND·FL.

house, from the foundation to dinner, by telephone, to be delivered that afternoon: labour was to be had at the command of a button, without reference to cost or social organization. In a fifth scene depicting the future, a human figure reduced to an eyeball, an ear, a nose, and a hand (that is, to pure sensation) ascended to a modernistic suburban tract in the clouds while a narrator intoned that future people would have 'Time for interest in government, in community, in the group. Time to plan for our community. At last Man is freed . . . freed in time and space' [126].[30]

The annihilation of time and space had once seemed the province of massive, all-pervasive machines and engineering structures. In Rohde's vision, speed and power led to the annihilation of the entire material world. Barely perceptible personal technologies substituted buttons and electronics for tangible objects. Outlandishly sophistic-ated technologies were literally placed in every one's hands.

This vision of an ephemeral future landscape has been remarkably tenacious. In Depression-era versions, needlessly complex devices replaced ordinary, perfectly adequate mechanical or manual tech-niques, as in one World's Fair demonstration house where a glass wall between the living-room and garden disappeared at the push of a button, rather than opening on hinges or tracks. In the 1990s cyber-fantasies of the electronic eradication of time and space predicted an end to the need (and possibly the desire) for direct human contact. Public space will be reconstituted on-line. In every case, the abundance of material goods would, paradoxically, produce a dematerialized world.

A recurrent pop-culture image of the humans of the future placed bald, bulbous, brain-laden heads atop useless, toothpick bodies. In a 1970s televised presentation of Ray Bradbury's popular novel *The Martian Chronicles* (1958), one such family sat in lightweight pedestal chairs, surrounded by clouds, receiving nutrition and entertainment from small hand-held devices like television remote controls. In this brand of technocratic futurism there was no place for architecture or decorative furnishings. Technology's role in protecting human life and comfort and in extending human capacities had become so pervasive that it was no longer visible—not the supplement but the whole environment. The technological colonization of the world that had filled the earth with such substantial monuments as suspension bridges and dams and with oceans of consumer durables had reached a strange impasse, one that vaporized the world's materiality.

This was a depressing prospect, one that might prompt even the most optimistic technological utopians to entertain doubts about the value of material progress as a path to social perfection. Perhaps this was the reason that Henry Dreyfuss's 'Democracity' exhibition, 'a perfectly integrated future metropolis' housed in the New York World's Fair's theme centre, the Trylon and Perisphere, downplayed technology in favour of a pastoral landscape derived from English anti-urban theorist Ebenezer Howard. Small commuter suburbs were scattered around a central, formally planned business and cultural centre, buffered from it by green spaces. In Democracity, the 'march of men and women, singing their triumph' was 'the true symbol of the

126 Gilbert Rohde
'Man Freed in Time and Space', design for Community Interests Pavilion, New York World's Fair, 1939.

KING KONG © 1933 RKO PICTURES, INC.

127

King Kong, 1933.

Nature battles technology atop
New York's newly completed
Empire State Building.

World of Tomorrow'.[31] A *Life* magazine article that was evidently influenced by Democracity added that in the future the happiest people would live in small light-industrial and agricultural villages. 'They do not care for possessions . . . they are not attached to their homes and hometowns, because trains [and] express highways get them across America in twenty-four hours.'[32]

These visions of the future, technological or not, evaded important questions. What sorts of social relationships would characterize the new society? The world's fairs of the 1930s provoked bitter struggles over racial discrimination in employment and visitation, yet political, racial, and cultural differences had no place in the fair's principal exhibits. Behind the political and social neutrality of futurist rhetoric lay a vision of an international patriarchal technocracy that promised to enrich Americans, bringing the exotic to their doorsteps, but at an unexamined cost. What would be the structure of political authority, beyond the celebration of a vaguely defined 'democracy'? What would the future family be like? Like Fuller, most fair planners implicitly accepted the traditional gender roles of middle-class white society, where men worked for wages while women tended house and minded children. Technology offered new ways to fill these traditional roles, but said nothing about new roles. Yet the international scope of the technocratic vision—among other things, Mrs Modern's telephone bringing her exotic woods from the East Indies—implied a global reordering that technocratic futurists declined to address.

The social evasiveness of technocratic consumerism was captured in the memorable closing scene of *King Kong* (1933) [**127**]. After the ape had fallen from the Empire State Building, a newly constructed engineering marvel, one character observed that 'the airplanes got him'. No, said another, 'It wasn't the airplanes—'twas beauty killed the beast.' The men whose technology had brought beauty and beast together in the hope of financial gain looked on the fatal encounter of beastly nature and feminine culture ruefully, as disinterested observers.

Money

5

The Political Economy of Architecture

A thousand years ago the Anasazi, ancestors of the modern-day Pueblo Indians of New Mexico and Arizona, lived in underground pit houses, in small, person-sized caves, in dwellings built in the openings in cliffs, and in free-standing houses of all sizes. Of all their varied types of architecture, it is the ruined 'great houses', enormous free-standing or cliff-face structures, that have intrigued successive waves of newcomers from the time the Navajo arrived six or seven centuries ago and claimed the Anasazi great houses as an ancestral homeland. Although we now understand that these buildings comprised a relatively short-lived episode in the long Anasazi-Pueblo history, they seem to represent something essential about Anasazi culture.

The problem is to understand why they were constructed. Most commentators have decided that they were communal dwellings of some sort. Since 1844, when Josiah Gregg first described Chaco Canyon, New Mexico, to the European-American world, the Anasazi great houses have been described as lost cities, villages, and apartment houses. Pueblo Bonito (910–1110), one of nine great houses in Chaco Canyon, is the best-studied of the great houses, and lends itself to this interpretation [128]. The building was pushed back against the north wall of the broad, shallow canyon like most of its neighbours. Its curved multistorey rear wall sheltered a central plaza divided down the middle, enclosed along the straight side by a low file of rooms, and punctuated by a number of sunken round rooms. The architecture of Pueblo Bonito has been interpreted as a schematized representation of a large community and its subdivisions. If formal analogies between the Anasazi great houses and contemporary pueblos are reliable, the divided plaza may reflect social organization into kinship-based halves, or moieties, each focused on one of the two large round rooms, which are believed to be kivas (sunken ceremonial chambers) like those now in use among Anasazi descendants. The smaller kivas may be evidence of further social subdivision. This view is reasonable, but difficult to do much with because it focuses on Pueblo Bonito in isolation and on an interpretation by analogy between architectures and societies separated by hundreds of years.

Detail of 143

It may be more fruitful to ask about the society that produced the great houses than to try to determine the uses of their individual parts. Using this strategy, archaeologists have examined the Anasazi great houses in the context of other Anasazi buildings and of the natural and human-made landscape they occupy. They believe that the adoption of agriculture some time between 700 and 1000 CE and a resulting change in social and domestic patterns led the Anasazi to abandon their traditional single-room, semi-subterranean pit houses in favour of above-ground housing with several more specialized rooms. The round subterranean kiva may preserve the form of the older pit houses as a reminder of origins.

The Anasazi great houses grew slowly over several centuries from small-scale beginnings. Pueblo Bonito began as a small elliptical arc around the beginning of the tenth century, and was enlarged to its present form in three principal stages between 1020 and 1130 [**129**]. As the building was enlarged, the workmanship improved. The earliest stages of Pueblo Bonito were cobbled together of shoddy stonework reinforced with mud and earthfast stakes, while the final stages were built of carefully shaped and fitted, dry-laid stonework.

The increase in scale may reflect an environmental change. From the early tenth to the twelfth century, summer rainfall was more plentiful and more regular than it had been before. In response to this unaccustomed abundance, groups of people began to concentrate at critical water junctions, for example where streams ran into the

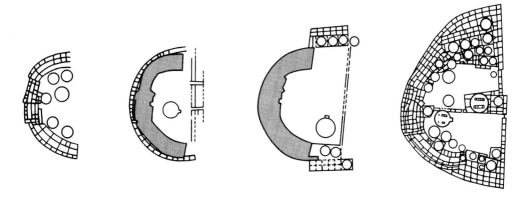

canyon, and built small communal houses at those points. This may have marked the beginning of canyon-wide efforts to make the land more productive through communal run-off irrigation systems, and of a political structure to carry out the project. The great houses were the residences of these newly gathered and organized people.

This argument founders on archaeological evidence that relatively few people resided in the great houses at their peaks. Across the canyon from the great houses, though, there were many much smaller ones, never more than one storey tall, that contained a few rooms and a couple of kivas. According to the archaeologists, these small houses teemed with people. In addition, there were several extremely large kivas, such as the so-called Casa Rinconada, sitting alone in the middle of the canyon between the great houses and the small ones. Taken together, these great houses, small houses, and isolated great kivas suggest a highly complex settlement system serving a stratified society. They imply that the great houses were begun as small communal residences during times of abundant rain and economic surplus, but were enlarged to their exceptional form during times of scarcity, perhaps by an élite who were able to gain control of water resources and food and thus to solidify their power and to demand support from the population at large. The great houses may not have been communal residences at all, but special places like palaces or public buildings, where rulers lived and 'taxes' collected from subjects were stored.

Recent discoveries support this view of a diversified and stratified Anasazi society and landscape. Aerial photographs have revealed a series of long, very wide, straight roads with scraped surfaces that led from Chaco to a series of outlying great houses similar to those in the canyon but slightly later in date [130]. The roads often ended directly in front of these outliers, which were accompanied by their own small houses and great kivas. Some of the great houses, like the so-called Aztec Ruins (1111–15) at Aztec, New Mexico, were comparable in size to the Chaco Canyon buildings, but most were quite small, 'great' only

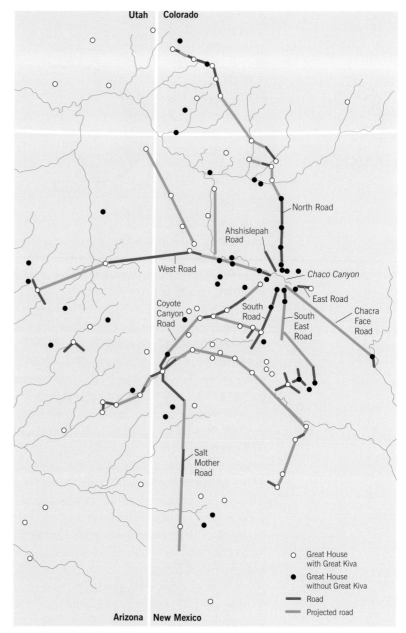

in comparison with their satellites.[1]

This regional system, which archaeologists call 'the Chaco Phenomenon', began to disintegrate around 1140. Possibly the political system was unable to respond to an exceptional period of drought. Whatever the case, the network collapsed and great houses ceased to be built, although they continued to be used. The population of Chaco Canyon dropped, while power shifted to distant Anasazi centres such as Mesa Verde, Colorado. In fact, the Mesa Verdeans occupied Chaco as a kind of colony of their own in the thirteenth century, altering the existing houses and building some new ones of a different form.

A traditional interpretation of the great houses would treat them as housing for static communities whose religious, social, and cultural values are revealed by their physical remains. Naturally the Anasazi great houses were shaped by such values, but from a vantage point many centuries later it is very difficult to deduce them from physical form. Yet whatever its symbolic meaning, architecture is rooted first of all in the everyday world of work and the economy. Empirical data about environment, landscape, and population, derived from archaeology, encourage us to understand the Anasazi great houses as monuments of a society that created a distinctive landscape during two centuries of prosperity, then abandoned it when the economy would no longer support it. The people and the culture survived, the ability to build grandly did not.

Proximity

Architecture is a phenomenon of political economy. The flow of money makes building possible and desirable. It is equally important to understand that buildings and landscapes are commentaries on political economy, not merely its translation into bricks and mortar. That is, raw economic power is filtered through the economic beliefs of builders and users, giving the landscape a variety that would not exist were it a simple vector of monetary forces.

Consider the commercial city, whose varied forms embodied equally varied conceptions of economic life. The Puritan port of Boston was founded in 1630 at the tip of the Shawmut Peninsula. A large hill called the Trimountain filled most of the west side of the Peninsula while the shoreline on the low eastern side was mostly

131

Boston in 1640.

Reconstructed plan.

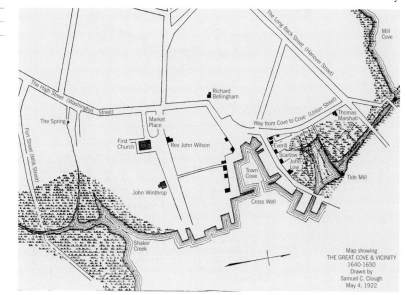

132 John Bonner

Boston, Massachusetts, 1722
This was the first published map of the city. Along with the key to the city's public buildings, Bonner has listed the city's major fires and small-pox epidemics as a kind of testimony to Boston's urbanity.

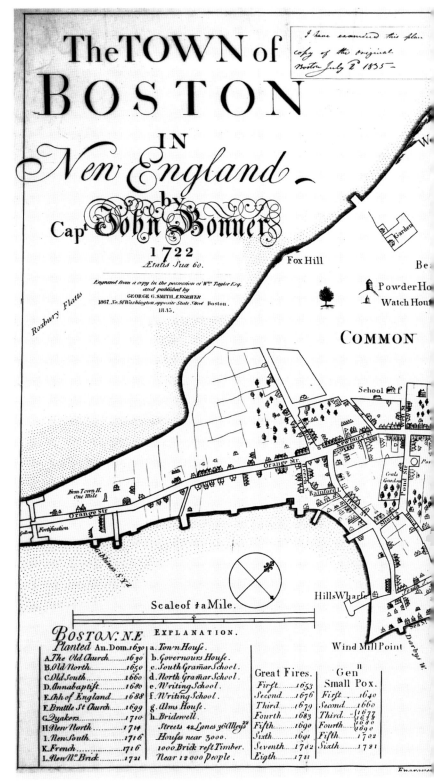

I have examined this plan copy of the original Boston July 2 1835 —

The TOWN of
BOSTON
IN
New England
by
Capt *John Bonner*
1722
Ætatis Suæ 60.

Engraved from a copy in the possession of Wm Tayler Esq.
and published by
GEORGE G. SMITH, ENGRAVER
1867 No.9 Washington opposite State Street Boston.
1835.

Roxbury Flatts

Fox Hill

Be

Garden

Powder Ho

Watch Hou

COMMON

School

From Town H.
One Mile

Orange Str

Orange Str

Fortification

Newbury

Orange Str

Rainford

Goals
Garden

Hills Wharf

Wind Mill Point

Scale of ¼ a Mile.

BOSTON: N.E
Planted An. Dom. 1630

A. The Old Church....1630
B. Old North............1650
C. Old South............1660
D. Annabaptist..........1680
E. Ch of England........1688
F. Brattle St Church....1699
G. Quakers.............1710
H. New North...........1714
I. New South...........1716
K. French.............1716
L. New N. Brick........1721

EXPLANATION.

a. Town House.
b. Governours House.
c. South Gramar School.
d. North Gramar School.
e. Writing School.
f. Writing School.
g. Alms House.
h. Bridewell.
Streets 42 Lanes 36 Alleys 22
Houses near 3000.
1000 Brick rest Timber.
Near 12000 People.

Great Fires.	Gen^ll Small Pox.
First....1653	First....1640
Second...1676	Second...1660
Third....1679	Third....1677 1680
Fourth...1683	Fourth...1689 1690
Fifth....1690	Fifth....1702
Sixth....1691	Sixth....1721
Seventh..1702	
Eigth....1711	

Engraved

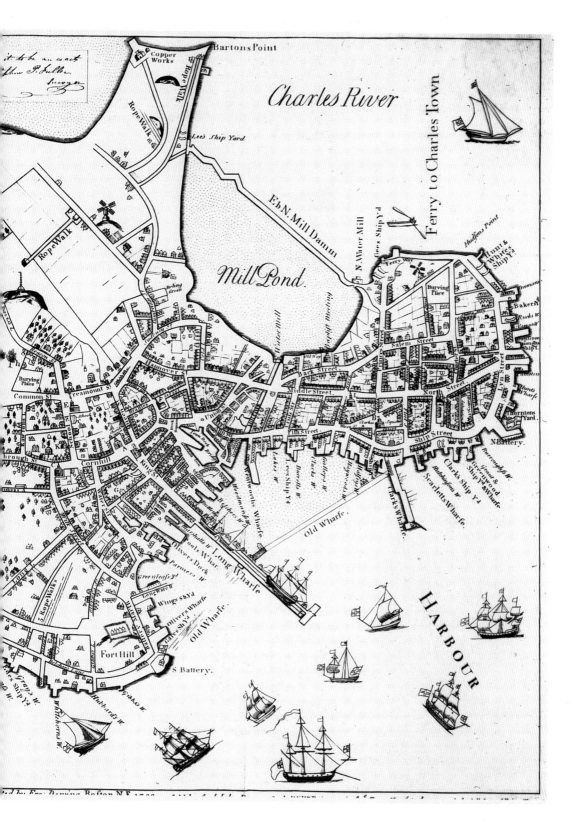

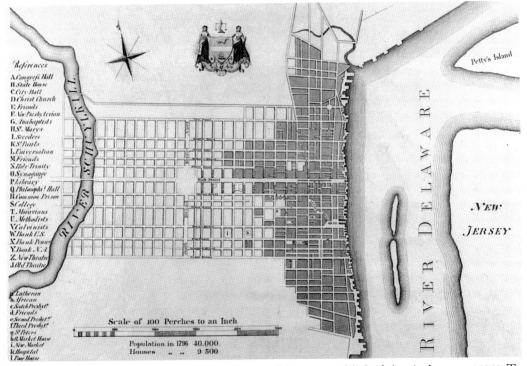

References

A. Congress Hall
B. State House
C. City Hall
D. Christ Church
E. Friends
F. New Presbyterian
G. Anabaptists
H. St. Mary's
I. Seceders
K. St. Paul's
L. Universalian
M. Friends
N. Holy Trinity
O. Synagogue
P. Library
Q. Philosophl Hall
R. Common Prison
S. College
T. Moravians
U. Methodists
V. Calvinists
W. Bank U.S.
X. Bank Penn
Y. Bank N.A.
Z. New Theatre
A. Old Theatre

a. Lutheran
b. African
c. Scotch Presbyt
d. Friends
e. Second Presbyt
f. Third Presbyt
g. St. Peters
h. Market House
i. New Market
k. Hospital
l. Poor House

Scale of 100 Perches to an Inch

Population in 1796 40,000.
Houses   ,,   ,,   9,500

133

Philadelphia, c. 1807.

The official, rectilinear plan of
the city contrasts sharply with
the pattern of urbanization
(shaded sections), which
stretches along the Delaware
River beyond the boundaries
of the Penn-Holme grid. By the
time this map was drawn the
secondary squares had
disappeared. They were
restored in the early 19th
century.

swampy, so a small navigable cove established the city's centre [131]. To
one side, a broad marketplace provided sites for the market-house, the
first meeting-house (which served both for religious and for secular
gatherings), and the houses of the governor and minister. At right
angles to the market-place a road ran along the waterfront from the
neck of land that connected the Peninsula to the mainland to the
industrial district at the north end of town, beyond Town Creek. A
century after its founding, the city had grown considerably, but
remained faithful to this spatial framework [132]. The market-place
was now called King Street. A new Colony House (1711) stood at its
head, and Long Wharf (1710), which replaced the town cove as the
focus of maritime activity, extended King Street's axis into the harbour.
The open land of the Peninsula had been subdivided except for a
remnant known then, as now, as the Common, but the road to the
Neck remained the spine of the city. In short, the city was shaped by a
T-shaped armature formed by the intersection of the Long Wharf and
King Street with the road to the Neck.

It might be possible to see this 'unplanned' or 'organic' city as a
product of the accidents of geography, except that many other early
American waterfront cities based on formal plans grew in a similar way.
William Penn and his surveyor Thomas Holme planned Philadelphia
on a grid organized around five squares and stretched between the
Schuylkill and the Delaware rivers, and imagined that the entire
platted city would develop evenly [133]. Penn and Holme designated

the central square as the site of the principal public buildings, and the other four squares as the nuclei of élite neighbourhoods. They assumed that commercial waterfronts would develop along both rivers.

The built city was much different from the planned city. Most development stretched along the Delaware River and extended inland along the perpendicular spine of market houses and public buildings running down the centre of High (now Market) Street. The result was a parabolic pattern of construction draped around a T-shaped armature very much like Boston's. Urbanization did not reach the Schuylkill River for 150 years after the city was founded. By then, Philadelphia had already spilled far beyond its northern and southern political boundaries.

For all their apparent differences, Boston and Philadelphia were shaped by the same understanding of urban life and economy. The key concept was proximity. Business was imagined as a set of personal connections or encounters. The most important urban space was the nearest one, for tradespeople depended on the street for direct physical contact with potential customers.

The sense of business as a personal transaction requiring physical proximity remains a powerful vernacular principle of urban planning. Prosperous nineteenth-century merchants opened up their establishments to the street physically, through the used of piered shop-fronts fitted with full-height doors or, in the case of luxury goods, with large plate-glass windows. They commandeered the sidewalk as display spaces for their wares [134]. Their commercial heirs are to be found in ethnic neighbourhoods in contemporary American cities, along the congested walkways of Philadelphia's Italian Market or Grant Avenue in San Francisco's Chinatown, or among the gated but façadeless restaurants and groceries of Latino neighbourhoods in Los Angeles and San Francisco [135]. Through it all, vendors remain constant figures of the streetscape, despite two hundred years of official opposition.

The building blocks of the commercial city—the central business district, the specialized retail or manufacturing neighbourhood and the tall office building, the shopping arcade, the department store, and the mall that imitate them—are all products of the traditional belief in proximity. Even post-war Los Angeles, long seen as a city that grew by scattering bedroom suburbs from its downtown, owed much to the habit of proximity.[2] The Los Angeles basin might be read as a series of small 'colonial' cities that grew up around important industries that required large amounts of land and consequently located outside the urban core [136]. The most important were the aircraft manufacturers that came to Los Angeles just before World War II and dominated the southern California economy until the 1990s. As aircraft building reorganized from the small-scale hand construction of individual

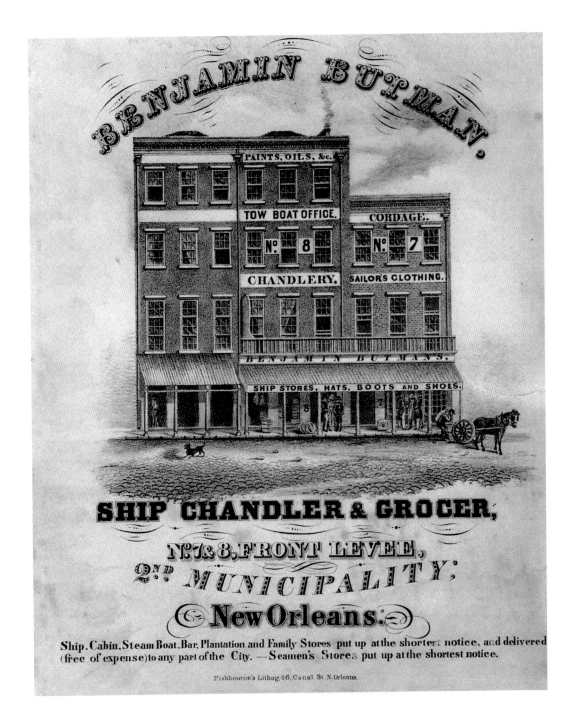

BENJAMIN BUTMAN.

PAINTS, OILS, &c.

TOW BOAT OFFICE.

CORDAGE.

Nº 8

Nº 7

CHANDLERY.

SAILOR'S CLOTHING.

BENJAMIN BUTMAN'S.

SHIP STORES, HATS, BOOTS AND SHOES.

SHIP CHANDLER & GROCER,

Nº 7 & 8, FRONT LEVEE,

2ND MUNICIPALITY,

New Orleans.

Ship, Cabin, Steam Boat, Bar, Plantation and Family Stores put up at the shortest notice, and delivered (free of expense) to any part of the City. — Seamen's Stores put up at the shortest notice.

Fishbourne's Lithog. 46, Canal St. N. Orleans.

The granite-piered shop-front, invented in Boston in the late 1820s, enabled the entire ground storey to be opened up to the street. Awnings claimed the sidewalk as display space for merchandise.

machines to assembly-line mass production, it required more space and larger numbers of less-skilled workers. The so-called Big Six, the major aircraft manufacturers in the city, all built new plants along a ten-mile radius from downtown Los Angeles. With government encouragement, 'community builders' such as the Marlow-Burns Company and Kaiser Community Homes created houses and shopping districts to accommodate these new workers. These new subdivisions were organized as self-contained economic units, not as suburbs focused on a distant downtown. Like the builders of colonial Boston and Philadelphia, the community builders of wartime Los Angeles understood urban economic life as an essentially local phenomenon.

System and Flow

Since the early nineteenth century the proximate model has coexisted with others that envisaged the economic city differently. In the eighteenth century some powerful merchants began to understand economics as a system. As they saw it, their fortunes were dependent on connections beyond their control and beyond their sight, not just on the territory of the shop and the space adjacent to it, or on face-to-face transactions with people who happened to move through it. Adam Smith's famous metaphor of the invisible hand was only one of many ways of describing this new conception of the economy.

This sense of interconnectedness had a direct effect on American urban space beginning in the early nineteenth century. For people who understood trade as a system, an economically effective urban space was one of connection and comprehensive order. The age-old grid became an emblem of the systematic character of the city. As urban reformers articulated it in the early nineteenth century, the idea of the grid challenged the assumption of proximity. Within its frame, each cell was discrete, self-contained, geometrically perfect, structurally separate, but related to every other space, not just to those immediately adjacent to it. The urban grid was conceived like a modern spreadsheet (which is, in fact, a grid). Every site had an address that could be mapped within the larger whole and in relation to every other site. In early nineteenth-century terms the grid permitted separation and classification of urban activities. Its co-ordinated independence was the spatial equivalent of political republicanism's co-ordination of individual and community, but it also commodified space, making it possible to assign each parcel a value comparatively and to sell it.

The grid was an organizing device that proved seductive at every scale, from the shelving of a shop to the double-loaded corridor of a prison or a hotel, all the way up to the national land survey established by the Northwest Ordinance of 1787. Reformers sought to restore damaged urban grids like Philadelphia's and they gridded new cities and new parts of old cities, as the government of New York City did in

its additions of 1797 and again on a grandiose scale in the state-funded
Commissioners' Plan of 1811, which projected a network of 200–by–
800–foot blocks over most of the island of Manhattan.

The grid implied a dynamic system of movement. In 1824, a group
of Philadelphia investors, including the architect John Haviland, combined to build a new shopping arcade at the western edge of the city's
business centre [**137**]. Shop-fronts lined the avenues of the gridded
interior to make the Arcade a miniature genteel shopping district
within the larger city. But Haviland and his partners had in mind a
more active sense of system than the classificatory grid. To its

investors, the Arcade's location at the western edge of the city was in keeping with the westward movement of commerce in the country as a whole. Niches on the front were intended to be fitted with iron figures of commerce and navigation. On the necking of each pier was a mask of Mercury (the Greek god Hermes), the god of roads, doors, boundaries, and lucky finds, and the protector of travellers and all who had dealings with strangers [**138**]. In soliciting a charter from the state legislature, the investors presented the Arcade as part of the system of internal improvements, an 1820s policy for developing a national economic infrastructure through the partnership of government and business. Reliefs of the coats of arms of the state and of the city (which included a figure holding a plan of the city's grid) were mounted on the façade.

This sense of the city as the nexus of a dynamic network was particularly seductive to builders in the early twentieth century, when the growth of government control over land use and the development of ever-larger tracts by single corporations encouraged a conception of the relationships in terms of urban flow rather than of static relationships. In the first decade of the century, Daniel Burnham produced a series of city plans that started from the idea of systematic circulation. They ranged from his work for the Macmillan Commission (1902), a congressional body charged with restoring and rationalizing the plan of Washington, to his collaboration with architect Edward Bennett

136

World War II-era communal development in Los Angeles in relation to the Big Six aircraft corporations. Westchester, Westside Village, and Toluca Wood were three early Marlow-Burns communities built to serve aircraft workers.

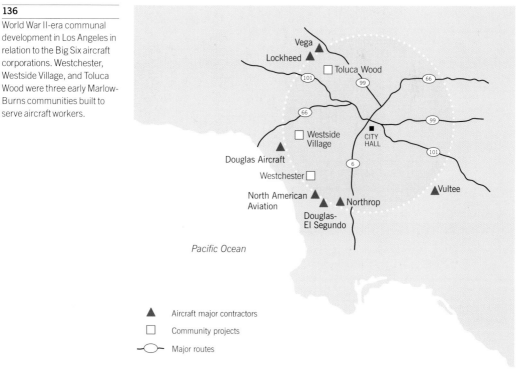

▲ Aircraft major contractors

□ Community projects

─○─ Major routes

on the monumental *Plan of Chicago* (1909), commissioned by the Merchants' Club, a businessmen's organization that merged with another, the Commercial Club, to carry off the project. While artist Jules Guérin's lush colour renderings emphasized the visual qualities of the plan, particularly of its monumental classical civic core near the shores of Lake Michigan, its most important attribute was Burnham's and Bennett's effort to convey the idea of the planned city as a system of integrated systems [**139**]. As a hygienic system, the city was united by a chain of parks connected by green parkways that ran along the lake and circled through the neighbourhoods. As an economic system, the plan was organized by land-use zoning. As a transportation system, the plan linked a lake-front harbour and railroads to a network of radial streets and circumferential boulevards that tied the city unit together. Finally, Burnham and Bennett acknowledged the inseparability of city and hinterland in their concept of 'Chicagoland', a regional system graphically emphasized by a Guérin bird's-eye view.

Little of the Chicago plan was constructed, nor were any of the other grand plans of the early twentieth century ever fully realized. We must look to the work of individual entrepreneurs for the effects of the idea of the urban system on the real city. Commercial developers took the notion to heart, though in ways that had very different con-

137 John Haviland

Philadelphia Arcade, 1824–6 (demolished 1863), Philadelphia.

Rental plan, 1826.

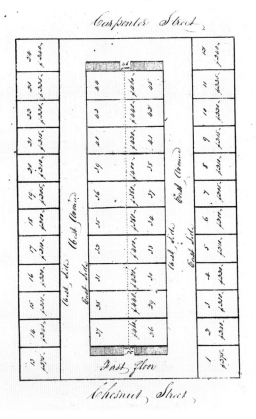

ARCADE, PHILADELPHIA.

sequences for the city than the grand planners envisaged.

Downtown Cleveland clustered around Public Square until Burnham produced the Group Plan (1903) for a U-shaped mall flanked by monumental public buildings, to be built off the north-east corner of the square. This civic centre turned its back on the square, the traditional business district, and faced Lake Erie. The north opening would be closed by an equally monumental railroad station.

Before the Plan was fully implemented, however, a local firm of real-estate developers, the Van Swearingen Brothers, began to rework the south-east corner of the square in a manner very different from Burnham's static civic centre. Their project, the Terminal Tower Complex (1916–34), designed primarily by Burnham's successor firm, Graham, Anderson, Probst and White, was anchored by three build-

**139 Daniel H. Burnham and
Edward H. Bennett**

Plan of Chicago, Ill., 1909.
This diagram illustrates the
general plan for street
circulation and parks in
relation to the areas covered
by industries and
manufacturers, and shows the
railroad lines as well.

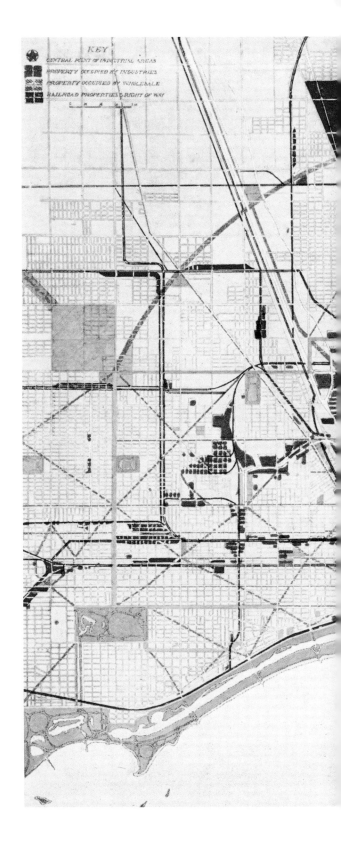

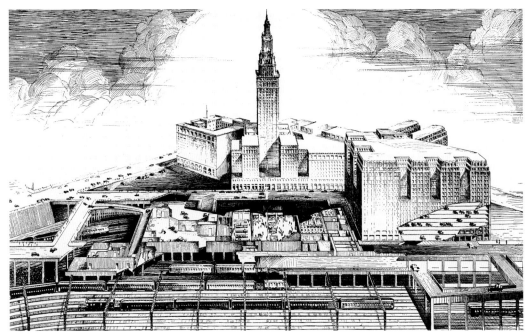

ings fronting the square: Hotel Cleveland (1916–18) and Higbee's Department Store (1930–1) flanked a central office building, Terminal Tower (1923–30) [**140**] [**141**]. Behind them, on the bluff above the Cuyahoga River, rose three linked office buildings known collectively as the Prospect Buildings (1928–30) and a post office (1932–4). Two other sites on the triangular tract were left vacant upon the developers' bankruptcy.

Although it stood on the Public Square, the Terminal Tower Complex made even less reference to the traditional downtown than the Group Plan had. With its hotel, offices, and department store, it was a self-contained enclave—'Vans' Super-City', the local newspaper called it.[3] Its isolation was sealed by the least visible part of the complex: Cleveland Union Terminal (1928–30), the multi-level transportation terminal that gave the project its name and its justification, after the Van Swearingen Brothers engineered a 1919 referendum that formally changed the site of the city's passenger station from the lakefront to Public Square [**140**]. Automobile parking was provided in the Prospect Buildings, which stood over the terminal. Long-distance trains departed from one level, while the Van Swearingens' Shaker Heights Rapid Transit line (1920) commenced its journey eastward from another. The Rapid, as it was known, carried passengers to the developers' Shaker Heights suburb (1905) just beyond the eastern edge of the city. Where the streetcar entered Shaker Heights, the brothers built Shaker Square, a local shopping district with an inn, a department store, and a theatre, all constructed in a Colonial Revival style that complemented the predominantly English vernacular style of most of the tract's single-family houses [**142**].

The Van Swearingen Brothers understood that residential districts, transit, hotels, offices, and shopping were all part of the urban system that made the city work. Paradoxically, by providing all these facilities within their own self-contained projects, they contributed to the breakdown of the larger city system. It was possible to do all one's business and return home without ever setting foot in the city itself. Their actions, together with the contemporary concentration of cultural institutions on the eastern boundary of the city (the art museum and historical society, followed by an art school and a music conservatory, constructed adjacent to Western Reserve University and Case Institute of Technology), led to the dismemberment of the formerly prosperous industrial city. The systematic urban vision embodied in the linkage of spaces, services, and transportation in the Van Swearingen Brothers' development was undermined by the nostalgic architectural imagery of Shaker Heights and Shaker Square, a white ancestral homeland built beyond the reach of the city's enormous population of European immigrants and the post-World War I influx of African Americans from the South, and eventually defeated by the project's economic failure.

The sprawling, little-known Terminal Tower Complex provided a prototype for such projects as New York's Rockefeller Center (1926–35) and Cincinnati's Carew-Netherland Plaza Complex (1930–1), a 'city within a city' containing a hotel, offices, and shopping arcade.[4] At Rockefeller Center, the developers recognized that the fiscal health of their property depended on that of the surrounding neighbourhood. They attempted to integrate the Center into its neighbourhood by routing the city's streets, along with pedestrian walkways and underground shopping streets, through the complex, as well as by staging

141

Terminal Tower Complex.
Sketch site plan, *c*.1980.
The Midland, Guildhall, and
Republic buildings collectively
comprise the Prospect
Buildings.

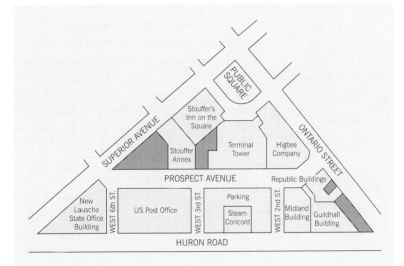

142 Small and Rowley

Shaker Square, 1929, Shaker Heights, OH.

The Van Swearingen Brothers' shopping centre, serving their élite suburb, was connected to the Terminal Tower Complex by a rapid-transit line whose tracks are visible in this photograph.

public events to draw in passers-by and by refusing to accept rental applications from tenants of nearby buildings to avoid undermining the neighbourhood. They bid unsuccessfully for a long-distance transportation link for the Center, a transcontinental bus terminal, but settled for symbolizing international trade by naming several of the buildings in the complex for foreign nations.

Like the Terminal Tower Group, the Rockefeller Center was a scale model of a city-system. However, a real city is controlled by many people and many corporations. Individuals' successes and failures alter the mixture but not the entire city. By contrast, these megadevelopments rose or fell according to the fortunes of a single corporation. The Van Swearingens failed before they completed their project, and it was only the Rockefellers' willingness to continue pouring money into Rockefeller Center during the Depression that kept it afloat. Moreover, the diversity of a real city was sacrificed to corporate considerations of profit and public relations. The seedy elements that every city has and needs—the zones of transition and humble services that accommodate the poor workers who make a city function—were excluded from these sanitized mini-cities. It was too tempting to think entirely in terms of visual composition, as the designers of the artistically ambitious Rockefeller Center sometimes did. Visual composition disastrously dominated the Empire State (or Rockefeller) Plaza (1962–78) at Albany, designed for the state during Nelson Rockefeller's governorship by some of the Rockefeller Center architects [143]. In Albany, Rockefeller Center's attempt at urban integration was jettisoned in favour of its obsession with formal massing. The result resembles an extra-terrestrials' colony dropped on an earthling city.

The Social Life of Work

It is easier to describe imaginative models of commerce than it is to separate them in practice. The office building is a case in point. Although architectural historians have been fascinated with the tall office buildings of the late nineteenth century and have spilled much ink in attempting to identify the first 'true' skyscraper and to claim it for Chicago or New York, these famous structures were one phase in a long-term development that can be traced back to the rapid urbanization of the post-Revolutionary era. Each spurt in urban growth stimulated an intensification in land values. During the 1880s, the decade traditionally associated with the construction of the first skyscrapers, Chicago's population doubled, from half a million to 1.1 million people. During that same period, land values soared from $130,000 per acre to $900,000 per acre, and reached $1,000,000 per acre by 1891.[5] Land values were products of the traditional belief in proximity, which in turn created a 'necessity' to build more intensively.

Yet this cultural construction of economic life was only part of the story of the office building. Equally important were the role of the business enterprise in a consumer society and, most of all, the social relations of work. Like a family house, the office building claimed a place in the larger society for business enterprises and symbolized the life inside it.

The traditional proximity-based commercial enterprise was conducted by a merchant assisted by one or two clerks and copyists, working out of a one- or two-room office called a counting-house. The business's success depended on the merchant's memory, bolstered by a few simple quasi-systematic records that served as *aides-mémoires*. As firms grew larger and their affairs more scattered, and as merchants came to accept a systematic interpretation of business, they generated more records, more kinds of records, and eventually more analytical records, technologies of memory that extended human capacities beyond their innate limits.

Variations of the merchant-clerk space—a single shared room or a pair of rooms, one for the boss and one for the employees—have served small businesses ever since. Speculative office buildings of the late nineteenth and twentieth centuries, for example, were built around single rooms and the so-called T-plan suite [144]. An outer room for reception and record-keeping led to a pair of inner offices for executives.[6]

For the largest organizations, though, the simple counting-house was quickly outmoded. In his United States Treasury Building (1836–42) at Washington, Robert Mills introduced a double-loaded corridor lined with small offices for the first large bureaucratic organization in the nation [145]. Mills's building was, in effect, a grid. The architect understood office work as a series of identical, interchange-

143 Harrison and Abramowitz

Governor Nelson A. Rockefeller Empire State Plaza, 1962–78, Albany, NY.

able tasks and provided identical, interchangeable spaces, each defined by a single groin vault and intended to hold two clerks, through which the department could distribute and redistribute its employees at will. In fact, the Treasury Department was still organized on the older merchant-clerk model. Each subdivision was run by an executive supported by a principal clerk and two or three sub-clerks and messengers. Treasury officials protested the lack of differentiation in the offices as well as their small size, both of which interfered with these work habits. They also complained of a lack of light and of Mills's failure to provide storage space for the records the clerks generated. The Treasury Building was formed around light courts that, when it was completed in 1869, formed a squared figure eight whitewashed on the interior to reflect light into the offices. However, the low vaulted rooms, especially on the portico-shaded east side, were so dark that some clerks on the upper floors were reputedly forced to use candles at mid-day.

Mills's Treasury Building depicted his conception of bureaucratic work, the social life of the office, rather than the abstract system of the economy. Its great East Colonnade along Fifteenth Street monumentalized the modular interior organization of structure, space, and

144 Graham, Anderson, Probst, and White
Straus Building, 1924, Chicago, Ill.
Advertisement for office space, showing T-plan office.

This Suite at $130 a Month
in Chicago's Finest Office Building

145 Robert Mills

United States Treasury
Building, 1836–42,
Washington, DC.

Plan, c. 1840, showing Mills's
projected north and south
wings bracketing the original T-
shaped building.

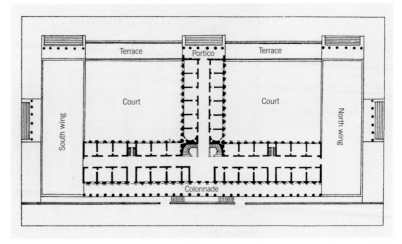

work (as well as providing auxiliary circulation to the offices, Mills said) [**146**]. Private businesses adopted the new models of work more hesitantly, but by the middle of the century, led by the railroads, corporations had begun to rationalize their record keeping and increase their staffs. Like Mills, they began to shape their offices from the inside out, building up from the basic spatial unit of work to the whole building. They tended to prefer large open rooms with adjacent executive offices, as at the Larkin Building [**107**]. Even though electric lights were available after 1879, natural light continued to be the principal source of illumination for another sixty years; so, like the Treasury Building, later office buildings were constructed as shallow slabs, often arranged around light courts. Twenty-five to twenty-eight feet was the rule of thumb for the maximum distance of any work space from a window. Structural bays and lighting needs thus created modular office spaces analogous to those in the Treasury Building.

The Public Life of Business

In the 1850s, Philadelphia historian John Watson looked about him and discovered '*A city building on the top of the former!*' These overbearing new buildings broke through 'the former *line* of equality, and beauty' that had formerly characterized the city: 'all is now self-exalted, and goes upon stilts' [**147**].[7] The tall buildings of the 1860s and 1870s took a step beyond the buildings Watson denounced, and the first skyscrapers yet another. Still, late-nineteenth-century skyscraper architects, developers, and interested observers believed that the new buildings were something qualitatively different from their predecessors. These relatively modest buildings of ten to fifteen storeys seemed outscaled and to herald a new kind of life to novelists like Henry B. Fuller, whose *The Cliff-Dwellers* (1893) and *With the Procession* (1895) portrayed the intense new life of skyscraper Chicago. They inspired the first popular futurists, men and women such as New York's

King Camp Gillette, who envisaged ever taller, denser, more congested cities. And they inspired architects and clients to consider the visual presence of their buildings in the new commercial city.

In a famous essay, 'The Tall Office Building Artistically Considered', the Chicago architect Louis H. Sullivan aestheticized the functional requirements of the skyscraper: it needed a storey below ground and an attic for mechanical services, an elaborate ground floor and a mezzanine for consumer-oriented businesses, and an indefinite number of tiers of offices.[8] At the time he wrote, Sullivan had already created several formulae for tall buildings, none of which was consistent with any other or with a literal interpretation of his maxims, but all of which generally satisfied them. However, he sometimes claimed that he had discovered the definitive version in the course of designing the Wainwright Building (1890–1), a speculative office building in St Louis [**148**].

The Wainwright Building is a tall block with a decorated ground floor addressed to passers-by and set off by a belt course from a grid of piers with recessed spandrels that mark the office floors. A deeply projecting cornice and a highly embellished frieze give the building presence in the skyline. Sullivan sought a visual embodiment of commercial life that would set the office in the context of the consumer city. The repeated windows take their 'cue from the individual cell . . . and we . . . make them look all alike because they are all alike'.[9] Like the columns of Mills's Treasury Building, Sullivan's repetitive quasi-classical piers dignify the repetitive spaces of office work, justifying its presence in the heart of the genteel downtown. As in the Treasury Building, also, the practical requirements of clerkship created a disjunction between the blockish mass of the façade and the irregular broken interior. Sullivan's building formed a capital F around glazed-

brick light courts that honoured the accepted depth for the penetration of natural light [**149**]. The offset west wing protected those offices' access to light even if another tall building were built adjacent to it. But all this was fronted by the shopfronts and elaborate main entrance. Sullivan fused Mills's interest in the metaphorical expression of bureaucratic work with the sense of the city as a social system made up of workers and consumers. In doing so, he acknowledged the civic presence of business enterprise.

Sullivan's essay treated the design of the tall building as though it offered the architect a free hand. In fact, aesthetics were constrained by technical requirements, economics, law, and architectural convention. In early twentieth-century New York, where developers were likely to build on relatively small lots, the preferred shape was a tower [**150**]. In Chicago, thin slabs on long narrow lots or cubic, cliff-like buildings with light courts on quarter-block lots (similar to the Wainwright Building) were most common. Within these norms, fiscal and legal requirements were responsible for much of a building's external massing. The urge to use land intensively was tempered by the relative costs of building and the state of the current rental market.[10] These, in turn, were subject to the zoning laws that city governments passed as they considered the effects of tall buildings on land values, city services, and the quality of life. New York's 1916 zoning law is the most famous, but other cities enacted zoning ordinances as well. The widely admired massing of the Empire State Building and other set-back New York skyscrapers of the 1920s and 1930s derived from this calculus of lot coverage, rental values, building costs, and the legally permissible 'zoning envelope' or spatial volume allowed by law, as they intersected with traditional rules of thumb for the penetration of natural light and with the progressive reduction in the size of elevator banks and service core at higher floors [**151**]. In Chicago, on the other hand, zoning laws

149

Wainwright Building.

Typical floor plan.

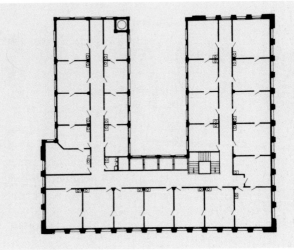

150 Napoleon Le Brun and Sons

Metropolitan Life Insurance Building, 1909, New York.

To the left of Metropolitan Life's tower, based on the Campanile in Venice, is McKim, Mead, and White's Madison Square Presbyterian Church (1903–6; demolished), which borrowed its imagery from the Pantheon.

151 J. L. Kingston

'Study of Economic Height for Office Buildings' within the confines of New York zoning law, 1930.

adjusted cornice heights according to vacancy rates and, after 1923, permitted the construction of towers on a small part of the site, creating a very different typical skyscraper, a blocky building topped with a spindly tower.

The tall office building, particularly as formulated in the classic skyscrapers of the 1920s and 1930s, had great cachet that sometimes overrode practical considerations. An elegant, distinctive speculative office building commanded more rent than a plain one. Silhouette; entry, lobby, and elevator ornament; even such mundane features as rest-rooms attracted tenants and so received close attention from architects and developers. For a governmental agency or a business corporation, a striking building created an impression of power and stability and gave it a memorable image or logo, just as an impressive headquarters building did for a manufacturing concern. For this reason, corporations often built larger buildings than they could occupy themselves, and rented out the surplus space. This was an old habit, widely practised among both business firms and institutions

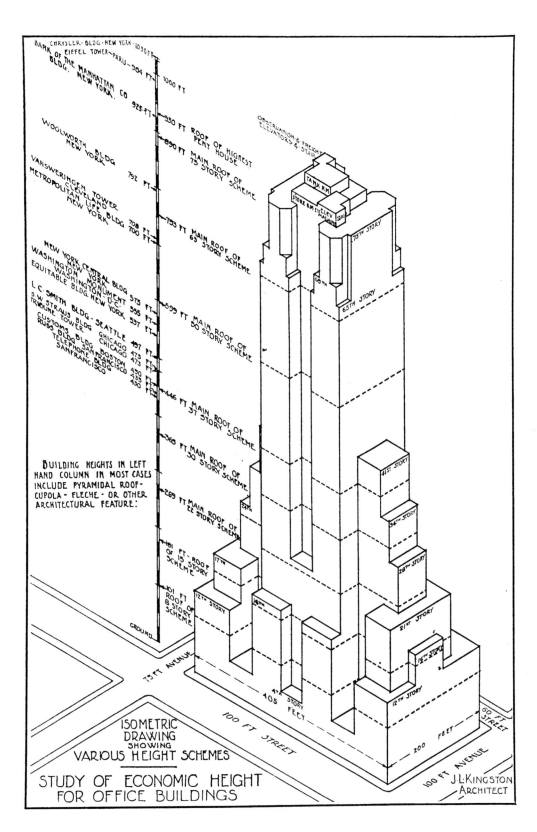

CHRYSLER · BLDG · NEW YORK · 1030 FT ·
BANK OF EIFFEL TOWER — PARIS — 984 FT
BANK OF THE MANHATTAN CO 925 FT
BLDG. NEW YORK

WOOLWORTH BLDG
NEW YORK 792 FT

VANSWERINGEM TOWER
CLEVELAND 708 FT
METROPOLITAN LIFE BLDG 700 FT
NEW YORK

NEW YORK CENTRAL BLDG 575 FT
NEW YORK
WASHINGTON MONUMENT 555 FT
WASHINGTON · D·C·
EQUITABLE BLDG. NEW YORK 537 FT

L·C· SMITH BLDG · SEATTLE 497 FT
S·W· STRAUS BLDG CHICAGO 475 FT
TRIBUNE TOWER CHICAGO 473 FT
CUSTOMS BLDG BOSTON 473 FT
RUSS BLDG SAN FRANCISCO 450 FT
TELEPHONE BLDG 435 FT
SAN FRANCISCO 430 FT

1000 FT

930 FT ROOF OF HIGHEST
PENT HOUSE

890 FT MAIN ROOF OF
75 STORY SCHEME

753 FT MAIN ROOF OF
65 STORY SCHEME

599 FT MAIN ROOF OF
50 STORY SCHEME

446 FT MAIN ROOF OF
37 STORY SCHEME

360 FT MAIN ROOF OF
30 STORY SCHEME

269 FT MAIN ROOF OF
22 STORY SCHEME

181 FT · ROOF
OF 15 STORY
SCHEME

101 FT
ROOF OF
8 STORY
SCHEME

GROUND

BUILDING HEIGHTS IN LEFT
HAND COLUMN IN MOST CASES
INCLUDE PYRAMIDAL ROOF-
CUPOLA - FLECHE - OR OTHER
ARCHITECTURAL FEATURE ·

OBSERVATION & FREIGHT
ELEVATORS & STAIR

TANK RM
STORE RM ELEV
MACHINE STAIR

75TH STORY

65TH

65TH STORY

41ST STORY

34TH STORY

28TH STORY

24TH

21ST STORY

18TH STORY

17TH

12TH STORY

16TH

12TH STORY

4TH STORY
405 FEET

75 FT AVENUE

100 FT STREET

200 FEET

60 FT STREET

100 FT AVENUE

ISOMETRIC
DRAWING
SHOWING
VARIOUS HEIGHT SCHEMES

STUDY OF ECONOMIC HEIGHT
FOR OFFICE BUILDINGS

J·L· KINGSTON
ARCHITECT

such as fraternal associations, private libraries and trade associations, which often occupied only a single floor of their large and sumptuous headquarters and leased out the rest. The construction of skyscrapers continued this practice.

In the end, the skyscraper's metaphorical power outweighed its economic rationale. Journalist W. J. Cash's observation of interwar Southern cities was true of the entire country outside the largest cities. 'For every real new skyscraper plastered with mortgages,' he wrote, 'ten imaginary ones immediately leaped up in the mind of the secretary of the Chamber of Commerce and his Rotarian followers.'[11] The lone early twentieth-century skyscrapers in small cities, like the skyscraper city halls in such places as Oakland (1914), Los Angeles (1926–8), Buffalo (1929–31), Kansas City (1937), Richmond (1971) and even the Corbusian slabs of New Orleans' Civic Center (1956–9), as well as the skyscraper state capitols in Nebraska (1922–32) and Louisiana (1931–3), had less to do with with economics and land-use restrictions than with the celebration of efficiency, modernity, and progress [44].

The skyscraper's visual cachet was apparent in the contemporaneous construction of skyscrapers in both the New York and the Chicago styles in a single city, Philadelphia, during the late 1920s and early 1930s. At the same time, the Philadelphia Saving Fund Society built a very different headquarters, on Market Street near City Hall [152]. Though emphatically unSullivanian in appearance, the PSFS Building followed his formula closely: a two-storey base contained shop fronts and a monumental banking room on the mezzanine. A grid of office floors (alternating two-room and T-plan suites) was capped by the mechanicals, hidden inside a colossal sign bearing the initials by which the bank was known. The imagery of urban process closely resembled Sullivan's as well. The elegant, highly polished marble of the base gave an air of luxury to the consumers' street. Its curved corner embodied the dynamics of the street, incorporating a sense of flow that continued to the escalator that carried one up to the banking room and the banks of elevators to the upper floor, which were called out by being incorporated into a dark-coloured spine that contrasted with the cladding of the offices. The giant PSFS sign was redundant, for the appearance of the building itself was enough to make the bank's headquarters stand out from the rest of the Philadelphia skyline.

Most of PSFS's brother corporations in the 1920s and 1930s preferred traditional or 'modernistic' classicism. The choice was careful, not the unthinking reaction or lack of imagination that Sullivan labelled it in his bitter old age. Since the mid-nineteenth century architectural writers such as Robert Dale Owen had promoted classicism as a flexible, modular architectural language, the visual equivalent of the grid (as Robert Mills understood). In addition, classical architecture carried the imprimatur of western élite culture, dignifying

Philadelphia Saving Fund
Society (PSFS) Building,
1929–32, Philadelphia.

commercial pursuits that might otherwise seem suspiciously tawdry and giving them an aura of stability in a volatile economy. In constructing a tower headquarters based on the Campanile at Venice, the Metropolitan Life Insurance Company boasted that the building was 'designed in the Early Renaissance style of northern Italy—a style combining dignity with refinement, and of a flexibility readily adaptable to the exacting commercial requirements of the day', just what one would presumably want from a prosperous but responsible insurance corporation [150].[12]

Such corporate palaces served a dual purpose that addressed the presence of the business corporation in public life. By cloaking themselves in an architecture widely celebrated as the highest cultural expression of humankind, they boldly claimed a privileged role in public life. The power to build in the classical mode, to present a quietly confident appearance to the public, lent the large corporation an authority that contrasted conspicuously with smaller businesses that continued to resort to startling signs and other strident devices to establish their presence in the commercial environment.

Inside, corporate 'home offices' offered a model of work life based on the idea of the home-like world that Frank Lloyd Wright had evoked in the Larkin Building [107]. Historian Angel Kwolek-Folland has described the seigneurial domesticity of managerial offices decorated with fireplaces and panelling. They contrasted sharply with the machine-dominated spaces of the clerical staff. As the outer office came to be more dominated by machines and the task of clerk lost the prestigious skills associated with it, the office came to be populated, but not run, by women.

The home-like world of the large corporation, as the Larkin Building showed, was predicated on surveillance with a very particular content. The executive paterfamilias watched and 'protected' his female employees from the vantage point of his den-like office. The women were further protected by segregation from men in their job assignments and work locations. The close co-operation and shared quarters of the old merchant-and-clerk of a century earlier gave way by the turn of the century to a broad gulf in status, pay, spatial accommodations, and architectural decoration that separated executive and secretary. Even the little T-plan office was gendered, with the outer, publicly accessible office occupied by female clerks and the inner, buffered, windowed offices the domain of male managers [144].

It was only after World War II that the introduction of efficient air-conditioning and fluorescent lighting freed corporate architects from some of the spatial and technical constraints of the early twentieth-century office building. Compared to prewar skyscrapers, the new office buildings of the 1950s offered enormous amounts of unencumbered floor space that accommodated a quantum leap in bureaucracy.

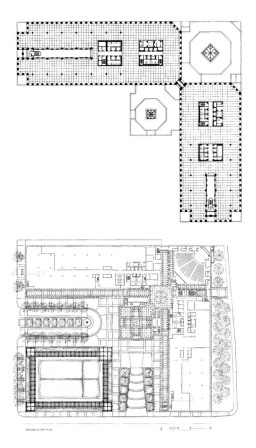

GROUND FLOOR PLAN

One study found that between 1940 and 1960 the average number of white-collar employees and the average floor space per firm doubled.[13] Expanses of glass now spoke of modernity and cultural authority. The 1970s and 1980s added idiosyncratic prismatic or historicist massing, but glass retained its cachet: a designer of a 1980s corporate head-quarters confessed to fears that a stone-clad building 'might not be modern enough'.[14] The task of the newest buildings remains the same as that of their predecessors of a hundred years earlier: to establish presence in the city by great height or distinctive appearance and to arrange the social relations of the office in a way that reinforces corpor-ate authority.

The techniques by which these ends were achieved have been remarkably stable for the past century. Even classical skyscraper massing was reappropriated in the 1980s. In expanding the Procter & Gamble World Headquarters (1982–5) in Cincinnati, the architects Kohn Pedersen Fox Associates placed two blunt towers on top of an L-shaped office slab [153]. There was no spatial necessity to build towers: the building occupies a small part of a two-block site and the slabs and the towers alike contained open work floors that differed little except in their floor areas [**154**]. Instead, the towers are obviously meant to become familiar images of a powerful corporation, and to be seen from a distance in the context of older, similarly shaped towers in the skyline such as the Central Trust Tower (1913), Cincinnati Gas and Electric Company (1929–30) and especially the nearby Times-Star Building (1930), which the Procter & Gamble building resembles most closely.

Procter & Gamble's claim to public authority on its own terms is unmistakable. The towers hide behind a formal garden that takes a two-block bite out of the downtown grid while the public street between the blocks is paved to match the garden, claiming it as corporate territory. Indeed, the garden is chained off when the building is closed. As one critic noted, 'those who stroll through the pergolas and parterres understand that they are guests of the company'.[15] The entry and the elaborate atrium (which resembles the public lobby of one of Chicago's most elaborate 1930s skyscrapers, the Board of Trade Building) are meant, like the towers, to be viewed from beyond the street-front guard shack.

On the interior the familiar cubicled open floors of the modern corporate office are organized so that every employee has a view. This is an explicit effort to avoid hierarchy, and is matched by the declared lack of differentiation in status from floor to floor. Yet the upper floors of the towers are finished more cheaply, and the corporation's executives shield themselves from egalitarianism by remaining ensconced in the upper floors of the old building.[16]

The Moral Authority of Capitalism

Since the late nineteenth century the architectural claims of the corporation have been underpinned by assumptions about the role of capitalist enterprise in the moral order of the world. These assumptions were laid out most explicitly in a spectacular world's fair, the World's Columbian Exposition, held in Chicago in 1893. Many of the city's major businessmen, assisted by some of the nation's most prestigious commercial architects working under the supervision of Daniel Burnham, shaped the celebration, which opened a year after the anniversary it was intended to commemorate.

The fair was an international exposition of a type that had been inaugurated at London's Crystal Palace exhibition of 1851, a display of the products of human ingenuity in industry and agriculture. Like the Olympic Games, which began a few years after the World's Columbian Exposition took place, the veneer of co-operation barely concealed an atmosphere of intense competition. The host country expected to 'win' and arranged the grounds to establish a home-field advantage for its own goods and culture.

Early on, the planners decided that the Chicago fair would have a formal, architecturally impressive Court of Honor, the famous 'White

City', at its centre [**155**]. It would be cloaked in the visual language of Renaissance classicism, which they believed represented the highest human achievement to date. The White City was a meditation on the place of the United States in world history, offered as evidence of the nation's claim to be the new pinnacle of culture.

The layout of the fair was carefully arranged to assert this claim over and over. A series of dichotomies, of near and far, formal and picturesque, classical and non-classical, serious and playful, told the story of the American past and predicted a glorious cultural future based on the nation's economy. As visitors moved farther from the Court of Honor, they moved away from its monumental unity and backwards in historical and cultural time. Beyond it was an area planned in a picturesque manner around a lagoon and containing the state and international exhibitions [**156**]. The former, modelled on well-known historic buildings, depicted the United States as it was in 1893 and as it had been in the past [**46**]. From the lagoon, one moved on to the Midway Plaisance, a slightly disreputable zone of fun that also represented the cultural past. It was run by the fair's Department of Ethnology and Archaeology and contained both formal ethnographic exhibits and pseudo-ethnographic commercial displays. The long narrow strip of the Midway was arranged as an 'ascending scale . . . starting with the lowest specimens and reaching continually upward to the highest stage', in the words of the organizers.[17] That is, the darkest-skinned peoples were placed at the far end and the lightest-skinned 'Teutons' adjacent to the lagoon area. The Women's Building stood at the intersection of the two.

Visitors to the World's Columbian Exposition were invited to understand the White City against this backdrop. The architecture

155 Daniel Burnham, chief planner

World's Columbian Exposition, 1893 (demolished 1894), Chicago, Ill.

The Court of Honor, or White City, is in the left foreground, with the less exalted portions of the fair stretching away to the Midway Plaisance at the rear, marked by the Ferris Wheel.

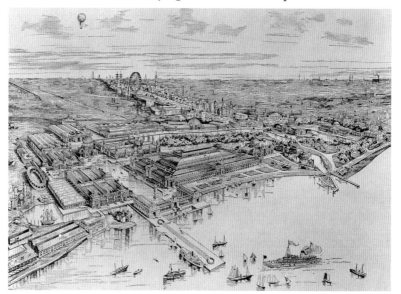

World's Columbian Exposition.
Souvenir Map. The Court of
Honor is in the lower centre,
adjacent to the pier, with the
Lagoon above it and the
Midway Plaisance at the upper
left.

offered a vision of future perfection, but contained the industrial products of the present-day United States. Viewers were encouraged to equate the material variety with cultural achievement. In that context, the whiteness of the White City was even more striking and multivalent. The visually white 'city so holy and clean' was also morally white, in contrast to the sinful moral and cultural titillation of the Midway Plaisance, and it was racially white.[18] The White City was a dangerous and self-indulgent fantasy, but one given persuasive force by its tangibility.

The Spatial Economy of Consumption
If the World's Columbian Exposition was competition presented as co-operation, it was also a festival of consumption disguised as a celebration of production. The exhibits focused on end-products not on processes, on the oceans of industrial and agricultural goods available to consumers in industrial societies. They also offered a glimpse of the intangibles that consumers' economic power could command, including access to the cultures of non-western people.

In that respect, the time-worn comparison of the World's Columbian Exposition to a department store is an apt one. For all its high-blown claims, the fair was a consumerist spectacle that skillfully employed the spatial techniques developed on the streets of the commercial city. Like the department store, the fair combined compression of scale with profusion of goods to overwhelm the visitor. It collected the industrial and agricultural products of a nation in a single confined space, then laid it out in a classified, systematic manner that created an impression of totality.

By the same token, consumer retailers implied that the finite selection of goods made and offered for sale in the market-place encompassed the entire world of possibilities, the entire scope of possible desires. The mixture of goods in a department store or the mixture of shops in an arcade or a shopping mall were carefully calculated to create this impression. Each reinforced the other, making the whole seem larger than its parts. The encompassing vantage point was crucial to this impression: on the interior of a shopping arcade, one could see all the shop fronts. On the interior of a department store, a kind of institution invented in France and imported to the United States in the third quarter of the nineteenth century, an open court or rotunda permitted the shopper to take in many of the displays at once. Twentieth-century department stores added escalators for the same purpose.

At the same time, the inclusivity of the consumer landscape was selective: it appeared to be a totality, but it reduced a world of possibilities to those that were appropriate to the desired audience. The investors in the Philadelphia Arcade (1824–6) were deeply divided over the issue of permitting lottery shops to rent space in the building [**137**]. Those who opposed the shops believed that they drove away genteel customers. Equally important, lottery outlets subverted the mechanism of desire and disappointment, which was fuelled by the association of mundane goods with higher values. At the Arcade, space for the Philadelphia (formerly Peale's) Museum was added at the last minute to serve this purpose. It was arranged according to intersecting moral and scientific classifications of people, plants, and animals. This museum of the unbuyable gave an impression of comprehensiveness that rubbed off on the museum of the buyable on the two lower floors. In addition, it dignified a visit to the Arcade as an edifying experience, rescuing it from the taint of mere consumerist luxury that republicans feared.

The prestigious architectural ornament of the Arcade's exterior was equally vital to the goals of the developers [**138**]. It associated the ephemeral act of consuming widely available goods with a fixed, exclusive, and presumably enduring élite. The temple form of a shopping arcade, the cast-iron façade of a late nineteenth-century department store that resembled a Renaissance palazzo, the classical decoration of a corporate headquarters all conveyed their messages through indirection. This was the critical difference between the World's Columbian Exposition and a skyscraper or a retail shop. The fair's architecture proclaimed a direct link between American industrialism and the high

157 Edward B. Delk and Edward Tanner, initial architects for the J. C. Nichols Company

Country Club Plaza, 1922–, Kansas City, Mo.

Plan c.1950.

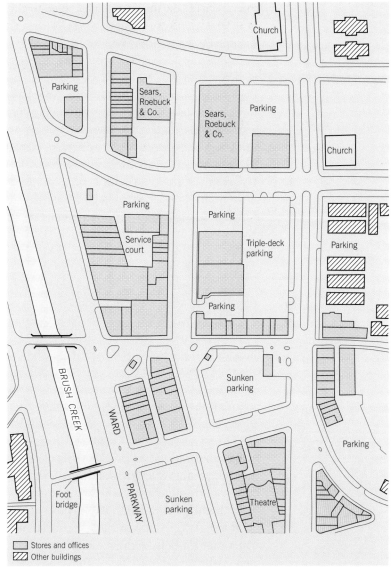

culture of Europe. No arcade or department store explicitly promised that shopping in its temple or palazzo made the consumer a Roman citizen or a Florentine banker. Such a claim would be rudely dismissed. Instead, consumerist architecture is the architecture of the wink and the gentle nudge in the ribs. Élite values and consumer goods are connected only obliquely. It is an architecture of inflection: by juxtaposition a little of each rubs off on the other. Élite culture is made more accessible and consumption more dignified.

The term *inflection* is borrowed from Robert Venturi's tract *Complexity and Contradiction in Architecture* (1966), which argued for architectural design that was not self-contained, but inflected, or affected visually by its context. In the same way, the psychological meanings of consumerist images are affected by their contexts. To put it another way, consumerism works to the extent that it is not rational, systematic, or transparent, that it does not make explicit promises of personal transformation, but to the extent that it offers fragmented, indirect, allusive, connections between hard goods and intangible desires.

Twentieth-century merchandisers inherited and continued to refine the techniques of compression and profusion, totalization and selection, juxtaposition and inflection. In Kansas City developer J. C. Nichols began in 1906 to build a series of subdivisions known collectively as the Country Club District, an upper-income enclave segregated by class, race, and, in its early decades, religion. In the early 1920s Nichols determined to create a regional shopping centre that would be the tip of a pyramid of various sized, carefully distributed shopping nodes that his company had scattered through the Country Club District since its inception [157]. This artificial downtown, Country Club Plaza, employed all the techniques of the shopping arcade, the department store, and the world's fair. It was a miniaturized city that, in Nichols's words, would create 'the orderly effect so generally praised in Paris and other European cities'.[19] The uniform one-to-two-storey heights and the quasi-Mediterranean style linked the disparate stores together [158]. The shops were carefully co-ordinated by type and restricted by the Company in the kinds of inventory they could stock, to minimize competition among them and maximize profit to the Company, which collected a percentage of their income.

The presentation was as refined as the selection. 'Screaming advertisements, hideous combinations of color, flaming advertising lettering across an otherwise pleasing storefront or plate glass window', all staples of the nineteenth-century urban shopping district, were strictly prohibited.[20] Instead, the architecture juxtaposed the goods on sale with the gentility and exoticism associated with the Spanish Renaissance and Baroque architectural forms chosen as 'the most adaptable and elastic for our purpose'.[21] So Kansas City's gentry shopped among the domes and towers of an Andalusian city. Where the world's fair exhibited foreign peoples as a sign of American culture's buying power, at Country Club Plaza painted-tile vignettes casually reminded shoppers of the reach of their own. In one, a peasant toiled along a road beside a Mesoamerican pyramid, his back bent over with the burden of dozens of pots that, one assumed, would end up on the shelves of the Plaza.

Nichols believed that his best and most desirable customers were those who could afford to travel to the Plaza by car. Over 50 per cent of the land in the Plaza was given over to roads and parking. After a year, automobile traffic was so great that a parking garage was built. At Country Club Plaza and its successors, the consumerist techniques of

158
Country Club Plaza.

the shopping arcade were folded into the desire to create an improved city of a particular sort, one that adapted urban methods and forms to the automobile.

Post-war shopping-centre and, later, shopping-mall developers were equally faithful to the old retailing lessons of profusion, juxta-position, and refinement. Guided by market research and sociological data that stereotyped target audiences, developers controlled the mix of shops in their new retail centres even more closely than in the Philadelphia Arcade or Country Club Plaza. They also endorsed Nichols's desire to create an automobile-friendly city without sacrificing urban qualities. In designing the influential Northgate Regional Shopping Center (1947–51) in Seattle, John Graham and Company studied downtown Seattle. They noticed that large depart-ment stores acted as magnets that drew people back and forth among the smaller businesses, and they structured their shopping centre in the same way [**159**]. A double row of stores faced one another across a pedestrian mall. Large 'anchor' department stores were separated by speciality shops. Viewed from the outside, across their acres of parking lots, these buildings now appear to be anti-urban assaults on the city. The designers, however, saw them from the inside, as quintessential (if perfected) urban spaces organized around an internal street.

In short, suburbanizing developers believed they were revitalizing the city. Ironically, given the mall's association with the automobile, their vision turned on a downtown without cars. In part, the planners'

objection to the automobile was practical: how could one accommodate cars within the traditional relationship of shop-front to street? The
answer was to turn the street inside away from the car. At Northgate,
not only were cars barred from the shopping street, but an underground service tunnel allowed delivery traffic to be separated from
both pedestrians and their automobiles.

The issue was more than a logistical one. Early shopping-centre
designers also sought to create a pedestrian-scaled urban community
that would encourage face-to-face contact. Pioneering shopping-
centre designer Victor Gruen, who was responsible for Northland
Shopping Center (1954), Detroit, and Southdale (1956), Edina,
Minnesota, the first enclosed, air-conditioned mall, wanted them to
have a civic presence—to be urbane as well as urban—by housing many
of the public rituals of traditional downtowns.

The nostalgia was genuine and at the same time it was part of the
selling process—by definition, the two are inseparable in the production of consumer desire. The idealized community of the mall juxtaposed the buyable and the unbuyable in yet another way. As Peale's
Museum did in the Philadelphia Arcade, public dances, children's-
choir performances and Santa Clauses marked the shopping mall as a
communal site that transcended merchandising. In recent years,

nostalgic images of old-time merchandising and sanitized vendors' carts reminiscent of the laissez-faire downtown street incorporated into modern malls have been added to the repertoire [**160**]. They transform shopping into a communal rite, a part of the national heritage.

In the mid-1950s Gruen brought this nostalgic urbanism back into the city, a process that he described as repaying the city for its lessons with the fruits of shopping-centre wisdom. His 'City X' project for Fort Worth (1956) proposed to turn that city's deteriorated downtown into a lucrative shopping centre, surrounded by concentric highways and satellite parking to 'repel the invasion of mechanical hordes into those areas where they create havoc.'[22] The plan was rejected by the voters, but Gruen was able to build something like it in Kalamazoo, Michigan (1959) and Fresno, California (1961).

Urban revitalization schemes of the 1970s and 1980s incorporated the same nostalgic concept of the pre-automobile city. Faneuil Hall Marketplace, Boston, was built around the city's nineteenth-century public market [**161**]. Cities established these institutions to distribute vital provisions while controlling hygiene, prices, and sources (sellers had to be local people). Quincy Market (1825), the main building, is a magnificent granite neo-classical building constructed on filled land adjacent to the eighteenth-century market house, Faneuil Hall. It had been an urban revitalization scheme in its own right, intended to dignify the city's ordinary commerce. The market continued to function in its original manner until the 1970s, when it was gentrified. The new

160 Rouse Corporation, developer; Frank Gehry, architect

Santa Monica Place, 1979–81, Santa Monica, Calif.

Interior.

161 Alexander Parris

Quincy Market, 1825, Boston. This rendering shows the early 19th-century market hall after it was reworked, beginning in 1971, by Benjamin Thompson & Associates for the Rouse Development Corporation, to create Faneuil Hall Marketplace, the first of the 'festival market-places' that became so popular in the 1980s and 1990s.

facility was a fragmented parody of the old, offering a carefully controlled mix of food and luxury goods. True to the consumer process, the fragment claimed to be the whole: it stood for the old-time city that tourists come to experience, evoking its grittiness without the grit. As Gruen hoped the downtown mall would be, Faneuil Hall Marketplace and its imitators, called 'festival market-places', have become models for the redevelopment of ageing downtowns as consumerist ancestral homelands, using historic architecture as the stage setting for a sanitized version of urban life in the past.

Consuming Architecture

While architecture can be a tool or catalyst of consumerism, it is itself a commodity. In the United States, a basic human necessity—housing—has been distributed almost exclusively on an ability-to-pay basis. For example, many nineteenth-century Southern planters and nearly all slaves occupied single-room houses, but in the slaves' houses many families were typically crammed into one room. Among late nineteenth- and twentieth-century urbanites, lodgers competed for space on undivided floors or platforms or at best slept in hammocks in the cheapest flop houses, a term used to describe lodging-houses that had no beds or other permanent fixtures. Cubicle hotels were the first step up: the rentable space was gridded off by thin half-height partitions [162]. As one ascended the social scale to the middle- and upper-class hotel or apartment house, the partitions became higher and thicker, the separations greater.

In addition to simple shelter, money buys individuality, the integrity of person and property essential to the middle-class self-conception. Lodgers in cubicle hotels had to put their clothes under chairs to prevent their being hooked by other guests 'fishing' over the partitions. At the opposite extreme, one of the first American luxury hotels, Boston's Tremont House (1829), advertised sound-proofing that protected its guests even from being aware of others.

Architecture has always been alienable property. In the nineteenth century it became a consumer commodity, with all that implies about the relationships among money, objects, and selfhood. The marketers of houses have depended on the consumerist juxtaposition of commodities and values, the buyable and the unbuyable, as much as those in the shopping arcade or the festival market-place have. In a typical sales pitch, the Aladdin Company of Bay City, Michigan, the early twentieth-century manufacturer of prefabricated Aladdin Redi-Cut Houses, advertised its bungalow 'The Pasadena' as 'a home of sunshine, flowers, trees and foliage . . . California—its sunshine and flowers veiled in blue sky—is evident in its every line'. Of 'The Sunshine', the copywriters wrote that 'Individuality is portrayed in all its lines and it is distinctly American in character.'[23]

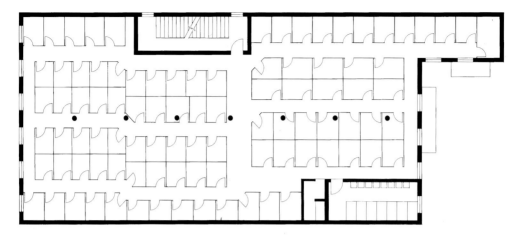

162

Kenton Hotel, *c.*1900, New York.

Sketch plan of a lodging-house's grid of cubicles. There is a shared lavatory in the rear corner.

163 Revere Copper Company

'After Total War Can Come Total Living', *Revere's Part in Better Living* no. 10 (1943).

This was one of a series of pamphlets published by Revere Copper and Brass Incorporated to remind consumers of its participation in wartime production and its intended return to manufacturing consumer goods after the war.

In 1918, it cost $1655–$2096 to buy a little bit of California in 'The Pasadena', exclusive of the prices of lot and assembly, while 'The Sunshine's' distinctly American individuality set one back $2099. These prices were lower than the average cost of housing in 1918. In that year, median income was $1140 per annum, just enough pay for one of these modest but distinctly middle-class Aladdin houses on standard mortgage terms. Theoretically, 60 per cent of American wage-earners could have afforded these models, although only 46 per cent of Americans nationwide (and less than 25 per cent in most cities) actually owned their own houses.[24] In a society that has defined the house as the principal sign of self, the ability to consume shelter carries great weight in defining one's social existence.

The difficult relationship between consumption, identity, and citizenship became a topic of public discussion during World War II, when so much of the nation's productive capacity was turned to military purposes. During the war domestic consumption was depicted as something selfish, to be put aside for the benefit of the war effort. Yet consumption seemed also to be the foundation of American strength: personal buying created national economic growth that could be channelled into the war effort and then back to consumer production. By implication, military research during the Defense Emergency would repay national self-discipline and deferred gratification with a richer post-war life [**163**].

Many architects saw their war work in this light. The migration of labour to military-related industries created a demand for quick, efficient, cheap housing. The Lanham Act of 1940 committed $150 million (and ultimately $3 billion) to the Federal Works Agency to build housing for war-workers. One beneficiary was William Wurster, commissioned to design 1,677 war-worker houses for Carquinez Heights, on the San Francisco Bay. Wurster specified flat roofs to streamline construction by allowing floors and ceilings to be con-

"After total war
can come total living"

structed in the same ways, and he arranged the houses in long north-south rows to eliminate yardwork for 'busy workers'. He hoped to derive lessons for postwar building from this effort. When he was offered a companion commission for Chabot Terrace (1943), he insisted on being allowed to experiment with the form and structure of twenty-five of the houses for future reference [**164**].

Wartime construction such as this, as well as experimentation with new materials and manufacturing procedures, stood in ambiguous relationship to consumption. It fuelled a kind of futurist speculation in magazines and museum exhibitions focused on the marvellous 'House of 194x' that would inevitably be constructed after the war. Speculative builders like Marlow-Burns, Kaiser Community Homes, and Joseph Eichler on the West Coast and Levitt and Sons on the East Coast made fortunes by applying less glamorous but very lucrative wartime methods to streamline and cheapen construction to accommodate hordes of returning veterans who needed houses.

Yet the wartime techniques expected to provide plentiful houses for middle-class consumers were by-products of interwar research to provide housing at or below the threshold of consumption. Between the world wars, design and planning professionals like Catherine Bauer, whose *Modern Housing* (1934) introduced American readers to the plight of their lower-class neighbours, advocated European social housing of the 1920s as a model for the United States. At the same time, research agencies, notably the National Forest Products Laboratory, began a search for the 'minimum house', shifting the focus

164 William Wurster

Chabot Terrace, 1943, Vallejo, Calif.

Experimental war-worker housing.

from comfortable housing to the lowest acceptable standard. Elaborate machinery with moving walls allowed National Forest Products Laboratory researchers to discover the smallest possible space in which one could live what middle-class officials believed was a decent life. The solution was a square house of relatively small dimensions, with four rooms and a bath.

These results were in turn incorporated into Farm Security Administration housing for farm workers in the western states during the 1930s, and carried over into war-worker housing [165] [166]. These government projects were celebrated in an influential 1944 exhibition of 'good architecture' in the United States, *Built in USA since 1932*, shown at the Museum of Modern Art, New York. Curated by Bauer's sister Elizabeth Mock, the show juxtaposed these minimal houses for the poor to Fallingwater, Rockefeller Center, and the great public works of the Tennessee Valley Authority.

In short, builders for post-war middle- and upper-middle-class buyers drew inspiration and practical advice from housing stripped of the symbolic content cherished by the middle class. Worker-housing appealed to a long strain of Protestant asceticism in American culture, intersecting with modernist visual austerity. Many architects and housing theorists (as opposed to private developers) were uncomfortable with the consumer dimension of the single-family house. Since the late nineteenth century housing reformers and designers had chosen to see human society and human interaction as an intangible process. They emphasized domestic space—the creation of family settings that would encourage the 'proper' kinds of social and family life and personal development—over crass architectural display.

This ambivalence about housing and social life, domesticity and community planning, was evident even in the most appealing social housing projects. The Carl Mackley Houses (1933–4) in Philadelphia, built (with assistance from the Public Works Administration) by the

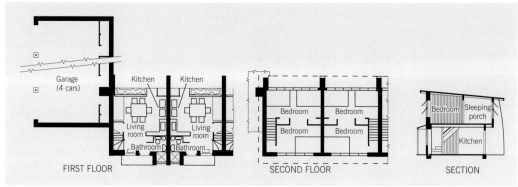

FIRST FLOOR   SECOND FLOOR   SECTION

166

Chandler Farms.

Plans and section of two units.

Full Fashioned Hosiery Workers Union whose members worked in nearby textile mills, are a case in point. The architects organized the long narrow buildings parallel to the contours of the slope on which they were built, after the manner of German social housing of the 1920s [**167**]. The project presented as idealized a portrait of urban activity and community as any skyscraper. The buildings were massed close to the street to maintain an urban appearance and density greater than that of the surrounding neighbourhood of row houses, and store fronts were set into the basements along the pedestrian level. Multiple circulation levels allowed automobiles to enter below-grade parking courts around the perimeter. Such elements as passageways through the ranks of buildings, play spaces on the roof, laundry rooms on the upper floors, a park-like open space, and a community centre with a swimming-pool promoted a good social life through constant contact among neighbours. The plentiful public spaces stood in telling contrast to the individual apartments, which adhered quite closely to the minimum-house standard [**168**]. The planners were more interested in teaching residents the value of communal life than in private pleasures.

The Carl Mackley Houses remain a pleasant and well-kept environment, one of the best of the social housing schemes, but they made no concessions to the values of a consumer society oriented towards the house as an embodiment of personal identity. Indeed, housing reformers of the inter-war and post-war period often expressed contempt for such materialism. In *Toward New Towns for America* (1957), his summary of the work of the Regional Planning Association of America in which he had played a central role, Clarence Stein bitterly denounced 'the fallacy of the American faith, almost a religious belief, in what is called "home ownership"', a phrase that Stein always set off in ironic quotation marks. The truth of the mortgage system (the twentieth-century invention that enabled so many Americans to buy houses) was that '"home-ownership" for those with low incomes is a myth'.[25] He believed that the poor would be better advised to rely on the benevolent intentions of philanthropists.

To some reformers the materialism of home ownership seemed suspect even for the well-off. William Wurster, who married Catherine Bauer, is a good example. Bauer pushed the California architect towards social housing such as Carquinez Heights and the Valencia Gardens public housing project (1943) in San Francisco, but most of his practice was devoted to middle- and upper-middle-class houses. Still, Wurster declared in *House and Garden* in 1946 that 'it is fun building to a minimum and I feel sure it is a national duty to do so'.[26]

Housing Non-Consumers

The ambivalence about consumption and identity was most evident in the long sad story of housing for those too poor to consume on their own (as opposed to those who needed help, like the working-class residents of the Carl Mackley Houses). Did they have a right to consume if they did not produce? To put it another way, did they have a social existence? The issue was complex and emotion-laden, involving the most deep-seated values of American society. European-American Christian tradition taught that God had created economic hierarchy. Poverty was inescapable, but so was the duty of Christians to help the poor. The growth of capitalist and consumer ideologies in the middle of the eighteenth century generated a new view of poverty. While there were a few worthy poor—people who couldn't help themselves, such as widows, orphans, and the ill—most poor people were so-called sturdy beggars whose poverty was the result of personal failure or indolence. They could be better off if they chose to be. Historian Michael Katz argues that Americans became entangled in untenable distinctions between the worthy and the unworthy poor and repeatedly decided that it was better to oppress the worthy poor than to risk being taken advantage of by the unworthy. In a statement that could as easily have been written in the 1990s, the Philadelphia Guardians of the Poor in 1836 opposed outdoor relief, or cash payments to the poor: 'The pauper is as comfortably housed, clothed and fed as his more frugal and industrious neighbour', which removed the incentive to work harder and demoralized the industrious. Instead, they should be housed in almshouses which, 'except to the worthless, conveys a sense of degradation'.[27]

In housing, the result has been to reinforce the economic principle that only those who can pay should have pleasant physical surroundings: anything more robs the industrious. Since the early nineteenth century, public-welfare officials have assumed that housing for the poor, whether in almshouses or public housing, should involve no excess expenditures or gratuitous physical amenities and that it should be disciplinary, instilling identity through enforcing desirable behaviour. The poor should have only what they could win and hold in the marketplace.

167 Oskar Stonorov and Alfred Kastner
Carl Mackley Houses, 1933–4, Philadelphia.
Axonometric view.

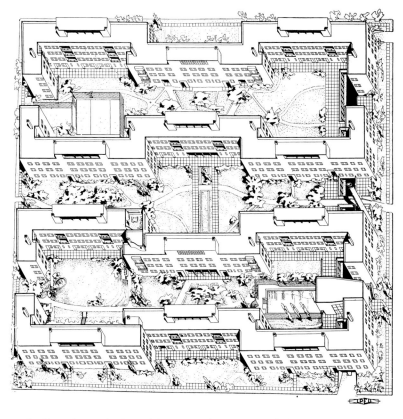

In fact, the majority of the poor always existed that way, in 'market' housing such as tenement flats and rentals, alley and court housing inside blocks, and in urban residential hotels [**162**]. Yet social and housing reformers were unable to accept these accommodations. To be sure, the tenement-house reforms of the late nineteenth century and the campaigns against court and alley housing and single-room occupancy hotels in the twentieth century exposed genuine problems of hygiene, fire safety, and structural integrity, but, under the influence of middle-class notions of domesticity and the connection of housing with selfhood, reformers were equally concerned with the forms of social life that went on in tenement apartments and hotel rooms. (In the latter instance, they were as opposed to upper-class residence in luxury hotels as they were to working-class residence in flop houses.) These kinds of market-based accommodation were inferior because they were not matched on a one-to-one basis to the consumer. They lacked the elements of personal discipline and individual identity that constituted proper housing—separation of domestic functions, restriction of residence to family members, privacy for residents of different ages and sexes—yet inability to pay for such amenities was the source of the problem in the first place.

Those lowest on the housing scale were thus trapped between the

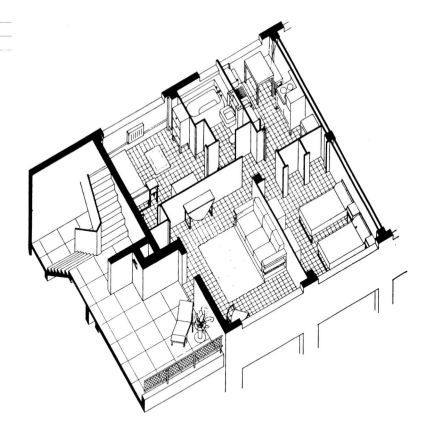

reformers' moralistic ideals. On the one hand, the places they could afford to live were socially unacceptable because they were not individualized enough. On the other, reformers and public officials were constrained from providing the types of housing they approved because it was socially unacceptable to give such things to those who could not afford them. Even in the twentieth century, when federal and urban governments intermittently accepted their responsibility to provide housing for the poorest Americans, market ideologies crippled their efforts. The great urban renewal projects of the 1950s and 1960s were driven by downtown real-estate needs. As suburban development and its attendant shopping-centres and malls drew business from the city centres, developers and public officials turned to wholesale re-development of the downtowns to resuscitate their investments. To clear land, making it available for profitable commercial projects and emptying it of poor citizens whose presence might undermine efforts to attract tenants and customers, mass housing was built out of the way of new development, at the cheapest possible price. This usually meant the construction of high-rise housing on small lots, a policy generally opposed by architects but pushed by merchants and redevelopment agencies. The result was housing that would have warmed the hearts of the Philadelphia Guardians of the Poor, housing that, in the words of

Progressive Architecture editor Thomas Fisher, was 'stripped of most amenities and shrunk to the meanest proportions'.[28]

Critics of modern architecture and public housing made the Pruitt–Igoe Houses (1950–4) in St Louis the most notorious of these projects, but they were by no means the only one [**169**]. As Katharine Bristol and Roger Montgomery have demonstrated, Pruitt–Igoe's problems derived from racism and from the conception of housing as a pendant to commercial development. Pruitt–Igoe was built to move the poor away from prime centre-city real estate. While the architects argued for a mixture of low-, mid-, and high-rise towers, the federal agency that oversaw the project insisted on the construction of thirty-three high-rise towers for economy's sake. For the same reasons, amenities such as play areas and landscaping were omitted and the buildings were made of the cheapest materials and with fittings that often broke the first time they were used. In the long tradition of expecting paupers to pay for their own relief, the Federal Housing Act of 1949, under which the houses were built, stipulated that the project must operate on the income it produced. The state of the post-war housing market and racial relations relegated Pruitt–Igoe to the poorest African-Americans, whose rents, pro-rated to their incomes, were incapable of supporting maintenance.

169 Kleinweber, Yamasaki, & Hellmuth

Pruitt–Igoe Houses, 1950–4, St Louis, Mo.

The houses when they were new. The more familiar photograph of the demolition of these houses in 1976 has become a triumphant symbol of the follies of public housing and modern architecture. The firm that designed these houses, which epitomized the urban renewal schemes of the 1950s, has successfully made the transition to 90s-style redevelopment: it is now HOK, whose subsidiary HOK Sports is a popular designer of downtown baseball stadiums.

170 Venturi and Short

Vanna Venturi House,
1959–64, Chestnut Hill, Pa.

Pruitt–Igoe and such contemporaries as the Bay Street Public Housing (1950), San Francisco, Schuylkill Falls (1953–5), Philadelphia, and the Robert Taylor Homes (1960–2), Chicago, combined the mean-spiritedness inherited from the nineteenth century with pseudo-social-scientific notions of poverty as a pathology that public housing must address. In a consumer society, where identity was based increasingly on possessions and material imagery, housers, politicians, and voters assumed that their poor neighbours were a different sort of people, people who needed behavioural modification, people for whom the mechanisms of consumption were irrelevant or even out of place. Yet they continued to insist that the mechanisms of the market, which were driven by consumption, were the only acceptable solution. This is not to say that the poverty could be eliminated by providing bigger apartments or beautiful architecture. Even in generous-spirited housing, architects continue to betray a sense that the poor are qualitatively different, as two contemporaneous buildings by Robert Venturi's office illustrate.

Venturi made much of allusive qualities of the Vanna Venturi House (1962), built for his mother in the genteel Philadelphia suburb of Chestnut Hill [**170**]. The broad roof and prominent 'chimney' were classic signs of domesticity, but the chimney was not what it seemed and the sheltering gable was split down the middle. Similarly, the vestigial classical pediment and belt course were broken by off-the-rack windows. To the architect, these decorative elements were

171 Venturi and Rauch, Cope and Lippincott

Guild House, 1960–3, Philadelphia.

ironized and subverted by their context, yet the result was classic consumerist architecture, a series of fragmented images that juxtaposed values, exalting cheap materials through association with prestigious antique classical architecture and in the process celebrating middle-class domesticity.

On the surface, Guild House (1960–3), elderly housing built by the Society of Friends in the context of the otherwise-grim East Poplar urban renewal project at the edge of Center City Philadelphia, employed many of the same ironic devices and the same visual motifs as the Venturi House [**171**]. The curved pediment and yawning entry of the latter find their complements in the façade of Guild House, while the minimalist frieze recalls the house's equally perfunctory belt course. In a famous reading of the building, Venturi and two co-authors, Denise Scott Brown and Steven Izenour, described Guild House as 'an imitation palazzo' made of ordinary materials and stock components. They went on to praise, ironically, 'the exceptional and fat column' and 'the luxurious glazed brick' at the entrance, along with the veined marble 'that developers apply at street level to make their apartment entrances more classy and rentable'. The façade was capped by a 'flourish', a gold-anodized aluminium television antenna, which was both an evocation of a modernist sculpture and a poor substitute for an 'open-armed, polychromatic, plaster madonna' that would have been rejected by the Quaker developers. They labelled the developer's aesthetic that Guild House parodied ugly and ordinary, but consonant with the 'inevitable' plastic flowers that the residents placed in their windows.[29] The whole was intended in some way to express the lives of the elderly.

Both the Venturi House and Guild House used the same techniques of consumerist fragmentation, juxtaposition, and allusion. Yet Venturi's mother's house, however ironized, enshrined a respectful middle-class self-definition, while the Guild House ironized but endorsed a view of its aged tenants as the detritus of consumer society, prey to the developer's tawdry deceptions and enslaved to television. In that respect, despite its concern for alleviating some of the starkness of the neighbouring public housing for other non-consumers, Guild House shared the ambivalence about consumption and about the identities of non-consumers in a consumers' world that have permeated housing reform for two hundred years.

Art

Many Americans who could not name a building by Frank Lloyd Wright or pick the man out of a police line-up are certain that he was a great artist, one of a chain whose genius defines the history of architecture. Others—scholars as well as laymen and -women—understand architectural history as a parade of styles that can be recognized by diagnostic visual features, like birds, then checked off on a life list: Prairie, International, Classical, Neo-classical, Modern, Moderne, Post-Modern (but so far no Post-Moderne), Deconstructivist, and Everything Revival. Given the great diversity of American buildings, landscapes, builders, and users, how have we come to see architecture as an art organized by the co-ordinates of artist-architects like Wright and of visual styles? Why do we prefer to think of architecture primarily as an art, rather than as technology, a social act, a work of the intellect, or a commodity? To understand this state of affairs, we need to examine the histories of the concepts of art, architect, and style. Although none of them constituted *the* history of American architecture or its all-pervasive matrix, all have deeply affected the making of the landscape and the stories written about it.

Architects and Builders

Every building, large or small, high or low, is designed. Someone, or some group of people, decided what it should look like. Long before the appearance of a self-identified architectural profession, most American cultures recognized some of their members as specialists with superior skills or knowledge of building, yet their roles varied from culture to culture. Building required craft, mathematical, engineering, theoretical, aesthetic, political, and even ritual or magical expertise, combined in ways that were incompatible with any contemporary definition of the role of the architect. Moreover, these qualifications were distributed among builders and clients in ways that differ from contemporary practice. For example, women made and maintained Plains Indian tipis, often under the direction of a skilled older woman. The completed tipi was sometimes painted by its residents, working under the direction of a specialist in painting whose skills included translating traditional forms and the vision experiences

Detail of 184

and animal guardians of the household's warrior into an appropriate design as well as physically outlining the images on the skin or canvas surface.

The familiar distribution of tasks among architect, builder, and client in contemporary architecture is a relatively recent one that began to take shape in the United States in the late eighteenth century. Before then, responsibilities for building and design among European Americans were widely distributed. While some people built their own houses and a few more people constructed their own farm- and out-buildings, most construction was performed by people who made all or part of their livings as builders. Their skills and their scale of operations varied widely, ranging from small craft workers who restricted them-selves to equally small building and repair jobs to large-scale contrac-tors or 'undertakers'. These were rich men with big businesses such as Virginia's Mourning Richards who, in the mid-eighteenth century, contracted simultaneously to build five churches and one house, spread over a hundred-mile territory. In the rural South, wealthy planters such as Thomas Jefferson and Landon Carter trained slaves as skilled work-men to work on their own properties, and occasionally bid on public construction contracts to be completed by their plantation crews.

The most prosperous undertakers employed large numbers of workers, white and black, slave, indentured, and free. William Buckland, who was trained in England as a joiner (a maker of furniture, panelling, and other fine woodwork), emigrated to North America as an indentured servant to work at George Mason's Gunston Hall (1755–8), Fairfax County, Virginia, and built up a business in Virginia and Maryland after he had obtained his freedom. At the time of his death in Annapolis in 1774 Buckland owned the services of convict house-carpenter and joiner Samuel Baily, a carver, an adult male slave, and an African-American boy.

In urban areas, skilled building workers were elaborately organized. Craftsmen were trained through apprenticeship and in the short-lived schools sometimes taught by senior builders. Craft organizations disciplined the trade. The Carpenters' Company of the City and County of Philadelphia, founded in 1727, was the most famous of a number of builders' guilds that proliferated in the Quaker City and could be found in other large cities as well. As with its brother organ-izations, the key to the Carpenters' Company's power was its price-book, ostensibly published to ensure that 'every gentleman concerned in building may have the value of his money, and that every workman may have the worth of his labour'.[1] In fact, the company's control over measuring, the practice of evaluating finished work according to the price-book, allowed it to dominate the building industry even though less than a quarter of the 450 carpenters resident in Philadelphia at the end of the eighteenth century belonged to it. The book was secret and the company required that members' copies be returned at their resignations or deaths. According to architect Benjamin Henry Latrobe (no friend of the Company) the use of the price-book served to discourage carpenters from undertaking any novel work, such as his own, not encompassed in it.

Full-time builders such as Buckland and the members of Carpenters' Company designed buildings based on their craft training and architectural handbooks and treatises imported from England. In addition, genteel dabblers who owned a few handbooks and some strong opinions about proper taste sometimes contributed to design as well. One such was Joseph Brown, a professor at Rhode Island College (Brown University) in Providence, who has traditionally been credited as the architect of that city's First Baptist Church (1774–5), assisted by his copy of James Gibbs's *Book of Architecture* (1728). Brown was appointed, along with carpenter Jonathan Hammond and housewright Comfort Wheaton, to make a design for the church. Brown and Hammond travelled to Boston to see its churches and meeting-houses 'and to make a memorandum of their several dimensions and forms of architecture'. A design was created by grafting plates in Gibbs's book, notably an alternative design for the tower of St Martin-in-the-Fields Church (1726), London, on to traditional New England meeting-house forms. The committee's plan was drawn, and the church was built, by carpenter James Sumner of Boston. The First Baptist Church typified the way that major buildings were designed in colonial America, as a negotiation among clients and builders, assisted by publications and by the examples of standing structures. Design began when the building was first contemplated and reached a turning-point when the contract was drawn up, but it continued throughout the construction process, as a collective action.

Why Architects?

Colonial builders were knowledgeable people who took pride in their work even though few can be identified by name. Historians have wasted gallons of ink debating whether any of them was a 'real' architect. Was the first American architect the Newport sea captain Peter Harrison, who was given that title by his biographer? Was it William Buckland? Thomas Jefferson? Or John Hawks, who was trained as an architect in England and came to North Carolina in 1764 to construct Tryon Palace at New Bern? Even though Hawks was paid as an architect and given exclusive charge of design and construction of Tryon Palace, his claim to the title was nominal. Design is only incidentally important in distinguishing architects from others involved in building. The architect is more aptly defined by a particular relationship to the construction of buildings and to the public.

Sociologists define a profession as a full-time occupation that has its own training schools, a professional organization, licensing and other forms of community recognition, a code of ethics, and the right of self-governance. From this point of view, architecture did not become a fully-fledged profession until well into the twentieth century. But the drive towards professionalization occupied the entire course of the nineteenth century, and it revolved around the two principal elements of the sociologists' definition: autonomy, or self-definition, and packaging, or public recognition of the architect's distinctive claims.

The struggle to establish the architectural profession was a contest for control of the entire building process. All the things that had formerly been done to construct a building before the advent of the architect continued to be needed, but the would-be architect proposed to realign the process of negotiating and constructing a building in order to interpose himself between the client and the builder. This new player wanted to substitute complete professional control for the negotiation of design and construction, excluding both client and builder. Such a reorganization would separate headwork from handwork, on the one hand, and production from consumption on the other.

The architectural profession as Americans know it began to take shape in mid-eighteenth-century England. Beginning with Hawks, immigrants trained in England and France as professional architects and engineers found their way to America. In a letter to an aspiring architectural student, the English-trained architect Benjamin Henry Latrobe, who arrived in Virginia in 1796, proclaimed himself 'the first who, in our Country has endeavored and partly succeeded to place the profession of Architect and civil Engineer on that footing of respectability which it occupies in Europe'.[2]

Among the early professionals, Latrobe articulated ideals of professionalism that accorded most closely with the modern sociological definition. In 1806, he detailed them for the benefit of his protégé, Robert Mills. The architect, Latrobe said, was an impartial intercessor between architect and client. He knew the entire building process and should supervise it all. His time and ideas were his wares, and he should make this clear by retaining control of his drawings, and by allowing no changes to his design without his consent.[3]

Latrobe's letter illuminated the problems of the so-called 'market professions' in early-nineteenth-century America, those, like architects and physicians, who trafficked in arcane knowledge. How could someone attract business who had nothing tangible to sell? When a builder was hired, he left behind a house that did not exist before he arrived. The architect's skill produced nothing so palpable as the builder's physical craft did. A house could be built without his services and, in the eyes of most clients and builders, to no discernible disadvantage.

The professional aspirations of the market professions rested on a 'negotiation of cognitive exclusiveness', meaning that the professional needed to convince prospective clients that he possessed knowledge essential to them that could be obtained nowhere else.[4] For engineers, for example, part of the value of building daring suspension bridges was that they were clearly works that were beyond the capacity of non-engineers. This was much harder to demonstrate with respect to the aesthetic and spatial abstractions of architecture.

The key problem for architects, in other words, was that the process of establishing professional standing was necessarily two-sided. To his perpetual frustration, Latrobe never understood that it was not enough simply to declare himself an architect and expect clients to flock to his door. Potential clients must in turn acknowledge the existence and value of the practitioner's skills. This negotiation affected the claims that architects made for their profession, as they attempted to characterize their expertise.

'Cognitive exclusiveness' implies that professionals must present themselves as a recognizable, predictable body. To establish this impression, early-nineteenth-century American architects codified the disparate fragments of architectural knowledge into a science. Bits of architectural history, borrowed from the ancient Roman architectural theorist Vitruvius by way of European handbooks, served to establish architectural science as an unbroken tradition with deep historical roots. Common builders' practices were systematized and recast in an invented jargon to exoticize them. For example, John Haviland taught the readers of his *Builder's Assistant* (1818–21) that 'Dividing wood, by cutting away a very thin portion of the material of equal thickness throughout, to any required extent, by means of a thin plate of steel with a toothed edge is called SAWING, and the instruments themselves [are] called SAWS.'[5] Architects sought to carve a niche for themselves by claiming a more complete or higher order of mastery of architectural science than building craftsmen. The architect understood the whole process, the builder only his part of it.

In addition to standardizing architectural knowledge, architects (like other professionals) sought to standardize themselves, to create a mode of acting that was recognizably architectural through fashioning a professional consciousness. A short-lived Association for the Advancement of Architectural Science in the United States (later named the American Institution of Architects), founded in 1836 by prominent practitioners from New York and Philadelphia who were later joined by others from New England and the South, was succeeded in 1857 by the hardier American Institute of Architects, inaugurated by many of the same men. As Thomas U. Walter noted in an 1879 presidential address to the second organization, 'Whatever promotes the consolidation of the profession tends to lead the public to a higher appreciation of architectural genius.'⁶

Another way to standardize professional identity was through licensing to screen out those who did not meet accepted standards of education, expertise, and demeanour. The first licensing law was passed in Illinois in 1897, largely through the efforts of Peter B. Wight, an architect turned terracotta-fireproofing manufacturer and critic, and Dankmar Adler, Louis Sullivan's partner. Licensing came slowly, state by state, as disagreements over standards of training and apprenticeship pitted old-style architect-carpenters and architects trained as apprentices against those educated in architectural schools and colleges.

Architecture as a Business

In the early nineteenth century, as now, many architects worked for builders rather than supervising them. Pre-Civil War architects often became entangled with speculative builders in what would now be called 'design-build' schemes, conducted on such shaky (and sometimes shady) financial grounds that they almost inevitably went bankrupt. John Haviland's participation in the Philadelphia Arcade (1824–6) strained his finances to the point that he embezzled money from the construction of the United States Naval Hospital (1826–9) at Portsmouth, Virginia, which ruined his career. After the failure of a speculative housing scheme, Thomas U. Walter left Philadelphia for Washington one step ahead of his creditors. Robert Mills encountered similar difficulties in Baltimore.

As the century progressed, architects tended to abandon direct involvement in building, and until very recently professional codes of ethics explicitly forbade such ventures. At the same time they came to understand that whatever else an architectural practice was, it was foremost a business. The stereotypical division of architectural firms into design and business partners first appeared in the late nineteenth century when architectural offices began to be organized more like contemporary business enterprises. Burnham and Root's offices in the Rookery Building, Chicago, contained private rooms for the two partners (John Wellborn Root, the design partner, also had a private studio), as well as one for the chief engineer, the top executives of the company [172]. There was a library, elaborately decorated in the style of seigneurial domesticity favoured in corporate offices of the era, and serving as a genteel sales room. In keeping with the architect's stance as a mediator between builder and client (as well as with the customs of social class), there were separate waiting-rooms for clients and contractors. The office superintendent's room occupied the centre of the space. It was adjacent to a clerk's room, in the old merchant-clerk pattern, but also to a large drafting room, the equivalent of the open clerical floors of large corporations. As with a corporation, several

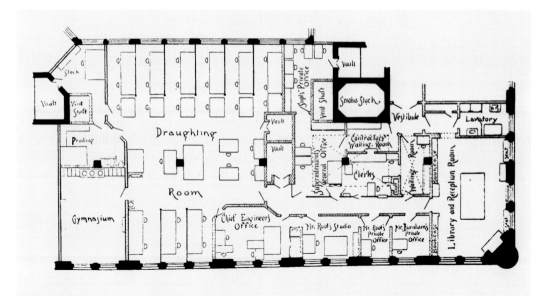

Labels visible in the floor plan:
Stock · Vault · Vent Shaft · Printing · Draughting · Room · Gymnasium · Chief Engineers Office · Mr. Root's Studio · Mr. Root's Private Office · Mr. Burnham's Private Office · Library and Reception Room · Bookcase · Waiting Room · Contractors' Waiting Room · Superintendent's General Office · Clerks · Vault · Supt's Private Office · Vent Shaft · Smoke Stack · Vestibule · Lavatory

172 Burnham and Root

Architectural Offices,
c.1888–9, Rookery Building,
Chicago.

vaults protected the firm's drawings, its paper assets.

The most successful architectural firms of the turn of the century were those who were able to organize successfully along the lines of the division of labour, establish managerial hierarchy, and institute business practices that closely resembled those of the corporate world. This helped them to manage large practices with many employees efficiently and it established a common ground for dealing with large corporate clients. It served the additional purpose of bolstering client recognition of professional claims to cognitive exclusiveness. The New York firm of McKim, Mead, and White was among the firms that were organized in a manner that paralleled the corporate offices they served. There were eighty-nine professional staff in 1909, and probably more than a hundred employees overall [173]. In 1913, McKim, Mead, and White moved into spacious new quarters in the Architect's Building on Park Avenue in New York. By that time all the founding partners except Mead were dead. The office was equipped with the most up-to-date record-keeping technologies, which were set in the middle of the floor and divided the enterprise into production and administrative segments. At the administrative end, the executives' offices were arranged around a private corridor, behind a suite of reception rooms opening off the entry hall. At the other end was the open drafting room.

Skidmore Owings and Merrill, founded in 1936, dwarfed even the largest turn-of-the-century firms. They aspired to emulate medieval master builders and in the process integrated more and more of the building process into their purview, including design, structure, production management, interior design, graphic presentation, technical research, and mechanical engineering. (Many of these tasks had been

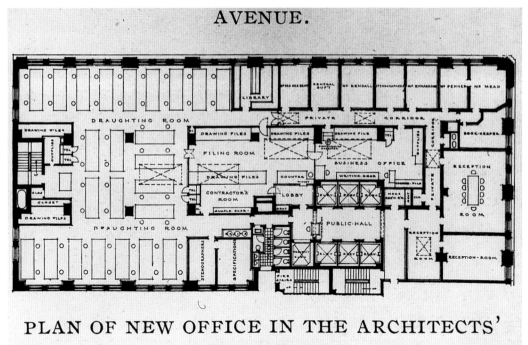

PLAN OF NEW OFFICE IN THE ARCHITECTS' BUILDING.

173 McKim, Mead, and White

Architectural Offices, 1913, 101 Park Avenue, New York.

thrown off by architects in the nineteenth century to clarify the public perception of the profession.) By 1958, the firm operated four offices totalling over a thousand employees.

In the long run, the architect's claims for the distinction between design and building were bolstered by the growing separation of head-work from handwork in all segments of the American economy. That is, the profession's role developed in tandem with the reorganization of labour occasioned by the industrialization of building and the articulation of a capitalist economy in the United States. Large-scale production of all sorts needed close co-ordination, which argued for the centralization of decision making and a finer division of labour. For this reason, architects succeeded more easily in making their claims for a role with public and corporate buildings than with private and domestic ones.

Like the most successful producers of consumer goods, large, centralized, corporate architectural firms offer a highly polished, high-quality, predictable product. John Graham, architect of the Northgate Regional Shopping Center, understood architecture as a form of merchandising, a collective effort directed toward speed and cost-effectiveness, designed to deliver an attractive product to the customer at an attractive price.[7] Just as the centralization of labour gave the industrialized building landscape a sameness, so has the commercialized centralization of design.

This is not necessarily an indictment. In consumer goods, we don't want every dress or shirt to be original, but we would like them all to be good. We do want a certain number of them to be original, and that leads to another strain in the story of professionalization.

Architecture and Social Class

As a market profession architecture, like medicine and law, had inherited a measure of cultural, intellectual, and social prestige that antedated professionalism. Unlike medicine and law, but like art, architecture also enjoyed a special status arising from its traditional role as a vehicle of social identity and from the metaphorical power of architecture as a symbolic or sign system. As a result of its expressive capacities, architecture transcended the instrumental values of the other market professions: it could claim to be an art. This provided another avenue for distinguishing the architect's profession from the builder's craft.

Architects quickly realized that architectural science was a dead end. The kinds of knowledge it encompassed could be mastered by anyone. Many early nineteenth-century architects began their careers as builders and wrote handbooks for other builders who aspired to make the same leap. By the 1830s and 1840s they began to guard their knowledge more jealously. When he considered the possibility of writing a handbook (which he did several years later), young Philadelphia architect Thomas U. Walter decided against it: 'don't think I'll ever make a book,' he wrote in his journal; 'was I ever to attempt it I might give every man an opportunity of buying for a few dollars, all the brains I've got.'[8] A few years later, Walter admitted that the secrecy was pointless. 'A mere knowledge of those qualities that address themselves to the human reason, will never enable the Architect to rise superior to the rank of an imitative builder.' Instead, architects must appeal to their superior taste—'qualities in design which produce certain effects upon the mind, that are totally undefinable'—as their distinguishing characteristic.[9] Taste was a professional qualification not obtainable from books.

Architects claimed superiority to builders based on their taste, cultivated through special training, socialization, and immersion in architecture. Before the advent of the professional, however, taste had been an attribute of social class not training: by definition, gentlemen and -women were tasteful. The new architects were manufactured gentlemen who in turn sold their taste in a consumer economy.

There was more to the story than this, for the acquisition of architectural taste also conferred gentility on the architect. Architecture allowed architects and clients to define or redefine their social roles and prestige in a society where position was no longer based on inherited status. For architects, professional education, training, and accomplishments earned social status, and architects were intensely proud of it. Benjamin Latrobe insisted that he was a gentleman, which, he said, fitted him to address the architectural needs of other gentlemen better than builders were able to do. On being named a Professor of the Franklin Institute, Walter asked for a letter confirming the appointment, 'as I want to use the title, and I have a delicacy in doing so without written authority'.[10] Professional training allied architects with the emerging middle classes and distinguished them from working-class builders.

Increasingly, the road to a nineteenth-century professional career led through an undergraduate college or university, further barring working-class aspirants. This was less true of architecture than of other professions, for it remained possible until recently to bypass academic training but to be licensed as an architect after an apprenticeship in a professional office. Yet architecture schools have been ensconced in colleges since 1865, when the Massachusetts Institute of Technology began to train architects. William Robert Ware, founder of that programme, lamented that 'The profession is at present in the hands of mechanics' (artisans) who might be good at practical matters, but 'are ignorant of the higher branches of their calling' that only a collegiate education could convey.[11]

If architects sought social prestige through professional attainments, clients sought it through the high-status cultural capital to which architects offered access. This was the point of ornate turn-of-the-century corporate headquarters and of the mansions, clubs, churches, and other settings that corporate leaders commissioned. Early twentieth-century architectural journalist Charles Moore believed that the success of McKim, Mead, and White and similar firms in selling elaborate mansions to industrialists and capitalists like the Vanderbilts, Carnegies, Morgans, and Fricks, whose no-nonsense business tactics might make them appear to be immune to such luxuries, was a product of 'the rapid increase in wealth and the consequent desire of the traveled wealthy for a share in old-world art and culture'.[12]

In short, architects relied on pre-commercial and anti-commercial visual metaphors of gentility, culture, and art in pursuit of their professional goals. They alluded to aristocratic and pre-capitalist exclusivity to sell their products in a capitalist economy. The notion of style was indispensable for this purpose.

Style

In a renowned essay, the art historian Meyer Schapiro defined style as 'the constant form—and sometimes the constant elements, qualities, and expressions—in the art of an individual or group'.[13] In other words, style is a consistent pattern of making or acting. Schapiro's definition was as protean as it was concise, containing within it multiple, not necessarily compatible, meanings.

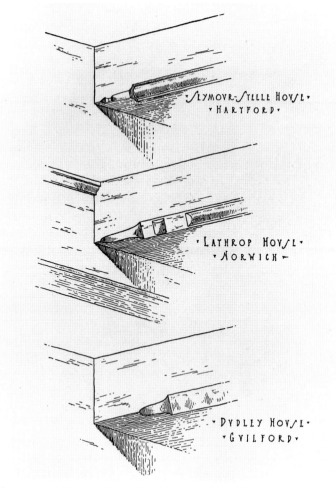

174 J. Frederick Kelly
Decorative chamfers and chamfer stops on three early 18th-century Connecticut houses, drawn by pioneering vernacular architecture scholar J. Frederick Kelly, 1924.

·SEYMOVR-STILLE HOVSE·
·HARTFORD·

·LATHROP HOVSE·
·NORWICH ·

·DVDLEY HOVSE·
·GVILFORD·

At its grandest scale, style is 'a manifestation of the culture as a whole, the visible sign of its unity'.[14] Since the eighteenth century Western high architecture has been dominated by two large patterns, the classical and the picturesque. The classical was regular, ordered, modular, symmetrical, balanced; it stressed unity and totality, and sought a rational response. The picturesque was less obviously ordered, asymmetrical, less obviously unified, often accretive; it aimed to elicit an affective response. These had nothing to do with the particular ornamental arsenal. A building with 'classical' ornament, such as San Francisco's Palace of the Fine Arts, could be picturesque in intent, while a building with 'picturesque' decoration, such as the Pennsylvania Academy of Fine Arts, might be classical in its ordering principles [81] [53].

These large-scale ordering patterns might be lumped under the rubric *Style*, with a capital *S*. They represent conscious attempts to address deep, often unarticulated, cultural principles for organizing and classifying experience. But Schapiro's phrase 'constant elements, qualities, and expressions' also points to a second aspect of style. In this second sense, style is a visual organizer, a conventional background or matrix for more explicit architectural expression. Archaeologists often use the term *style* in this manner, to refer to those attributes of an object's 'constant form' that order it but contribute nothing to its technological or symbolic function: they are matters of habit. The conventional manner of shaping an arrowhead or of inserting the last reed into the bottom of a basket are simply the ways the artisans learned to perform these necessary tasks. Similarly, architectural fieldworkers often remark on the careful finish of building parts never meant to be seen. There was no need for a rafter in an inaccessible attic to be adzed to a smooth finish, much less to be chamfered (to have its corner cut off at an angle), yet that was often done.

In the visible parts of buildings, small details of this sort abounded. Exposed beams were chamfered and sometimes given elaborate chamfer stops [**174**]. The edges of external weatherboards and internal sheathing in pre-industrial buildings were laboriously beaded; so were the joints of a matchboarding, a kind of machine-made interior wooden panelling used in stairways, kitchens, and other utilitarian areas of middle-class houses in the late nineteenth and early twentieth centuries. The milled quarter-round moulding remains a standard contractor's detail. These shapes are classical, but used in this fashion they are thoroughly conventional, nearly invisible details that serve as the background for more explicitly expressive forms. To the extent that they are noticed, the chamfered edge, the carefully levelled course of masonry, or the smoothly finished plaster wall signal to colleagues and clients the worker's craft. They locate the building in the realm of 'quality', satisfying the builder's and the client's sense of propriety and completion.

Style also denotes more self-conscious visual vocabularies that serve as 'signpost[s] or banner[s]' of the context in which we should view a building or a builder.[15] By choosing one visual vocabulary over another, designers or owners identify themselves as part of one social or aesthetic clique but not another, or annotate buildings and spaces as appropriate for a certain activity or inappropriate for another. In this sense, style delineates categories and distinctions. This facet of *style* encompasses the parade of named styles—Gothic, neo-classical, constructivist—alluded to at the beginning of this chapter, the visual lexicons popularly equated with the history of architecture. Named styles are as conventionalized as any other form of style. They can change capriciously and unpredictably, which makes them a vehicle for architectural fashion. In architecture as in any other aspect of popular culture, no one can guess what will be fashionable: one must keep a close eye on the scene to remain current. Thus knowledge of architectural fashion is presumptive evidence of membership in an aesthetic

175 Robert R. Taylor

Collis P. Huntington Memorial Academic Building, 1902–4 (destroyed), Tuskegee Institute, Tuskegee, Ala.

This building sums up the history of African-American education in the early 20th century. It was built at Booker T. Washington's Tuskegee Institute and named after a California railroad baron whose family also donated a library to Hampton Institute, another important school for African-Americans. The photograph was taken by Frances Benjamin Johnston, a pioneering female photographer who received several commissions from Hampton and Tuskegee to document black life in turn-of-the-century America.

élite. By the same token, allusions to aesthetic fashion can be useful in claiming social place. In an exclusionary society that pegged social worth to high culture, the builders of the Hampton Institute, an African-American college founded after the Civil War, engaged the New York society architect Richard Morris Hunt to design its first buildings in a current style indistinguishable from that of white colleges, while African-American architect Robert R. Taylor did the same for the Tuskegee Institute, another early black college [**175**].

Architectural fashions were just as capricious in the past as they are in the present, but the accidental conjunction of particular visual vocabularies with particular places or times invested historic styles with meaning in the eyes of later generations. From this point of view, for example, the middle ages were 'pious', so the Gothic style is particularly appropriate for churches and for houses (where private religious devotion is practised). The Egyptian style was appropriate for cemeteries because ancient Egypt was 'one vast cemetery', for medical schools, because Egyptian mummification was seen as a type of medical practice, and for prisons, because Egypt was seen as an oppressive place.[16]

This way of reading architecture—called 'associationism'—was particularly popular in the nineteenth century, when architectural theorists strove to systematize the use of historic styles for aesthetic expression. Contrary to the hopes of the more simplistic nineteenth-

century theorists, however, no such precision was possible. The essential arbitrariness of historic and contemporary styles renders visual forms too ambiguous for such enterprises, but it also gives them great symbolic potential.

The Haskell Stadium entrance arch (1926) at Haskell Institute (now Haskell Indian Nations University), Lawrence, Kansas, derives its power from this very ambiguity [**176**]. Why a triumphal arch? The Romans built triumphal arches to celebrate military conquests. The imagery seems puzzling here, in a monument donated by Alice Beaver and Agnes Track, two female Quapaw alumnae who had made fortunes in the Oklahoma oil boom. A standard answer would be to cite contemporary architectural fashion. High architects of the early twentieth century thought Roman imperial architecture appropriate to the dignity of a nation assuming the mantle of greatness. Triumphal arches to celebrate victories in the Spanish-American War and World War I were built all over the nation in the first decades of the century. So architectural fashion had something to do with it: it marked Haskell as a progressive place, in tune with the times. It is unlikely that a triumphal arch or the Roman style would have been chosen in 1876 or 1976.

Yet there is something puzzling about the women's choice to donate an imperial, erstwhile military monument such as this at Haskell Institute, which was founded in 1884 as a place to which the children of the defeated Indian nations of the central and western states were brought to learn white ways and, as just as important, to unlearn Indian ways. Richard Pratt, one of the founders of the Indian boarding-school movement, called on students to 'put aside Indian thoughts, and Indian ways, Indian dress, and Indian speech. We don't want to hold onto anything Indian.'[17] At Haskell children of all ages, organized in military fashion, received the rudiments of a European education while participating in forced labour on the school's farm. Many died under the rigorous conditions.

In the light of Haskell's genocidal enterprise, we are led to ask what triumph was celebrated by this arch. Did the choice of a classical style for the monument demonstrate that Alice Beaver and Agnes Track had put aside Indian thoughts and Indian ways? Part of our uncertainty arises from simplistic ideas of ethnic expression in architecture that have gained a foothold in recent decades. We have come to believe that members of ethnic minorities ought to evoke their traditional forms in their contemporary architecture. A museum should look like a long-house, a community centre like a tipi, or a gambling casino like a wigwam. From this point of view, ersatz Native American architecture, such as the Navajo-blanket pattern worked into the brickwork of Haskell's 1960s-era student union or the imitation totem pole that supports its portico is more authentic, more Indian, than a classical triumphal arch.

Our interpretation is further complicated by the stadium to which the arch is attached. A plaque on it identifies it as the gift of over a thousand Indians from more than fifty tribes. It is 'the largest and most unique Indian project ever attempted, and will stand as a monument built by the older Indians for the younger Indians yet to be educated at Haskell Institute'. To anyone acquainted with Chaco Canyon or the Hopewellian earthworks, the notion that a football stadium might be the greatest monument of Native American architecture seems comical. To appreciate the sentiment, it is important to understand the importance of Indian football in the early twentieth century.[18] Administrators at schools like Haskell and the Carlisle Indian School promoted football competition as a way of introducing Indians into white society. It had the additional advantage, in their eyes, of showing Indian students that they must compete with whites on white terms. To the white public, sport was one arena in which Indians could be allowed a modest role in the larger society. To both Indians and non-Indians the contests were played out in the context of the recent Indian wars. White newspapers described football games in terms of battles, referring freely to scalping, tomahawks, and savagery in their accounts. Many Indians also understood the games as recapitulations of the wars of conquest that would allow them to vindicate themselves on the proverbial level playing-field. Haskell and Carlisle teams regularly crushed opponents from the major white college football powers of their day.

The conventionality of architectural style and the arbitrariness of its associations fuse all these meanings indelibly to this simple, un-exceptional monument. When wealthy Indian alumnae of a school dedicated to eradicating their native culture pay for a triumphal arch in a classical style associated with centuries of European history and favoured by contemporary élite white builders, in order to celebrate Indian football victories, just as Indian football is beginning to lose its importance, we begin to understand the power of architectural style to create powerful and moving images without resorting to explicit messages.

The Architect as Artist

Architectural styles contribute to professional standardization by packaging buildings in familiar dress. Unlike the other market pro-fessions, however, architects developed an alternative strategy for establishing professional distinction, one that coexisted uncomfortably with the regularization of practice and practitioners that professions ordinarily prefer. This alternative strategy declared that architecture is an art. The architect assembles conventional formal elements in a distinctive manner that creates a unique relationship between the creator and the creation, one that cannot be replicated by clients, builders, or other architects. He creates a personal style that fuses cultural Style with rapidly changing architectural fashions.

Belief in the uniqueness of works of art was rooted in long-established myths. In European-American culture, as in many others, artistic creation has been equated with divine creation. God the Creator has often been depicted as an architect, and architecture conversely as a replica of the divine structure of the universe. In creating the world, God endowed it with some of his power: the world partakes of the divine. The almighty Architect and his creation are one.

This theological metaphor shaped the romantic notion of artistic genius that nineteenth-century architects borrowed and in turn bequeathed to their twentieth-century successors. The romantics assumed that artists infused their creation with their genius, which authenticated it as a unique, inimitable work of art. One might copy the form, but the artist's spirit would be absent.

These assumptions have become so deeply ingrained in the ways architects and their public think about the art of architecture that their intrinsic contradictions are rarely examined. First, the idea of the architect as artist conflicts with the standardizing tendencies of pro-fessionalism (as art-architect Frank Lloyd Wright acknowledged in distancing himself from the American Institute of Architects). Second, there is a limited market for this kind of architecture, and only

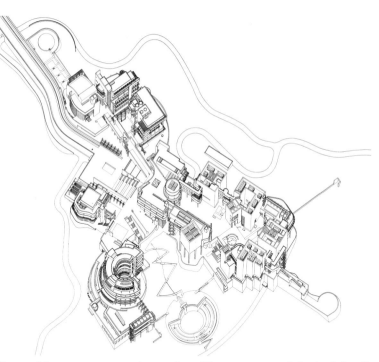

a few architects can succeed as artists. However, as sociologist Magali Sarfatti Larson has pointed out, the conspicuous minority of art-architects bolsters the position of the majority of ordinary practitioners by generating new forms to resupply the profession's visual stock and by serving as a kind of public-relations vehicle, imbuing the entire profession with the cultural prestige (as well as some of the utilitarian scorn) of art.

Third, the romantic conception of the artist assumes originality, but the social nature of architecture implies that the architect is in some ways a product of an era, a culture, a tradition, or at least a teacher. Architects commonly incorporate references to predecessors and contemporaries, acknowledging influences to define the context in which they want their work to be viewed, offering viewers a starting-point for interpretation.

The J. Paul Getty Center, designed by Richard Meier and recently completed in Los Angeles, draws much of its visual force from this sort of architectural genealogy [**177**]. The complex forms a kind of acropolis, an allusion reinforced by its podium, which resembles the Mycenaean wall on which the Athenian Acropolis stands, by the Pan-Athenian Way that winds up the hill, and even by the off-white cladding of the buildings.

These are merely the first of many visual references that enrich the work of the designer and the institution through association with prestigious architects and buildings of the past and the present. The Getty Center is an anthology of quotations from the canon of modern architectural history. Here is the glass tower from Fallingwater, or perhaps a corner of Walter Gropius's and Hannes Meyer's Fagus Shoe-Last Factory; there, the sinuous entrance façade of the museum recalls Wright's S. C. Johnson and Son Administration Building. The galleries cite John Soane's Dulwich Art Gallery explicitly and Louis Kahn's revered Kimbell Art Museum less directly. The ghost of the Kimbell appears again in the vaults of the tram stop, while the galleries of the museum wing stand in the court like the pavilions at the Salk Institute. The rounded corners, elegant pipe-railed stairs, and window bands evoke 1920s International Style modernism and the moderne architecture of 1930s Los Angeles.

A nineteenth-century associationalist would compose these visual references carefully to convey an explicit mood or a message. Meier juxtaposes slivers of the recent architectural past almost haphazardly. He ransacks the works of many past architects, including himself in an earlier incarnation, in a way that is informed by post-modern and deconstructionist theories of architecture. These theories stress the fragmentation of reference and understanding: a building is not a systematic treatise, but a layering of hints, allusions, and traces that circle around and continually redefine one another. There is no need for the allusions to be complete or to make sense. They are memories of the recent architectural past, not its documentary record. It is the nature of memory to distort forms, relationships and chronologies, to juxtapose fragments in a new way, to create something more vivid, and perhaps more real, than the original event or image. So Meier distorts the originals to which he is indebted. The ramp leading up to the Propylaeon at the Acropolis is here shifted off-centre, so that the final approach to the museum is misaligned with the path up the hill. The Salk-like galleries are canted as though a truck had careened into them. These techniques put Meier's mark on his borrowings, claiming them as his own art, much as Robert Rauschenberg once defaced a painting by Willem De Kooning to make the *Erased De Kooning* his own.

Meier's quotations legitimize his own work and that of his clients. The J. Paul Getty Foundation serves, as Charles Moore said of McKim, Mead, and White's work, to put a veneer of culture on a fortune. Once more, the architect serves as a merchant of respectability, the transformer of vulgar capital into cultural capital. No mere serviceable building could serve that purpose, and no one but a star architect, with all the prestige that conveys, could have made this building.

Styles of the Self

The architect's personal style is as important as visual style in the marketing of art-architecture. Those architects with the greatest

artistic reputations usually create distinctive personae that are as well
known to the public as their architecture. The California art-architect
Bernard Maybeck was often photographed dressed in a smock and
beret, surrounded by studio assistants clad in jackets and ties, an artist
among clerks [**178**]. Frank Lloyd Wright was a master of such imagery.
His photographs present him as an artist, clad in cape and beret, as a
beloved mentor surrounded by students, and as a powerful visionary
dominating the observer [**179**].

Wright reinforced his artistic persona with a self-conscious rhetoric
of integrity, embattlement, and singularity, created during the 1920s
and 1930s when commissions were few and writing projects corres-
pondingly numerous. Even more important were the stories told about
him, each of which was calculated to reinforce his public image. Some
were true, of course, such as the one about the dendriform (tree-
shaped) columns of the S. C. Johnson & Son Administration Building
(1936–9) at Racine, Wisconsin. The columns violated state building
codes and Wright was called on to demonstrate their stability [**180**]
[**181**]. A sample column was loaded to five times the anticipated load
and the building inspectors were satisfied. All very reasonable on both
sides, but as the story is customarily cast as a contest of rule-bound
bureaucrats with intuitive genius. Another tale recounts Wright's re-
fusal to work on the design for Fallingwater until the client motored up
the drive to his office. At the last minute, he quickly sketched the design, virtually as it was built. The implication is not that Wright had
been thinking about the design all along, but that he created a great

179

Frank Lloyd Wright, 1947.
The architect as visionary,
standing in front of a model of
a Wainwright-like building.

work in a flash of inspiration.

We might liken these to the *jatakas*, legendary stories that Buddhists tell about the Buddha. Architectural *jatakas* are parables about the nature of art and artists: they are signposts to understanding the designer's work. There are *jatakas* associated with most famous architects. The concrete reading-desk of Bernard Maybeck's First Church of Christ, Scientist (1910), in Berkeley is decorated with painted flowers. According to tour guides, Maybeck spontaneously seized paint and brush and turned the cracks of an imperfectly made pulpit into decorative assets. In a speech delivered at Brown University in the 1970s, Peter Eisenman spoke with glee of his clients' distress at being confronted with narrow doors, staircases that went nowhere, and other elements of an artistic work that infringed on daily life. One client had even lived in his basement for two years. Eisenman's story was a *jataka* about the integrity and will of the artist.

180 Frank Lloyd Wright

S. C. Johnson & Son
Administration Building,
1936–39, Racine, Wis.
Wright observes the test of his
dendriform column, in the
company of contractor and
client.

181
S. C. Johnson & Son
Administration Building.
Great workroom.

Jatakas cut both ways. They are often used by the sceptical to undermine cognitive exclusivity, exposing it as a hollow pretence. At the First Unitarian Church (1947), Madison, it is said, Wright one day demanded that the stone walls be totally rebuilt. Nothing was done before he returned, but the workers told the architect they had complied with his wishes. 'Much better,' he replied. Folklorist Archie Green, who worked as a carpenter in postwar Marin County, California, told of a crew of carpenters given the drawings for one of the first 'modern' houses in the region. On his first visit to the site the architect was shocked to discover that the builders had made his asymmetrical façade symmetrical, thinking there had been an error.

Wright's capes and berets, and Maybeck's smocks were part of the personal style of the artist-architect, drawn from a familiar repertoire of symbolic costume that characterized them for the general public, providing them with visibility, and often reputation, at the expense of their workaday colleagues. In the business-like architectural firms of the late nineteenth century, it was usually the artist whose reputation soared at the expense of the business partner, although both may have contributed to the firm's design work. Louis Sullivan is remembered instead of his partner Dankmar Adler. John Wellborn Root is remembered more fondly than his more corporate partner Daniel Burnham. Stanford White outshines his partners Charles Follen McKim (an equally prolific designer but not as publicly dissolute as White) and William Rutherford Mead.

The artistic persona and the professional persona seem to conflict: one promises individuality, the other predictability. Yet the two were not necessarily at odds. Henry Hobson Richardson was enormously successful because he combined the business tactics of Burnham and Root, personal social connections derived from his Louisiana roots and his Harvard education, and the self-presentation of the artist [**182**]. Yet design in the Richardson office was collaborative—necessarily so, in light of the enormous number of projects he undertook in his later years. According to his friend and first biographer Mariana Griswold Van Rensselaer, Richardson's office housed a score of workers of all levels of training, including 'an unusual number of students, working in an unusually independent way', the whole staff 'laboring together on work which had a single inspiration and a common accent, and each feeling a personal pride in results which the world knew as the master's only' [**183**].[19] Richardson's self-presentation gave the collective product of his office a recognizable identity. Charles Moore's Piazza d'Italia (1975–78), New Orleans, illustrates the same process in contemporary architecture. Masks of Moore [**184**] in the monument's frieze advertise it as a 'signature architect's' work. They also speak to Moore's limited involvement in its production, for they were included by his office staff as a surprise to him.

182

Henry Hobson Richardson, 1886, photographic portrait by George Collins Cox.

The architect as artist.

Offices of Henry Hobson
Richardson, *c.*1886.

Architectural historians customarily support the artistic model of architectural design. Architectural history reinforces the art-architect's claims to recognition by mapping professional work into the long, time-honoured history of the visual arts, reciting the *jatakas*, attaching single names to office products. Because large corporate firms, such as Albert Kahn's in the early twentieth century or SOM, Caudill Rowlett Scott, and HOK in recent years, prosperous architectural businesses with many clients, frankly acknowledged their complex corporate organizations, they are difficult to fit into the narrative of artistic creation.

Who is an Architect?

Why have art-architects—and architects in general—customarily been middle-class white men? Part of the answer is simple discrimination. Prospective women and minority architects were barred from schools and actively discouraged from entering the profession for many years. When aspiring architect Bertha Yerex Whitman sought to enter the University of Michigan school of architecture in 1914, its dean told her that 'we don't want you, but since the school is coeducational and state owned, we have to take you if you insist'.[20] She did. Paul R. Williams was advised by his high-school counsellor that blacks needed doctors and lawyers, but would never build elaborate houses or office buildings, and that he would have to rely on white clients if he became an architect.[21] He did.

Through persistence, however, women and some African-Americans trained and practised as architects beginning in the last quarter of the nineteenth century. Yet their opportunities were limited. Despite the example of domestic architect Frank Lloyd Wright's showcase career, success in the architectural profession typically depended on non-domestic work. The size and complexity of a building project, rather than aesthetics, impelled most clients to seek out architects. Women and minority architects often lacked access to a sufficiently large pool of predominantly white male clients to obtain this work. Women were denied access to the public arena on grounds of the traditional notion that publicity was demeaning. African-American architects were restricted, for the most part, to work for other African-Americans and, owing to the segregated nature of American society, their work remained as invisible to potential white clients as it has to historians.

As a result, it is possible to name early female and African-American architects but not to say much about them. Margaret Hicks's Cornell University student project for a workman's cottage was published without comment in the *American Architect and Building News* in 1878, but we know little more about her. Sophia Hayden, the first woman graduate of the Massachusetts Institute of Technology, designed the Women's Building at the World's Columbian Exposition. Shortly afterward, she had a nervous breakdown, married, and left the profession. Robert R. Taylor, an African-American architect trained at MIT, designed many of the buildings at Tuskegee Institute, Booker T. Washington's school for African-American students [175]. Julian Abele, another African-American architect, worked as a designer in the office of society architect Horace Trumbauer for his entire career, and played a major role in the design of the Duke University campus.

There are other names and works that could and should be excavated and brought to light, but this fill-in-the-blanks approach misses two larger points. First, many people who were interested in architecture were diverted to allied occupations as a way of evading restrictions. Amaza Lee Meredith, a young black woman, was hampered by both her race and her sex from entering the architectural profession, so she became an art teacher at Virginia State College, an African-American institution near Petersburg. However, Meredith maintained an active interest in architecture and designed a moderne house, one of the first in the state, for herself and her partner Edna Meade Colson [185]. Similarly, Catherine Bauer's early interest in architecture was channelled into planning and architectural criticism, where her influence on architecture, though great, was indirect.

Second, and equally important, the issue of who became an

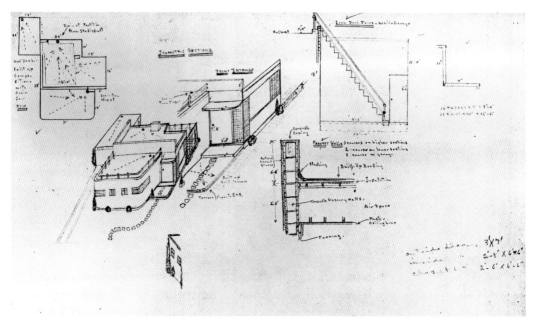

architect, especially who became a famous architect, was determined by social patterns that made architecture male and white even when overt discrimination ended. Here personal style intersected with cultural style, those habitual ways of acting or organizing ourselves that are based in deeply rooted, often unarticulated values. As members of a market profession, successful architects were those who fit the nation's social patterns most closely.

For example, Wright and Maybeck came from culturally ambitious middle-class families and found work among the same kinds of people. Wright was based in an upper-middle-class suburb of Chicago. When Maybeck worked in Berkeley, the city was becoming a middle-class bedroom community of post-earthquake San Francisco. Wright, Maybeck, and lesser lights such as Elbert Hubbard (a Larkin family relation, doyen of the Roycrofters arts and crafts community and, according to Reyner Banham, the man who taught Wright to dress as an artist) were the shamans of their communities, safely middle-class, surrogate wildmen in an increasingly corporate and business-dominated society.

In other arenas, architecture's long-established role as a sign and conveyor of social power encouraged the notion that an architect should be a strong-willed person capable of holding and dispensing power [**179**]. In the United States the prototypical strong-willed person has been white and male. Richardson's contemporary George W. Sheldon wrote of him that 'More than any other American architect, he had the personal power that can interest the capitalist, and provide the means for great undertakings.'[22] Frank Lloyd Wright's client William E. Martin of Chicago told his brother Darwin D.

Martin of Buffalo, a Larkin Company official and eventual Wright client, that

I have been—seen—talked to, admired, one of nature's noblemen—Frank Lloyd Wright. He is an athletic looking young man of medium build—black hair—(bushy, not long) about 32 yrs. Old.—A splendid type of manhood. He is not a fraud—nor a 'crank'—highly educated & polished, but no dude—a straight-forward business like man—with high ideals—I met his mother a beautiful type of woman. . . .

You will fall in love with him—in 10 min. conversation = he will build you the finest most sensible house in Buffalo = you will be the envy of every rich man in Buffalo it will be published in all the Buffalo papers it will be talked about all over the east. . . . I am not too enthusiastic about this—he is pure gold.[23]

In short, cultural style identified an architect as a man of a certain kind: white, middle-class, forceful—making it difficult to see women or members of ethnic minorities as real architects even when they did break into the profession. Wright's manly self-presentation contrasted with that of his one-time employee, Marion Lucy Mahony. After she was graduated from MIT, Mahony moved to Chicago to work for her cousin, Dwight Perkins, then joined Wright's office in 1895. During her time there, she became his major delineator: many of the most famous 'Wright' renderings, including the Hardy House and the 'Fireproof House for $5000', are hers [**186**]. One historian thought her 'perhaps more an artist than an architect' because architectural design was usually given to others in the office, while she was assigned mostly to do the furnishings for Wright's houses.[24] The assessment was self-fulfilling. The historian saw the pattern of work assignments as its own cause: if Mahony was given these tasks, it must have been because she was suited only to such work. More likely, her assignments were based on Victorian stereotypes of women's capacities—attitudes such as that expressed in the *Inland Architect* in 1884, when Lulu Stoughton Beem asserted that 'Women are naturally better judges of color, better in the blending of fabrics, besides knowing intuitively what is wanted in a house—wants too small for men to perceive.'[25]

The suspicion is reinforced by the comments of Mahony's colleague Barry Byrne, who described her as 'a thin, angular, shallow skinned person with a beak of a nose; she was so homely that she looked almost distinguished. She had a fragile frame and walked as though she were falling forward. She was a good actress, talkative, and when around Wright there was always a real sparkle.'[26] Byrne implied that Mahony was out of place and unwomanly in her homeliness and her presence in the office, but womanly in her talkativeness, her actress-like dissembling, and her inability to make her contribution spontaneously without being drawn out by the Master. Yet when Wright skipped town and Hermann von Holst took over the firm, Mahony was appointed chief designer. The work she did in that capacity was claimed either by Wright or by von Holst, who removed her name from much of it. In 1911, Mahony married another former Wright employee, Walter Burley Griffin, and spent the rest of her career collaborating on and rendering work under his name, a subordination she seems to have accepted with equanimity. 'I can never aspire to be as great an architect as he, but I can best understand and help him and to a wife there is not greater recompense', she wrote.[27]

Marion Mahony Griffin's standing in the architectural profession during her lifetime and her relative invisibility in the present, then, cannot be written off as simple discrimination. Her actions were shaped by her own culturally informed style as much as by the pre-conceptions of her colleagues. As a result her style of self-presentation as an architect was not the sort that won her individual recognition, nor is it clear that she sought it.

The architectural career of San Francisco Bay Area architect Julia Morgan, the first woman graduate of the College of Civil Engineering at the University of California and later a student at the École des Beaux-Arts, was also shaped by personal and cultural styles. After her return from Paris, Morgan worked for John Galen Howard, then maintained her own office from 1905 until her retirement in 1940. Morgan's practice fitted the traditional pattern of professional success. Like Maybeck, she worked primarily as a domestic architect at a time when the East Bay was being rapidly built up in the wake of the 1906 earthquake. Like Richardson, her social connections helped her: she was the product of an upper-middle-class Oakland family and obtained many of her early commissions from her family and friends. This tale has a gendered twist, for most of her work was domestic and most of her non-domestic work was obtained from woman-associated institutions, such as churches, women's colleges and women's sub-divisions of coeducational colleges, and the Young Women's Christian Association.

Historians make much of Morgan's self-effacing modesty, which is ingratiating when compared with the bluster of her male colleagues. It was rooted in the cultural styles of American class and gender relation-ships. Genteel people such as Morgan were trained not to call public attention to themselves; this was doubly true of women. Because Morgan was unwilling to be a public figure, she would probably have been forgotten were it not for her work at San Simeon (Hearst Castle, 1919–42). The association with the emphatically unretiring William Randolph Hearst and his palace kept her name alive until she began to receive feminist attention in the 1960s and 1970s. Even the Hearst Castle commission was obtained through her social and gender ties.

PLATE 67. PROJECT: CURTIS PUBLISHING COMPANY FIREPROOF HOUSE. PERSPECTIVE

Morgan worked first for Hearst's mother, Phoebe Apperson Hearst, who commissioned several houses and several buildings for the University of California from Morgan. At Hearst Castle, Morgan gladly subordinated her aesthetic identity and her declared aversion to ostentatious design to Hearst's demands, both from a sense of professional obligation and from respect for her client as a powerful man.

In short, those aspects of personal style derived from widespread cultural patterns have ensured that the invisibility of women and minority architects would be particularly long-lasting. If one cannot see them as architects, if one does not believe that they act like architects, no amount of architectural training can overcome it. Despite the strength of their work, both Mahony Griffin and Morgan were viewed as appendages of their male clients and associates. And acting like an architect has a deeply ingrained racial and gendered content: architects and the public alike have learned to judge the quality of design by the quality of the swagger [187] [188].

Morgan's approach to architecture adds another dimension to the discussion. Most of her domestic work was known for its careful planning and comfortable interiors. She rejected flashy or picturesque design. Her attitude might be set in the context of a statement published by the *American Architect and Building News* in 1876, four years after Morgan's birth.

First, the planning of houses, at least as far as the convenience of the arrangement is concerned, though a very necessary part of an architect's duty, is not architecture at all; and the ability to arrange a house conveniently does

187

Julia Morgan, photographed in
her Paris apartment, 1899,
aged 27.

not in the least make an architect. There are thousands of people who can
adjust the plans of houses to their own perfect satisfaction and convenience,
and who do it, but who yet are not architects.[28]

In support of the architectural profession's bid for cognitive exclusivity,
this architectural journal disowned that part of domestic architecture
that was the most important, the most jealously controlled by clients,
and, not coincidentally, that had been relegated to women architects.

Domestic architecture seemed appropriate to female architects
because it had already been claimed by laywomen as their own. As part
of their roles of protecting and nurturing their families, women
assumed responsibility for household hygiene and efficiency. Just as
exceptional women such as Catherine Beecher and Harriet Beecher
Stowe felt qualified to advise American women on the design of houses
and furnishings best adapted to women's experience and duties, so

Richard Neutra in Switzerland, 1919, aged 27.

After World War I the young architect continued to wear his military uniform, stripped of its insignia.

women living on remote farms confidently submitted plans of houses that they had built or dreamed of building for their own families to agricultural journals as their contributions to architecture.

Even where architects were employed, women's vested interest in domestic design was assumed. In William Dean Howells's *The Rise of Silas Lapham* (1885), a novel that centres around the construction of a new house for a family of Boston *nouveaux-riches*, Silas Lapham wants to build a house in the style of mid-century, but 'escaped from the master builder and ended in the hands of an architect', a man 'skilful, as nearly all architects are, in playing upon that simple instrument Man'. The architect does so by subtly enlisting the aid of Persis Lapham, who instinctively understands the architect's aesthetic when her husband does not, and who 'began to feel a motherly affection for the young man'. The overmatched Lapham is quickly manœuvered to adopt the architect's point of view.[29]

Giant Artichoke, *c.*1975,
Castroville, Calif.

Beyond Art

Architects can help to shape the landscape, but they can never control it as completely as they wish. Architecture is too diffuse. Every architect and every building belongs to several overlapping 'high' and 'vernacular' circles of architectural knowledge. These circles of architectural knowledge encompass technologies, social ideas, and meanings that are unaccounted for in, and often antagonistic to, art-architectural traditions. Furthermore, architects' control of building design is constantly challenged by non-architects. Doctors, jailers, teachers, asylum-keepers, and other specialists have published treatises containing detailed prescriptions for the architecture of their workplaces. Businessmen, industrialists, and other professional clients also assume that architects should be directed by non-architects. Architects confront similar resistance from potential domestic clients, who believe that their concerns are poorly addressed by professional practitioners.

Even in the matter of visual design, architects have been unable to establish a monopoly. If one of the functions of art-architecture is to define and restrict an arena of exclusive professional action, the project is doomed to fail. While access to words—architectural theory—can be protected by obscurity, visual and spatial forms cannot. They can easily be adapted to other systems of meaning outside the premises of art-architecture.

So popular designers—both professional architects operating outside the realm of art and non-professionals—often appropriate visual forms from the high tradition and jettison their theoretical rationales, transforming them into open-ended visual commodities. In this manner, eighteenth-century Americans abandoned the dogmatic theories of Anglo-Palladianism while retaining its visual forms as signs of social dominance [14]. Similarly, the ironic fragmentary pediments of the Vanna Venturi House now appear on shopping malls across the nation, offered without irony, as signs of up-to-date consumption [170]. They have escaped the circles of art.

Often popular builders anticipate the theories and techniques of art-architecture. The post-modern ironic stance and such of its visual strategies as dislocation through improbable juxtapositions, disparity of scale, and fragmentation have been part of popular architecture since the nineteenth century [189]. In fact, some of the roots of postmodern architectural theory lay in the study of roadside architecture of the automobile age. A seminal work of early postmodernism, Robert Venturi, Denise Scott Brown, and Steven Izenour's *Learning from Las Vegas* (1972), appropriated the lessons of this popular architecture for art-architects. In a sense, the authors attempted to reinforce cognitive exclusiveness by drawing the professional circle a little larger, laying claim to some appealing aspects of the American landscape that architects had previously overlooked or scorned. To do so, they reversed the relationship of popular and art-architecture, describing popular architecture as an essentially sound but imperfect subset of art-architecture—it was 'almost all right'. But the borrowed and vernacular forms in which popular architecture is cast are layered and intertwined in ways that achieve 'naturally' and 'collectively' what postmodernists and deconstructivists attempt to accomplish artificially and individually as works of art. The art-architect's imitations are too feeble to stand against the real thing.

As it has been defined in American architecture, to be an artist is to impose a vision, to subject others to individual genius or inspiration. Art-architecture is the quintessential gesture of consumer culture, a commodity made for a passive customer. But the landscape is too important a stage for human symbolic action and lay people are too jealous of their own prerogatives to sacrifice them to such a narrow and self-serving agenda. This account of architecture in the United States opened with an eighteenth-century folk house and closes with a giant artichoke. They can serve as intimations of the variety and range of human landscape in the United States, reminders that it cannot be explained by a single theory, accounted for by a single history, or controlled by a single profession or a single vision. It is our common property and we are the better for that.

Notes

Introduction

1. Rhys Isaac, 'The First Monticello', in Peter S. Onuf, ed., *Jeffersonian Legacies* (Charlottesville, 1993), 77–108.

2. Quoted in Herbert Muschamp, 'Eloquent Champion of the Vernacular Landscape', *New York Times*, 21 Apr. 1996, 36.

Chapter 1. An American Icon

1. Anna Thornton, 18 Sept. 1802, quoted in Merrill D. Peterson, ed., *Visitors to Monticello* (Charlottesville, 1989), 34–5.

2. Thomas Jefferson, *Notes on the State of Virginia* (1780), query XV.

3. Edwin Morris Betts, ed., *Thomas Jefferson's Garden Book, 1766–1824* (Philadelphia, 1944), 25–6.

4. Marquis de Chastellux, *Travels in North America in the Years 1780, 1781, and 1782* (1786), repr. in Peterson, ed., *Visitors to Monticello*, 12.

5. Although the English professional architect John Hawks arrived in North Carolina before the American Revolution, Latrobe, who believed himself to be the first American professional, was the first to commit the remainder of his life to establishing the profession in America.

6. Latrobe to John Lenthall, 3 May 1805, quoted in Talbot Hamlin, *Benjamin Henry Latrobe* (New York, 1955), 294.

7. Latrobe to Lenthall, 7 Jan. 1805, in *The Correspondence and Miscellaneous Papers of Benjamin Henry Latrobe*, John C. Van Horne, Jeffrey A. Cohen, Darwin H. Stapleton, Lee W. Formwalt, William B. Forbush III, and Tina H. Sheller, eds., 3 vols. (New Haven, 1984–8), ii. 6.

8. This paragraph is based on Colin Campbell, *The Romantic Ethic and the Spirit of Modern Consumerism* (Oxford, 1987) and Daniel Miller, *Material Culture and Mass Consumption* (Oxford, 1987).

9. Latrobe to Isaac Hazlehurst, 16 Jan. 1809, in Latrobe, *Correspondence*, ii. 693.

10. Andrew Jackson Downing, *The Architecture of Country Houses* (New York, 1850), 262–3.

11. Quoted in Gwendolyn Wright, *Moralism and the Model Home: Domestic Architecture and Cultural Conflict in Chicago, 1873–1913* (Chicago, 1980), 27.

12. *The American Woman's Home* was a reworking of Catherine Beecher's earlier *A Treatise on Domestic Economy* (1841).

13. Elizabeth Blackmar, *Manhattan for Rent, 1785–1850* (Ithaca, NY, 1989), 126–38.

14. Catherine Beecher, *A Treatise on Domestic Economy* (New York, 1977), 265.

15. Downing, *Architecture of Country Houses*, 295.

16. Ibid.

17. Frank Lloyd Wright, *An Autobiography* (New York, 1977), 166–7.

18. Ibid., 166.

19. Richard Meier, 'Smith House 1965', in *Five Architects: Eisenman Graves Gwathmey Hejduk Meier* (New York, 1975), 111.

Chapter 2. Community

1. *Francis Hopkinson's 'Account of the Grand Federal Procession Philadelphia', 1788*, ed. Whitfield J. Bell, Jr. (Boston, 1962), 10–11.

2. The term 'revitalization movement' was coined by anthropologist Anthony F. C. Wallace to describe the Iroquois Longhouse Religion discussed below. Anthony F. C. Wallace, *The Death and Rebirth of the Seneca* (New York, 1970).

3. Quoted in Perry Miller, *The New England Mind: The Seventeenth Century* (Boston, 1969), 436.

4. Thomas Hooker, *A Survey of the Summe of Church-Discipline* (London, 1648), 188. I am grateful to Robert St George for helping me locate this reference.

5. Quoted in Dora P. Crouch, Daniel J. Garr, and Axel I. Mundingo, *Spanish City Planning in North America* (Cambridge, Mass., 1982), 18.

6. The evasive terms *phenomenon* and *synthesis* are meant to indicate that Hopewell was neither a culture—a group of people sharing

most aspects of life ways and language—nor an empire—a territory under a single political regime. Yet people of many different societies and polities scattered over a wide area from present-day Kansas City to New York State and from the Great Lakes to Florida built very similar kinds of élite monuments.

7. Quoted in Robert S. Neitzel, *Archeology of the Fatherland Site: The Grand Village of the Natchez* (New York, 1965), 63.

8. Ibid., 80.

9. Daniel K. Richter, *The Ordeal of the Longhouse: The Peoples of the Iroquois League in the Era of European Colonization* (Chapel Hill, NC, 1992), 18–19. Anthropologists apply the term Iroquoian to people who lived all over the northeastern United States and adjacent Quebec and Ontario and who shared similar linguistic roots and cultural traits. 'Iroquois' refers more narrowly to the Five Nations (augmented by the Tuscarora, who moved from North Carolina and were invited to join the Iroquois League in the eighteenth century).

10. Virginia's 1701 state-house is sometimes said to have been the first building since ancient times to carry the name Capitol.

11. Thomas Crawford, quoted in Pamela Scott, *Temple of Liberty: Building the Capitol for a New Nation* (New York, 1995), 100.

12. Alexander later served as symbologist for the Oregon State Capitol, Rockefeller Center, and the Los Angeles Public Library.

13. Quoted in Eric S. McCready, 'The Nebraska State Capitol: Its Design, Background and Influence', *Nebraska History*, 55:3 (Fall 1974) 355–6.

14. Quoted in Frederick C. Luebke, ed., *A Harmony of the Arts: The Nebraska State Capitol* (Lincoln, Nebr., 1990), 38.

15. The concept of invented traditions was formulated in Eric Hobsbawm and Terence Ranger, eds., *The Invention of Tradition* (Cambridge, 1983).

16. Quoted in William J. Murtagh, *Keeping Time: The History and Theory of Preservation in America* (New York, 1988), 176.

17. R. T. H. Halsey and Elizabeth Tower, *The Homes of Our Ancestors, as Shown in the American Wing of the Metropolitan Museum of Art* (Garden City, NY, 1925), p. xxii.

18. Samuel Sewall, *The Diary of Samuel Sewall, 1674–1729*, ed. M. Halsey Thomas, 2 vols. (New York, 1973), i. 367 (26 Jan. 1696/7). Sewall alluded to the apostle Paul: 'We have a building of God, an house not made with hands, eternal in the heavens.' (Cor. 5: 1) Robert St George pointed out the relevance of this and other Biblical passages to me as sources of Puritan architectural metaphor.

19. Thomas R. Carter, 'Mansion on the Hill: The Mormon Temple at Manti, 1877–1888', paper presented at the annual meeting of the Vernacular Architecture Forum, Lawrence, Kan., May 1996.

20. Quoted in James F. O'Gorman, *The Architecture of Frank Furness* (Philadelphia, 1973), 34.

21. Lawrence W. Levine, *Highbrow Lowbrow: The Emergence of Cultural Hierarchy in America* (Cambridge, 1988), 133.

22. Abigail A. Van Slyck, *Free to All: Carnegie Libraries and American Culture, 1890–1920* (Chicago, 1996), 2.

23. Quoted in Erika Doss, *Spirit Poles and Flying Pigs: Public Art and Cultural Democracy in American Communities* (Washington, 1995), 199.

24. Reactions are detailed at length in Doss, *Spirit Poles*, 226, from which these quotes are taken.

25. Peter Calthorpe, *The Next American Metropolis: Ecology, Community, and the American Dream* (Princeton, 1993), 11.

26. Alex Krieger and William Lennertz, eds., *Andres Duany and Elizabeth Plater-Zyberk: Towns and Town-Making Principles* (New York, 1991), 21.

27. Quoted in Holly M. Rarick, *Progressive Vision: The Planning of Downtown Cleveland 1903–1930* (Cleveland, 1986), 24.

28. Krieger and Lennertz, eds., *Andres Duany*, 28.

Chapter 3. Nature

1. William Bradford, *Of Plymouth Plantation, 1620–1647*, ed. Samuel Eliot Morison (New York, 1967), 61–2.

2. Quoted in Fiske Kimball, *Domestic Architecture of the American Colonies and of the Early Republic* (New York, 1922), 11–12.

3. *Records of the Virginia Company*, iii. 522, quoted (and discussed) in Dell Upton, 'Ethnicity, Authenticity, and Invented Traditions', *Historical Archaeology*, 30: 2 (1996) 1.

4. William Cronon, 'Introduction: In Search of Nature', in William Cronon, ed., *Uncommon Ground: Toward Reinventing Nature* (New York, 1995), 35.

5. Mark Twain, *The Adventures of Huckleberry Finn (Tom Sawyer's Comrade)* (New York, 1884, 1951), 312.

6. Quoted in Stanley French, 'The Cemetery as a Cultural Institution: The Establishment of Mount Auburn and the "Rural Cemetery" Movement', *American Quarterly*, 26:1 (Mar.

1974) 48.

7. Andrew Jackson Downing, 'A Few Hints on Landscape Gardening', in Andrew Jackson Downing, *Rural Essays*, ed. George William Curtis (New York, 1853), 122.

8. Downing, 'On the Mistakes of Citizens in Country Life', in *Rural Essays*, 124.

9. Andrew Jackson Downing, *The Architecture of Country Houses* (New York, 1850), 345.

10. Downing, 'On Feminine Taste in Rural Affairs', in *Rural Essays*, 51–2.

11. Downing, 'The New-York Park', in *Rural Essays*, 147.

12. Frederick Law Olmsted and Calvert Vaux, 'Plan for Riverside, Illinois' (1868), in Leland M. Roth, ed., *America Builds: Source Documents in American Architecture and Planning* (New York, 1983), 193–4, 201; Laura Wood Roper, *FLO: A Biography of Frederick Law Olmsted* (Baltimore, 1973), 322.

13. Lewis Mumford, in Clarence S. Stein, *Toward New Towns for America* (New York, 1957), 15.

14. Stein, *Toward New Towns*, 195.

15. Bernard Maybeck, 'The Palace of Fine Arts', *Transactions of the Commonwealth Club of California*, 10:10 (1915) 369–74.

16. Frank Lloyd Wright, *The Natural House* (New York, 1970), 20.

17. This story is recounted in David G. DeLong, *Bruce Goff: Toward Absolute Architecture* (New York, 1988), 111.

18. Rousseau wished to analyse the problems of human institutions and to analogize about the education of children rather than to promote a revival of the primitive, but these nuances were lost in popular imagery of the noble savage.

19. Brad Collins and Juliette Robbins, comps., *Antoine Predock, Architect* (New York, 1994), 198–215.

20. Henry H. Saylor, *Bungalows: Their Design, Construction, and Furnishing* (New York, 1911), 5.

21. George F. Devereaux, 'In the Land of the Bungalow' (1929), quoted in Robert Winter, *The California Bungalow* (Los Angeles, 1980), 10.

22. Doye O'Dell and Rudy Sooter, 'Dear Okie' (Exclusive Records release 33X 1182–2, 1947).

23. William and Helga Olkowski, *The Integral Urban House* (1979), quoted in Dolores Hayden, *Redesigning the American Dream: The Future of Housing, Work, and Family Life* (New York, 1984), 48.

24. Sim Van der Ryn and Stuart Cowan, *Ecological Design* (Washington, 1996), 56.

25. Ibid., 24.

26. David W. Orr, *Ecological Literacy: Education and the Transition to a Post-Modern World* (Albany, 1992), 24.

27. Richard Register, *Ecocity Berkeley: Building Cities for a Healthy Future* (Berkeley, 1987), 8.

Chapter 4. Technology

1. Edward Waterhouse, quoted in Carl Bridenbaugh, *Vexed and Troubled Englishmen, 1590–1642* (New York, 1967), 101.

2. It is not possible to give a single date for the appearance of sawmills, which depended on each locality's developing a sufficiently large population to warrant the investment.

3. Early, hybrid rural examples published by Paul E. Sprague make the connection between balloon and Chesapeake framing evident, although this is not Sprague's conclusion (Sprague, 'Chicago Balloon Frame: The Evolution During the 19th Century of George W. Snow's System for Erecting Light Frame Buildings from Dimension Lumber and Machine-Made Nails', in H. Ward Jandl, ed., *The Technology of Historic American Buildings: Studies in the Materials, Craft Processes, and the Mechanization of Building Construction* [Washington, 1983], 35–61). The earliest reference to balloon framing in Chicago obviously refers to plank framing: 'many of them are what they call Balloon houses, that is built of boards entirely—not a stick of timber in them except for the sills' (Caroline Clarke to Mary Walker, 1 Nov. 1835, in Chicago Historical Society; quoted in Sprague, 'Chicago Balloon Frame', 36).

4. John D. Thompson and Grace Goldin, *The Hospital: A Social and Architectural History* (New Haven, 1975), 159.

5. Florence Nightingale, *Notes on Hospitals* (1859), 10; quoted in Thompson and Goldin, *Hospital*, 159.

6. Quoted in Robert C. Twombly, *Frank Lloyd Wright: His Life and His Architecture* (New York, 1979), 99.

7. Quoted in Reyner Banham, *The Architecture of the Well-Tempered Environment* (Chicago, 1969), 86. Although Wright sometimes claimed that his was the first 'air conditioned' building, it did not incorporate air humidity controls, which conventional definitions accept as one of the key attributes of true air-conditioning.

8. Quoted in Loren W. Partridge, *John Galen Howard and the Berkeley Campus: Beaux-Arts Architecture in the 'Athens of the West'* (Berkeley, 1978), 24.

9. This passage is based on G. J. Barker-Benfield, 'The Spermatic Economy: A Nineteenth-Century View of Sexuality', in Michael Gordon, ed., *The American Family in Social-Historical Perspective* (2nd edn; New

York, 1978), 374–402.

10. David E. Nye, *American Technological Sublime* (Cambridge, Mass., 1994), pp. xi–xx, 77 (quote).

11. Quoted in David P. Billington, *The Tower and the Bridge: The New Art of Structural Engineering* (Princeton, 1983), 80.

12. Ibid., 81. Roebling's statement echoed the theories of Viollet-le-Duc, who believed that the Gothic style was peculiarly appropriate to the visual expression of modern materials and structural systems.

13. Ibid., 123.

14. Ibid., 75.

15. Alan Trachtenberg, *Brooklyn Bridge: Fact and Symbol* (2nd edn; Chicago, 1979), 76.

16. Ibid., 18, 118.

17. Sim Van der Ryn and Stuart Cowan, *Ecological Design* (Washington, 1996), 7.

18. Quoted in Carl W. Condit, *American Building Art: The Nineteenth Century* (New York, 1960), 174.

19. Quoted in Esther McCoy, *Case Study Houses, 1945–1962* (2nd edn; Los Angeles, 1977), 118.

20. Ibid., 47.

21. Ibid., 71.

22. Raymond Loewy, *Industrial Design* (Woodstock, NY, 1979), 13.

23. Norman Bel Geddes, *Horizons* (Boston, 1932; repr. New York, 1977), 4.

24. Loewy, *Industrial Design*, 15.

25. Bel Geddes, *Horizons*, 3, 24.

26. [George F. Keck], *House of Tomorrow, America's First Glass House* (Chicago, 1933), quoted in Narciso G. Menocal, *Keck & Keck Architects* (Madison, Wis., 1980), 34.

27. Quoted in Helen A. Harrison, ed., *Dawn of a New Day: The New York World's Fair, 1939/40* (New York, 1980), 4.

28. Quoted in Nye, *American Technological Sublime*, 207.

29. Ibid., 219.

30. Quoted in Harrison, ed., *Dawn of a New Day*, 8.

31. Quoted in Nye, *American Technological Sublime*, 212.

32. Quoted in Joseph J. Corn and Brian Horrigan, *Yesterday's Tomorrows: Past Visions of the American Future* (New York, 1984), 49.

Chapter 5. Money

1. As with most Anasazi sites, 'Aztec' is a fanciful name first used in the nineteenth century (others have Navajo names). The Aztec great house had nothing to do with the Aztecs of central Mexico, whom it antedates.

2. This passage is based on Greg Hise, *Magnetic Los Angeles: Planning the Postwar Metropolis* (Baltimore, 1997).

3. Cleveland *Plain Dealer*, 19 Nov. 1928, quoted in Holly M. Rarick, *Progressive Vision: The Planning of Downtown Cleveland, 1903–1930* (Cleveland, 1986), 58.

4. John Emery, Carew-Netherland Plaza developer, quoted in John Clubbe, *Cincinnati Observed: Architecture and History* (Columbus Oh., 1992), 20.

5. Carl W. Condit, *The Chicago School of Architecture: A History of Commercial and Public Building in the Chicago Area, 1875–1925* (Chicago, 1964), 26.

6. Carol Willis has described the T-plan office and its architectural implications in *Form Follows Finance: Skyscrapers and Skylines in New York and Chicago* (Princeton, 1995), 24–30.

7. John Fanning Watson, *Annals of Philadelphia and Pennsylvania, in the Olden Time*, 2 vols. (Philadelphia, 1868), ii. 591.

8. 'The Tall Office Building Artistically Considered', *Lippincott's*, 57 (Mar. 1896) 403–9, repr. in Louis H. Sullivan, *Kindergarten Chats and Other Writings* (New York, 1979), 202–13.

9. Ibid., 205.

10. Chicago architect John Wellborn Root, best known for his aesthetic talents, considered at length such practical issues as the relationship of lot coverage to light in an important article, 'A Great Architectural Problem', *Inland Architect and News Record*, 15 (Jun. 1890) 66–71, in which he dismissed visual considerations as relatively unimportant and easily satisfied.

11. W. J. Cash, *The Mind of the South* [1941] (New York, 1991), 262–3.

12. Quoted in Angel Kwolek-Folland, *Engendering Business: Men and Women in the Corporate Office, 1870–1930* (Baltimore, 1994), 99.

13. Willis, *Form Follows Finance*, 135.

14. Alex Ward, quoted in Andrea Oppen-heimer Dean, 'Making a Nonentity Into a Landmark', *Architecture*, 74:11 (Nov. 1985) 34.

15. Daralice D. Boles and Jim Murphy, 'Cincinnati Centerpiece: Procter & Gamble's New Headquarters', *Progressive Architecture*, 66:10 (Oct. 1985) 75.

16. These aspects of the Procter & Gamble headquarters are detailed, ibid., 83; and in Dean, 'Making a Nonentity a Landmark', 37–8.

17. Quoted in Robert W. Rydell, *All the World's a Fair: Visions of Empire at American International Expositions, 1876–1916* (Chicago, 1984), 65.

18. *Daily Inter Ocean*, 26 Apr. 1893, quoted in Rydell, *All the World's a Fair*, 48.

19. Quoted in William S. Worley, *J. C. Nichols and the Shaping of Kansas City: Innovation in Planned Residential Communities* (Columbia, Mo., 1990), 247.

20. Ibid., 258.

21. Ibid., 275.

22. Quoted in Howard Gillette, Jr., 'The Evolution of the Planned Shopping Center in City and Suburb', *Journal of the American Planning Association*, 51 (Autumn 1985) 454.

23. Aladdin Company, *Aladdin Homes: 'Built in a Day'*, catalog no. 31 (Bay City, Mich., 1918), 19–20, 71.

24. Estimates of income distribution and housing costs are very difficult to make before the 1930s. These rough estimates are, frankly, cobbled together from the following sources: Wesley C. Mitchell, Willford I. King, Frederick R. Macaulay, and Oswald W. Knauth, *Income in the United States: Its Amount and Distribution, 1909–1919* (New York, 1921), 132–7, 144; *Historical Statistics of the United States: Colonial Times to 1970* (Washington, 1975), ii. 647; and estimates in Worley, *J. C. Nichols*, 184, 189–91. Aladdin offered houses at a range of prices from $555 to $5,880. In 1919, the steep post-war inflation in housing costs drove the price of The Pasadena up to $2,869 and The Sunshine to $2,994, representative of a general rise of about 50 per cent in the company's prices (Aladdin Company, *Aladdin Homes: 'Built in a Day'*, catalog no. 32 (Bay City, Mich., 1919), price list). They had returned to their original level by 1921.

25. Clarence S. Stein, *Toward New Towns for America* (New York, 1957), 35, 85.

26. Quoted in Greg Hise, 'Building Design as Social Art: The Public Architecture of William Wurster, 1935–1950', in Marc Treib, ed., *An Everyday Modernism: The Houses of William Wurster* (Berkeley, 1995), 154.

27. *To the Honourable the Senate and House of Representatives of the Commonwealth of Pennsylvania in General Assembly Met, The Memorial of 'The Guardians for the Relief and Employment of the Poor of the City of Philadelphia, the District of Southwark and the Townships of the Northern Liberties and Penn,' Respectfully Represents* . . . [Philadelphia, c.1836], n.p.

28. Quoted in Marta Gutman, 'Housers and Other Architects: Pragmatism and Aesthetics in Recent Competitions,' *Journal of Architectural Education*, 46:3 (Feb. 1993) 131.

29. Robert Venturi, Denise Scott Brown and Stephen Izenour, *Learning From Las Vegas: The Forgotten Symbolism of Architectural Form* (2nd edn; Cambridge, Mass., 1977), 90, 92.

Chapter 6. Art

1. *The Rules of Work of the Carpenters' Company of the City and County of Philadelphia 1786*, ed. Charles E. Peterson (New York, 1971), vii.

2. Benjamin Latrobe to Henry Ormond, 20 Nov. 1806, in *The Correspondence and Miscellaneous Papers of Benjamin Henry Latrobe*, John C. Van Horne, Jeffrey A. Cohen, Darwin H. Stapleton, Lee W. Formwalt, William B. Forbush III, and Tina H. Sheller, eds. 3 vols. (New Haven and London, 1984–8), ii. 680.

3. Latrobe to Robert Mills, 12 Jul. 1806, ibid., 239–45.

4. The phrase 'negotiation of cognitive exclusiveness' along with the term 'market profession', is derived from Magali Sarfatti Larson, *The Rise of Professionalism: A Sociological Analysis* (Berkeley, 1977).

5. John Haviland, *The Builder's Assistant*, 3 vols. (Philadelphia, 1818–21), ii. 53.

6. Thomas U. Walter, Thirteenth Annual Address to the American Institute of Architects, 19 Nov. 1879, Loose Sheets—AIA, Thomas U. Walter Papers, Athenaeum of Philadelphia.

7. Meredith L. Clausen, 'Northgate Regional Shopping Center—Paradigm from the Provinces', *Journal of the Society of Architectural Historians*, 43:2 (May 1984) 161.

8. Thomas U. Walter, Diary 1834–6, p. 36 (17 Jan. 1835), Thomas U. Walter Papers.

9. Thomas U. Walter, *Architecture Considered as a Fine Art*, lecture 6 of a series, Philadelphia, December 1841. MS, pp. 32–3, Thomas U. Walter Papers.

10. Walter to William Hamilton, 6 May 1854, Letters April-June 1854, Thomas U. Walter Papers.

11. Quoted in Joan Draper, 'The École des Beaux-Arts and the Architectural Profession in the United States: The Case of John Galen Howard', in Spiro Kostof, ed., *The Architect: Chapters in the History of the Profession*, (New York, 1977), 215.

12. Quoted in Andrew Saint, *The Image of the Architect* (New Haven, 1983), 83.

13. Meyer Schapiro, 'Style,' in A. L. Kroeber, ed., *Anthropology Today: An Encyclopedic Inventory* (Chicago, 1953) 287.

14. Ibid.

15. James R. Sackett, 'The Meaning of Style in Archaeology: A General Model', *American Antiquity*, 42:3 (1977) 370.

16. 'Rural Cemeteries', *North American Review* 53:113 (1842), quoted in Richard G. Carrott, *The Egyptian Revival: Its Sources, Monuments, and Meaning, 1808–1858* (Berkeley, 1978), 86.

17. Quoted in David Wallace Adams,

Education for Extinction: American Indians and the Boarding School Experience, 1875–1928 (Lawrence, Kan., 1995), 186.

18. My discussion of Indian football is based on Adams, *Education for Extinction*, 183–91.

19. Mariana Griswold Van Rensselaer, *Henry Hobson Richardson and His Works* (1888; repr. New York, 1969), 123.

20. Quoted in Doris Cole, *From Tipi to Skyscraper: A History of Women in Architecture* (Boston, 1973), 76.

21. Karen E. Hudson, *The Will and the Way: Paul R. Williams, Architect* (New York, 1994), 11.

22. George M. Sheldon, *Artistic Country-Seats: Types of Recent American Villa and Cottage Architecture with Instances of Country Club-Houses* (New York, 1886–7).

23. Quoted in Jack Quinan, *Frank Lloyd Wright's Larkin Building: Myth and Fact* (New York, 1987), 4–5.

24. H. Allen Brooks, *The Prairie School* (New York, 1972), 80.

25. Quoted in Gwendolyn Wright, 'On the Fringe of the Profession: Women in American Architecture', in Kostof, ed., *The Architect*, 282.

26. Quoted in Brooks, *Prairie School*, 79.

27. Marion Mahony Griffin, 'The Magic of America', MS, quoted in Susan Fondiler Berkon, 'Marion Mahony Griffin', in Susana Torre, ed., *Women in American Architecture: A Historic and Contemporary Perspective*, (New York, 1977), 79.

28. Quoted in Wright, 'On the Fringe of the Profession', 282.

29. William Dean Howells, *The Rise of Silas Lapham* (1885; repr. New York, 1949), 41–42.

List of Illustrations

The publisher would like to thank the following individuals and institutions who have kindly given permission to reproduce the illustrations listed below.

1. John and Mary Dickinson House. Salem County, NJ, 1754. Photo Dell Upton, Berkeley, CA.
2. Perkinsons, Chesterfield County, VA, late 18th century. Virginia Department of Historic Resources, Richmond, VA/photo Dell Upton.
3. Bronck Houses, Coxsackie, NY, (a) late 17th century; (b) 1738; (c) 1792; (d) mid-19th century. Drawing Dell Upton.
4. Thomas Jefferson: Monticello II, Charlottesville, VA, 1796–1809. Garden front. Photo Dell Upton.
5. Thomas Jefferson: Monticello II, Charlottesville, VA, 1796–1809. Ground floor plan with Monticello I superimposed. From W. H. Adams, *Jefferson's Monticello* (New York: Abbeville Press, 1983), 62.
6. Thomas Jefferson: Monticello II, Charlottesville, VA, 1796–1809. Exterior view from the south-east. Holsinger Studio Collection (9862), Special Collections Department. University of Virginia Library, Charlottesville, VA.
7. Thomas Jefferson: Monticello II, Charlottesville, VA, 1796–1809. Schematic view showing axial organization. Drawing Sibel Zandi-Sayek, Berkeley, CA.
8. Henry and Anne Saunders House, Isle of Wight County, VA, c.1795. Drawing Dell Upton.
9. Sites House, Rockingham County, VA, c.1800–10. Drawing Dell Upton.
10. Boardman House, Saugus, MA, 1687; lean-to, c.1696. Photo Dell Upton.
11. Boardman House, Saugus, MA, 1687. Plan. After A, Sorli in A. L. Cummings, *The Framed Houses of Massachusetts Bay* (Cambridge, MA: Harvard University Press, copyright © 1979 by the Presidents and Fellows of Harvard College), 24–25.

12. Prototypical Navajo conical forked-pole hogan. From P. Nabokov and R. Easton, *Native American Architecture* (New York: © Oxford University Press, 1989, and P. Nabokov and R. Easton), 327.
13. Thomas Jefferson: Monticello I, Charlottesville, VA, 1772. Massachusetts Historical Society, Boston, MA.
14. Mount Airy, Richmond County, VA, c.1754–64. South front. Photo Dell Upton.
15. Mount Airy, Richmond County, VA, c.1754–64. East front. Photo Dell Upton.
16. Charles Bulfinch: Swan House, Dorchester, MA, 1796. From F. Kimball, *Domestic Architecture of the American Colonies and of the Early Republic* (New York: Scribner's, 1922), 162. British Architectural Library, Royal Institute of British Architects (R. I. B. A.), London.
17. Speculative houses, Dayton, KY, c.1900. Photo Edward A. Chappell, Williamsburg, VA.
18. Catherine E. Beecher and Harriet Beecher Stowe: Design for an efficient galley kitchen, 1869. From C. E. Beecher and H. B. Beecher Stowe, *The American Woman's Home* (New York, 1869), 34.
19. Catherine E. Beecher and Harriet Beecher Stowe: Christian House, 1869. First-floor plan. From C. E. Beecher and H. B. Beecher Stowe, *The American Woman's Home* (New York, 1869), 26.
20. Frank Lloyd Wright: Herbert Jacobs First Residence, Madison, WI, 1937. Plan. S. 234. From W. A. Storrer, *The Frank Lloyd Wright Companion* (Chicago: University of Chicago Press, 1993), 242. The drawings of buildings by Frank Lloyd Wright used in this publication were prepared by William Allin Storrer under license from, and copyright by, The Frank Lloyd Wright Foundation © 1993. Requests for permission to reproduce these drawings should be addressed to William Allin Storrer c/o The University of Chicago Press.
21. Lamb and Rich: Henry R. Mallory House,

Bryam, CT, *c.*1885. From A. Lewis, *American Country Houses of the Gilded Age* (1886–87; Repr. New York, 1982 © Dover Publications Inc.), pl. 50.

22. John Calvin Stevens: James Hopkins Smith House, Falmouth Foreside, ME, 1885. From A. Lewis, *American Country Houses of the Gilded Age* (1886–87; Repr. New York, 1982 © Dover Publications Inc.), pl. 41.

23. Alexander Jackson Davis: Rotch House, New Bedford, MA, *c.*1845–47. Elevation. From A. J. Downing, *Architecture of Country Houses* (New York, 1850), 296. British Architectural Library, R. I. B. A., London.

24. Alexander Jackson Davis: Rotch House, New Bedford, MA. *c.*1845–47. Plan. From A. J. Downing, *Architecture of Country Houses* (New York, 1850), 297. British Architectural Library, R. I. B. A., London.

25. Frank Lloyd Wright: Frederick C. Robie Residence, Chicago, IL, 1908. Photo Richard Bryant/ Arcaid, London.

26. Frank Lloyd Wright: Robie Residence, Chicago, IL, 1908. First- (ground), second- (main), and third-floor plans. S.127. From W. A. Storrer, *The Frank Lloyd Wright Companion* (Chicago: University of Chicago Press, 1993), 127. The drawings of buildings by Frank Lloyd Wright used in this publication were prepared by William Allin Storrer under license from, and copyright by, The Frank Lloyd Wright Foundation © 1993. Requests for permission to reproduce these drawings should be addressed to William Allin Storrer c/o The University of Chicago Press.

27. Richard Meier: Smith House, Darien, CT, 1965. Entrance front. Photo Dell Upton.

28. Richard Meier: Smith House, Darien, CT, 1965. Ground, first and second floor plans. Richard Meier & Partners Architects. New York and Los Angeles.

29. Richard Meier: Smith House, Darien, CT, 1965. Site plan. Richard Meier & Partners Architects, New York and Los Angeles.

30. Plan of New Orleans, the Capital of Louisiana, 18th century. The Historic New Orleans Collection (acc. no. 1974. 25.18.25).

31. Common courthouse-square plans. After Edward T. Price, in E. T. Price, 'The Central Courthouse Square in the American County Seat' in D. Upton and J. M. Vlach (eds.), *Common Places: Readings in American Vernacular Architecture* (Athens, GA: University of Georgia Press, 1986).

32. Rock Springs Camp Meeting Ground, Lincoln County, NC, founded 1833. Site plan. Drawing by Carl Lounsbury, Colonial Williamsburg Foundation, Williamsburg, VA.

33. Balls Creek Camp Meeting Ground Catawba County, NC, mid-19th century. Photo Dell Upton.

34. Poverty Point archaeological site, West Carroll Parish, LA, *c.*1000 BCE. Reconstruction drawing of central district. From J. L. Gibson, *Poverty Point: A Culture of the Lower Mississippi Valley* (© Louisiana Anthropological Survey and Antiquities Commission, Baton Rouge, 1983), 8.

35. Newark Earthworks, Licking County, OH, *c.*200 CE. Survey drawing. From E. G. Squier and E. H. Davis, *Ancient Monuments of the Mississippi Valley* (Washington. DC, 1848), pl. xxv.

36. Monk's Mound, Cahokia, IL, *c.*1000 CE Aerial view. Photo Timothy Hursley, Little Rock, AR.

37. Tattooed Serpent's funeral, Grand Village of the Natchez, Natchez, MS, 1725. From A. Le Page du Pratz, *Histoire de la Louisiane* 3 (Paris, 1758), op. 55.

38. An Iroquoian house, *c.*900 CE. Reconstruction drawing. From M. Kapches, 'The Spatial Dynamics of Ontario Iroquoian Longhouses', *American Antiquity* 55/1 (1990), 50. © Society of American Archaeology.

39. 'Elevation des Cabannes Sauvages', Iroquoian longhouse, *c.*1720. Edward E. Ayer Collection (MS Map 150), The Newberry Library, Chicago, IL.

40. Sour Springs Longhouse, Six Nations Reserve, Canada, 1870s. Photo Frank Speck, 1943. Peabody Essex Museum, Salem, MA.

41. William Thornton, Stephen Hallet, Benjamin Henry Latrobe, Charles Bulfinch et al: United States Capitol, Washington DC, 1793–1916. Main floor plan, 1832–34. Drawing by Alexander Jackson Davis. Avery Architectural and Fine Arts Library (1940.011.00178), Columbia University, NY.

42. William Thornton, Stephen Hallet, Benjamin Henry Latrobe, Charles Bulfinch et al: United States Capitol, Washington, DC, 1793–1916. East front. Daguerrotype *c.*1846. Library of Congress, Washington, DC.

43. Thomas U. Walter: United States Capitol, Washington, DC, 1793–1916. Design for the new east front, 1855. Athenaeum of Philadelphia, Philadelphia, PA.

44. Bertram Grosvenor Goodhue, with Lee Lawrie, Hildreth Meiere, Augustus Tack, and Hartley Burr Alexander: Nebraska State Capitol and World War I Memorial, Lincoln, NB, 1922–32. Photograph *c.*1934. Nebraska State Historical Society (acc. no. C244.375), Lincoln, NB.

45. Bertram Grosvenor Goodhue, with Lee

New York.

74. Olmsted, Vaux and Company, *General Plan of Riverside, Illinois*, 1869. Courtesy of the Frances Loeb Library, Graduate School of Design, Harvard University.

75. Reginald D. Johnson and Wilson, Merrill, and Alexander (associated architects); Clarence S. Stein (consulting architect): Baldwin Hills Village, Los Angeles, CA, 1940–41. Photo Dell Upton.

76. Reginald D. Johnson and Wilson, Merrill, and Alexander (associated architects); Clarence S. Stein (consulting architect): Baldwin Hills Village, Los Angeles, CA, 1940–41. Plan. From C. S. Stein, *Toward New Towns for America* (University Press of Liverpool, 1951), 174.

77. Thomas D. Church: Donnell Garden, Sonoma County, CA, 1948–49. Site plan. From T. D. Church, *Gardens are for People: How to Plan for Outdoor Living* (New York: Reinhold Publishing Corporation, 1955), 231.

78. Thomas D. Church: Donnell Garden, Sonoma County, CA, 1948–49. View. From T. D. Church, *Gardens are for People: How to Plan for Outdoor Living* (New York: Reinhold Publishing Corporation, 1955), frontispiece.

79. Front Yard, Berkeley, CA. Photo Dell Upton.

80. Fay Jones and Associates: Thorncrown Chapel, Eureka Springs, AR, 1980. Photo Timothy Hursley, Little Rock, AR.

81. Bernard Maybeck: Palace of the Fine Arts, San Francisco, CA, 1915. Photo Dell Upton.

82. Frank Lloyd Wright: Fallingwater (Liliane S. and Edgar I. Kauffman, Sr, Residence), Bear Run, PA, 1935–36. Photo Scott Frances/Esto/Arcaid, London.

83. Frank Lloyd Wright: Fallingwater, 1935–36. Main level plan. S.230. From W. A. Storrer, *The Frank Lloyd Wright Companion* (Chicago: University of Chicago Press, 1993). The drawings of buildings by Frank Lloyd Wright used in this publication were prepared by William Allin Storrer under license from, and copyright by, The Frank Lloyd Wright Foundation © 1993. Requests for permission to reproduce these drawings should be addressed to William Allin Storrer c/o The University of Chicago Press.

84. Bruce Goff: Bavinger House, Norman, OK, 1950–55. Bruce Goff Archive, Ryerson and Burnham Libraries, The Art Institute of Chicago.

85. Henry I. Greber: J. C. Nichols Memorial Fountain, Kansas City, MO. 1950. Photo Dell Upton.

86. Antoine Predock: Centennial Complex,

American Heritage Center and Art Museum, University of Wyoming, Laramie, WY, 1986–93. Photo Timothy Hursley, Little Rock, AR.

87. Sioux Grass Dancers, Fort Yates, Dakota Territory, *c.*1888. © AZUSA Publishing Inc., Englewood, CO.

88. Charles F. Lummis: El Alisal (Charles F. Lummis House), Highland Park, Los Angeles, CA, 1897–1910. Photo Dell Upton.

89. Greene and Greene: Gamble House, Pasadena, CA, 1908. Rear. Photo Marvin Rand, Venice, CA.

90. Greene and Greene: Gamble House, Pasadena, CA, 1908. Photo Marvin Rand, Venice, CA.

91. Gustav Stickley: Open-air dining-room, 1909. From G. Stickley, *Craftsman Homes* (1909), 91. Avery Architectural and Fine Arts Library, Columbia University, NY.

92. George Fred Keck: Duncan House, Flossmoor, IL, 1941. From R. Boyce, *Keck & Keck* (New York: Princeton Architectural Press, 1993), 121.

93. Eleanor Raymond: Sun-heated house, Dover, MA, 1948. Photo courtesy Doris Cole (*Eleanor Raymond, Architect*, 1981).

94. Office of the State Architect: Bateson Building, Sacramento, CA, 1978. Photo Dell Upton.

95. Office of the State Architect: Bateson Building, Sacramento, CA, 1978. Isometric section. From S. Van der Ryn and P. Calthorpe, *Sustainable Communities: A New Design Synthesis for Cities, Suburbs, and Towns* (San Francisco: © Sierra Club Books, 1986), 18. Calthorpe Associates, Berkeley, CA.

96. Hidatsa twelve-post earth lodge, reconstruction drawing. From R. H. Lowie, *Indians of the Plains* (New York: American Museum of Natural History, 1954), 36.

97. Larger Wemp Barn, Fort Hunter, Montgomery County, NY, late 18th century. From J. F. Fitchen, *The New World Dutch Barn: A Study of its Characteristics, its Structural System, and its Probable Erectional Procedures* (Syracuse, NY: Syracuse University Press, 1968), 115.

98. Gedney House, Salem, MA, *c.*1665, addition, *c.*1700. A. Sorli in A. L. Cummings, *The Framed Houses of Massachusetts Bay, 1625–1725* (Cambridge, MA: Harvard University Press, copyright © 1979 by the Presidents and Fellows of Harvard College), 53.

99. Fairbanks House, Dedham, MA, *c.*1637. A. Sorli in A. L. Cummings, *The Framed Houses of Massachusetts Bay, 1625–1725*

(Cambridge, MA: Harvard University Press, copyright © 1979 by the Presidents and Fellows of Harvard College), 58.

100. Rich Neck Plantation Granary, Surry County, VA, early 19th century. Drawing Dell Upton. From Dell Upton, 'Traditional Timber Framing' in Brooke Hindle (ed.), *Material Culture of the Wooden Age* (Tarrytown, NY: Sleepy Hollow Press, 1981), fig. 8.

101. Balloon frame. From G. E. Woodward, *Victorian Architecture and Rural Art* (Watkins Glen, NY: © American Life Foundation, 1978).

102. Quonset hut, Z-Bar Ranch, Strong City, KS, *c.*1945. Photo Dell Upton.

103. Andrew Jackson Downing: Room without ventilation, mid-19th century. From A. J. Downing, *The Architecture of Country Houses* (New York, 1850), 466. British Architectural Library, R. I. B. A., London.

104. John S. Billings, M.D., with John R. Niernsee (consulting architect): Johns Hopkins Hospital, Baltimore, MD, 1876–85. Common ward. From J. S. Billings, *Description of Johns Hopkins Hospital* (Baltimore: Johns Hopkins Hospital, 1890), pl. 24. British Architectural Library, R. I. B. A., London.

105. John S. Billings, M.D., with John R. Niernsee (consulting architect): Johns Hopkins Hospital, Baltimore, MD, 1876–85. Isolating ward. From J. S. Billings, *Description of Johns Hopkins Hospital* (Baltimore: Johns Hopkins Hospital, 1890), pl. 28. British Architectural Library, R. I. B. A., London.

106. John S. Billings, M.D., with John R. Niernsee (consulting architect): Johns Hopkins Hospital, Baltimore, MD, 1870–85. Section of a common ward. From J. S. Billings, *Description of Johns Hopkins Hospital* (Baltimore: Johns Hopkins Hospital, 1890), pl. 23. British Architectural Library, R. I. B. A., London.

107. Frank Lloyd Wright: Larkin Company Administration Building, Buffalo, NY, 1903–4. Copyright © 1998 The Frank Lloyd Wright Foundation, Scottsdale, AZ.

108. John Galen Howard (architect); Dean S. B. Christy (consultant): Hearst Memorial Mining Building, University of California, Berkeley, CA 1902–7. Photo Dell Upton.

109. John Galen Howard (architect); Dean S. B. Christy (consultant): Hearst Memorial Mining Building, University of California, Berkeley, CA, 1902–7. Chimneys and ventilating cupola. Photo Dell Upton.

110. Louis I. Kahn: Richards Medical Research Laboratory, University of Pennsylvania, Philadelphia, PA, 1957–64. Photo Dell Upton.

111. John A. Roebling (chief engineer); completed by Washington Roebling and Emily Roebling: *The Great East River Suspension Bridge*, Brooklyn, NY, to New York, NY, 1869–83. The Brooklyn Historical Society.

112. Othmar Ammann (chief engineer); Leon S. Moissieff and Allston Dana (engineers); Cass Gilbert (consulting architect): George Washington Bridge, New York, NY, to Fort Lee, NJ, 1927–31. The Port Authority of New York and New Jersey.

113. Lacey V. Murrow (chief engineer); Leon S. Moissieff (consultant): Tacoma Narrows Bridge, Tacoma, WA, 1939–40. Washington State Historical Society Research Center, Tacoma, WA.

114. Rudoph M. Schindler: Lovell Beach House, Newport Beach, CA, 1926. Photo Dell Upton.

115. Richard Neutra: Lovell 'Health' House, Los Angeles, CA, 1927–29. Axonometric drawing by Jeffery B. Lentz, Historic American Buildings Survey, Library of Congress, Washington, DC.

116. Philip C. Johnson: Philip C. Johnson 'Glass' House, New Canaan, CT, 1949. Ezra Stoller © Esto, Mamaronek, NY. All rights reserved.

117. Rouse Corporation (developer); Frank Gehry (architect): Santa Monica Place, Santa Monica, CA, 1979–81. Parking garage, Photo Dell Upton.

118. Raymond Loewy: 'Evolutionary Chart of Design', 1930. From R. Loewy, *Industrial Design* (Woodstock, NY: Overlook Press, 1979), 76.

119. Julian Krupa: 'Cities of Tomorrow', 1939. From *Amazing Stories* (August, 1939). National Museum of American History. Smithsonian Institution, Washington, DC.

120. Norman Bel Geddes: 'Diagram Illustrating the Principles of Streamlining', 1932. From N. Bel Geddes, *Horizons* (1932: Repr. 1977. New York: © Dover Publications Inc.), 45.

121. R. Buckminster Fuller: 4-D Utility Unit (Dymaxion House), 1927. Buckminster Fuller Institute, Santa Barbara, CA.

122. R. Buckminster Fuller: 'Zeppelin Delivery of 4-D Houses', 1927. Buckminster Fuller Institute, Santa Barbara, CA.

123. George Fred Keck: House of Tomorrow, Century of Progress Exhibition, Chicago, IL, 1933. Exterior. Chicago Historical Society/ photo Hedrich-Blessing.

124. George Fred Keck: House of Tomorrow,

Century of Progress Exhibition, Chicago, IL, 1933. Plans. From N. G. Menocal, *Keck & Keck Architects* (Madison: Elvehjem Museum of Art, University of Wisconsin, 1980), 35. © State Historical Society of Wisconsin.

125. George Fred Keck: House of Tomorrow, Century of Progress Exhibition, Chicago, IL. 1933. Interior. Chicago Historical Society/ photo Hedrich-Blessing.

126. Gilbert Rohde: 'Man Freed in Time and Space', design for Community Interests Pavilion, New York World's Fair, 1939. Manuscripts and Archives Division, New York Public Library.

127. *King Kong*, 1933. © 1933 RKO Pictures Inc.

128. Pueblo Bonito, Chaco Canyon, NM, 910–1110 CE. Reconstruction. Reprinted with permission from *Mysteries of the Ancient Americas*, copyright © 1986 The Reader's Digest Association, Inc. Illustration by Lloyd Kenneth Townsend.

129. Pueblo Bonito, Chaco Canyon, NM. 910–1110 CE. Developmental sequence. From S. H. Lekson, T. C. Windes, J. R. Stein, and W. J. Judge, 'The Chaco Canyon Community', in *Scientific American* 259/1 (July 1988), 104. Courtesy of the Estate of Tom Prentise.

130. Chacoan road system and outlying great houses, New Mexico.

131. Boston, MA, 1640. Reconstructed plan. From W. M. Whitehill, *Boston: A Topographical History* (Cambridge, MA: Harvard University Press, 1959), 10.

132. John Bonner: Boston, MA, 1722. Map. Massachusetts Historical Society, Boston, MA.

133. Philadelphia, PA, *c*.1807. The Historical Society of Pennsylvania (Of. 610.17961), Philadelphia, PA.

134. *Benjamin Butman, Ship Chandler and Grocer*, New Orleans, LA, *c*.1860. The Historic New Orleans Collection (acc. no. 1955.52).

135. Wing Fat Market, Oakland, CA, *c*.1990. Photo Dell Upton.

136. World War II-era communal development, Los Angeles, CA. After Lisa Padilla and Greg Hise, Los Angeles, CA.

137. John Haviland: Philadelphia Arcade, Philadelphia, PA, 1824–26. Rental plan. The Historical Society of Pennsylvania (Burd papers, Am. 0364), Philadelphia, PA.

138. C. Burton: Philadelphia Arcade. Philadelphia, PA, 1831. Engraving. The Library Company of Philadelphia ((1). 1525.F.47d), PA.

139. Daniel H. Burnham and Edward H. Bennett, *Plan of Chicago*, IL, 1909. Chicago

Historical Society (qF38HP.B9.c.6).

140. Graham, Anderson, Probst, and White: Terminal Tower Complex, Cleveland, OH, 1916–34. Elevation and partial section. From *The Union Station: A Description of the New Passenger Facilities and Surrounding Improvements* (1930). Cleveland Public Library. By permission of Graham, Anderson, Probst, and White.

141. Graham, Anderson, Probst, and White: Terminal Tower Complex, Cleveland, OH, 1916–34. Sketch site plan, *c*.1980. Redrawn from Jim Toman and Dan Cook. *The Terminal Tower Complex* (Cleveland, OH: Cleveland Landmarks Press, 1980), 7.

142. Small and Rowley: Shaker Square, Shaker Heights, OH, 1929. Photo Dell Upton.

143. Harrison and Abramowitz: Governor Nelson A. Rockefeller Empire State Plaza, Albany, NY, 1962–78. Ezra Stoller © Esto, Mamaroneck, NY. All rights reserved.

144. Graham, Anderson, Probst, and White: Straus Building, Chicago, IL, 1924. From *Buildings and Building Management*, 25 (1925), 27. Avery Architectural and Fine Arts Library, Columbia University, NY.

145. Robert Mills: United States Treasury Building, Washington, DC, 1836–42. Plan. From R. Mills, *Guide to the National Executive Offices and the Capital of the United States* (Washington, 1841), 5.

146. Robert Mills: United States Treasury Building, Washington, DC, 1836–42. View. Photo Dell Upton.

147. Sloan and Stewart: Tower Hall, 518 Market Street, Philadelphia, PA, 1855–57. Photograph *c*.1898. The Print and Picture Collection, The Free Library of Philadelphia.

148. Adler and Sullivan: Wainwright Building, St Louis, MO, 1890–91. Photograph, *c*.1907. Missouri Historical Society, St Louis.

149. Adler and Sullivan: Wainwright Building, St Louis, MO, 1890–91. Typical plan. From L. H. Sullivan. *Kindergarten Chats and Other Writings* (New York, 1947: Repr. 1979 © Dover Publications Inc.), 204.

150. Napoleon Le Brun and Sons: Metropolitan Life Insurance Building, New York, NY, 1909. The Byron Collection, Museum of the City of New York.

151. J. L. Kingston: 'Study of Economic Height for Office Buildings' within the confines of New York zoning law, 1930. From W. C. Clark and J. L. Kingston, *The Skyscraper: A Study in the Economic Height of Modern Office Buildings* (New York: American Institute of Steel Construction, 1930), 15. British Architectural Library, R. I. B. A., London.

1947. © (1998) Pedro E. Guerrero, New Canaan, CT.

180. Frank Lloyd Wright: S. C. Johnson & Son Administration Building, Racine, WI, 1936–39. Photo courtesy of S. C. Johnson Wax, Racine, WI.

181. Frank Lloyd Wright: S. C. Johnson & Son Administration Building, Racine WI, 1936–39. Great Workroom. Photo Dell Upton.

182. Henry Hobson Richardson, 1886. Photographic portrait by George Collins Cox. Society for the Preservation of New England Antiquities, Boston.

183. Offices of Henry Hobson Richardson, c.1886. From M. G. Van Rensselaer, *Henry Hobson Richardson and his Works* (1888).

184. Charles Moore: Piazza d'Italia, New Orleans, LA. 1975–8. Photo © 1978 Norman McGrath, New York.

185. Amaza Lee Meredith: Azurest South (Meredith-Colson House), Ettrick, VA, 1939. Virginia State University Archives, Petersburg/courtesy Virginia Museum of Fine Arts, Richmond. Reprinted with permission of the publisher, from *The Making of Virginia Architecture* © 1992 Virginia Museum of Fine Arts.

186. Frank Lloyd Wright (architect); Marion L. Mahony (delineator): 'A Fireproof House for $5000', 1907. Copyright © 1998 The Frank Lloyd Wright Foundation, Scottsdale, AZ.

187. Julia Morgan, photographed in her Paris apartment, 1899, aged 27. University Archives, California Polytechnic State University (Morgan Collection IV/01/11/02/04), San Luis Obispo.

188. Richard Neutra in Switzerland, 1919, aged 27. Photo courtesy of Thomas Hines.

189. Giant Artichoke, Castroville, CA, c.1975. Photo Dell Upton.

The publisher and author apologize for any errors or omissions in the above list. If contacted they will be pleased to rectify these at the earliest opportunity.

Bibliographic Essay

The literature of American architecture is voluminous but unevenly distributed: some aspects have been over-studied, while others have been ignored. In this bibliographic essay I have tried to call attention to the principal sources of my arguments, including some non-architectural works that are essential for understanding the issues I raise, and to some other studies that have made significant intellectual contributions to American architectural history. Because it is a relatively easy task for interested readers to find monographs devoted to particular architects or buildings, I have cited them only when no broader work treats the same issues. The same principle governs the inclusion of primary sources.

Surveys

There is no shortage of chronological surveys of the architectural history of the United States. Neophytes should begin with Leland M. Roth, *A Concise History of American Architecture* (New York, 1979). William H. Pierson and William H. Jordy, *American Buildings and Their Architects* (Oxford, 1970– ; 4 vols. to date), a series of wide-ranging essays built around individual buildings and architects, is essential for more knowledgeable readers. However, no survey treats pre-Revolutionary American architecture adequately, so Dell Upton, 'Architecture: British', in Jacob Ernest Cooke, ed., *Encyclopedia of the North American Colonies* (New York, 1993) is a necessary starting-point for understanding Anglo-American colonial architecture.

Several excellent surveys depart from conventional approaches to the history of American architecture. Alan Gowans has written two very different ones: *Images of American Living: Four Centuries of Architecture and Furniture as Cultural Expression* (Philadelphia, 1964) links the history of architecture with that of furniture and the

decorative arts, and his more recent *Styles and Types of North American Architecture: Social Function and Cultural Expression* (New York, 1992) ranges far beyond the canons of high architecture to explore the social functions of visual design and formal type. Spiro Kostof, *America by Design* (Oxford, 1987) is a thematic treatment that synthesizes aesthetic and social history.

Traditional surveys are weakest in treating indigenous, folk, and vernacular architecture, so they must be supplemented with specialist works in these fields. Henry Glassie, *Pattern in the Material Folk Culture of the Eastern United States* (Philadelphia, 1968) was the primer for much of the contemporary study of folk architecture. The articles in Dell Upton and John Michael Vlach, eds., *Common Places: Readings in American Vernacular Architecture* (Athens, Ga., 1986); Robert Blair St George, ed., *Material Life in America, 1600–1860* (Boston, 1988); and Thomas Carter, *Images of an American Land: Vernacular Architecture in the Western United States* (Albuquerque, 1997) contain other seminal works by historians, folklorists, geographers, and architectural historians. Dell Upton, ed., *America's Architectural Roots: Ethnic Groups That Built America* (Washington, 1986) offers brief popular introductions to a number of folk architectural traditions in the United States. Finally, the articles in the Vernacular Architecture Forum's series *Perspectives in Vernacular Architecture* (6 vols. to date; various editors and publishers, 1982–) suggest the range of methods and subject-matter that characterize the most recent scholarship in this diverse field.

Peter Nabokov and Robert Easton, *Native American Architecture* (Oxford, 1989) is a unique synthesis of a century of scholarship on the indigenous architecture of the United States. It can be supplemented by the more detailed discussions of American Indian architecture and culture scattered through the

Smithsonian Institution's still-incomplete *Handbook of North American Indians* (9 vols. to date, 20 projected; Washington, 1978–), and the invaluable *Bulletins* and *Reports* of the Bureau of American Ethnology, published since 1879.

Chapter 1. The House as an American Icon
American Houses
The house has been the central preoccupation of American architects and historians, with the greatest attention paid to the single-family houses of middle- and upper-middle-class white Americans. Clifford E. Clark, Jr., *The American Family Home* (Chapel Hill, NC, 1986) is a historian's overview of the middle-class house, while architectural historian Gwendolyn Wright's *Building the Dream: A Social History of Housing in America* (New York, 1981) is more inclusive but more episodic. With the exception of Mark Alan Hewitt, *The Architect and the American Country House* (New Haven and London, 1990), almost no scholarly attention has been devoted to the monumental residences of the very rich.

Monticello
For the most part, studies of Thomas Jefferson's architecture stand in the interpretive shadow of Fiske Kimball's monumental *Thomas Jefferson, Architect* (Boston, 1916). Recent assessments of Monticello that enlarge on and sometimes diverge from the Kimball tradition include William Howard Adams, *Jefferson's Monticello* (New York, 1983) and Jack McLaughlin, *Jefferson and Monticello: The Biography of a Builder* (New York, 1988).

Susan R. Stein, *The Worlds of Thomas Jefferson at Monticello* (New York, 1993), discusses Monticello's furnishings and the uses of each of the house's principal rooms. The social practices that these spaces accommodated are brilliantly delineated in Mark Girouard, *Life in the English Country House, A Social and Architectural History* (New Haven and London, 1977).

The best discussions of Monticello's exterior landscape can be found in Rhys Isaac, 'The First Monticello', in Peter S. Onuf, ed., *Jeffersonian Legacies* (Charlottesville, Va., 1993) and William L. Beiswanger, 'The Temple in the Garden: Thomas Jefferson's Vision of the Monticello Landscape', in Robert P. Maccubbin and Peter Martin, eds., *British and American Gardens in the Eighteenth Century* (Williamsburg, Va., 1984). Charles A. Miller,

Jefferson and Nature: An Interpretation (Baltimore, 1988) sets Jefferson's gardening in its philosophical context.

The study of slave life at Monticello has just begun. The main source is Lucinda R. Stanton, ' "Those Who Labor for My Happiness": Thomas Jefferson and His Slaves', in Onuf, ed., *Jeffersonian Legacies*. This can be supplemented by Dell Upton, 'White and Black Landscapes in Eighteenth-Century Virginia', in St George, ed., *Material Life in America*, a discussion of the physical setting of slavery in Jefferson's Virginia, and by John Vlach's broader overview, *Back of the Big House: The Architecture of Plantation Slavery* (Chapel Hill, NC, 1993).

The Ordinariness of Architecture: Monticello's Context
Jefferson disparaged the aesthetic qualities and structural soundness of the architecture of his native state in a famous passage in *Notes on the State of Virginia* (1780). His remarks should be read in conjunction with the essays in Cary Carson, Ronald Hoffman, and Peter J. Albert, eds., *Of Consuming Interests: The Style of Life in the Eighteenth Century* (Charlottesville, Va., 1994), particularly Edward A. Chappell's 'Housing a Nation: The Transformation of Living Standards in Early America'. For specific regional and ethnic traditions, see Upton, ed., *America's Architectural Roots*; Upton and Vlach, eds., *Common Places*; Marcus Whiffen, *The Eighteenth-Century Houses of Williamsburg: A Study of Architecture and Building in the Colonial Capital* (rev. edn; Williamsburg, Va., 1984); Bernard L. Herman, *Architecture and Rural Life in Central Delaware, 1700–1900* (Knoxville, Tenn., 1987); and Abbott Lowell Cummings's monumental *The Framed Houses of Massachusetts Bay, 1625–1725* (Boston, 1979).

Design
Fiske Kimball stressed the role of architectural publications in shaping Jefferson's design, an emphasis he extended to all eighteenth-century American architecture in *Domestic Architecture of the American Colonies and of the Early Republic* (New York, 1922), a classic of American architectural history that is still worth reading. Kimball's analysis of the architecture of Jefferson and his contemporaries has not been refuted so much as it has been bypassed by more recent scholarship emphasizing the spatial characteristics and social use of colonial folk and high-style buildings. Henry Glassie, *Folk Housing in*

Middle Virginia: A Structural Analysis of Historic Artifacts (Knoxville, Tenn., 1976) presents a model of architectural design, derived from anthropology and linguistics, that stresses learning and applying principles over the imitation of published models. Another theme that runs through this and others of Glassie's works is the social isolation of domestic space, particularly as effected in the 'Georgian-plan house' (which he named). Girouard's analysis of similar phenomena among the English ruling élite has also influenced American scholars.

Consumption
For twenty years, historians and anthropologists have been preoccupied with consumption as an economic and a personal issue. The study of consumerism has attracted both historians and anthropologists over the last twenty years. Robert Bocock, *Consumption* (London, 1993), and Jean-Christophe Agnew, 'Coming Up for Air: Consumer Culture in Historical Perspective', in John Brewer and Roy Porter, eds., *Consumption and the World of Goods* (London, 1993) offers a way into the literature. The important essay by Cary Carson, 'The Consumer Revolution in Colonial British America: Why Demand?' in Carson *et al*, eds., *Of Consuming Interests* applies these insights to American material culture, and Timothy J. Breen's article in the same volume interprets the Revolution as a crisis of consumption.

From the anthropological viewpoint, Colin Campbell, *The Romantic Ethic and the Spirit of Modern Consumerism* (Oxford, 1987) and Daniel Miller, *Material Culture and Mass Consumption* (Oxford, 1987) are essential starting-points.

Architectural consumption is treated briefly in Dell Upton, *Holy Things and Profane: Anglican Parish Churches in Colonial Virginia* (New York, 1986; New Haven and London, 1997), while the specific role of William Buckland and Edmund Jenings in the design of Mount Airy is described in Charles E. Brownell, Calder Loth, William M. S. Rasmussen, and Richard Guy Wilson, *The Making of Virginia Architecture* (Charlottesville, Va., 1992).

The Republican House
Republicanism has been a central concept in early American historiography since the 1960s. Gordon S. Wood, *The Creation of the American Republic, 1776–1787* (Chapel Hill, NC, 1968) is essential, combining with Daniel T. Rodgers,

'Republicanism: The Career of a Concept', *Journal of American History*, 79 (1992) to follow the history of the idea in recent scholarship. For republicanism in architecture, see Dell Upton, 'Lancasterian Schools, Republican Citizenship, and the Spatial Imagination in Early Nineteenth-Century America', *Journal of the Society of Architectural Historians*, 55 (1996).

The New American House
The nineteenth-century American house has been intensively studied by historians and architectural historians. Vincent J. Scully, Jr., *The Shingle Style and the Stick Style: Architectural Theory and Design from Downing to the Origins of Wright* (rev. edn; New Haven and London, 1971) is an influential study of the aesthetics of late nineteenth-century houses, while David P. Handlin, *The American Home: Architecture and Society, 1815–1915* (Boston, 1979) treats the nineteenth-century house from the point of view of social and technological history.

In recent years, historians have explored the inner workings of these houses, while others have corrected previous scholars' over-emphasis on the freestanding suburban houses of middle- and upper-middle-class white Protestants. Colleen McDannell, *The Christian Home in Victorian America, 1840–1900* (Bloomington, Ind., 1986), for example, adds Catholics to the discussion, while Elizabeth Blackmar, *Manhattan for Rent, 1785–1850* (Ithaca, NY, 1989) discards the long-cherished equation of home with women, privacy, and unproductive labour and the workplace with men, public action, and productive labour first sketched in tracts by conservative nineteenth-century writers such as Catherine E. Beecher and Andrew Jackson Downing and accepted uncritically by so many modern historians.

Robert C. Twombly, 'Saving the Family: Middle-Class Attraction to Wright's Prairie House, 1901–1909', *American Quarterly*, 27 (1975) details Frank Lloyd Wright's loyalty to these ideals as an anti-urban gesture. Gwendolyn Wright, *Moralism and the Model Home: Domestic Architecture and Cultural Conflict in Chicago, 1873–1913* (Chicago, 1980), one of the best recent books on American architecture, analyses challenges and transformations to domesticity in Wright's city during the early years of his career. Dolores Hayden, *The Grand Domestic Revolution: A History of Feminist Designs for American Homes,*

Neighborhoods, and Cities (Cambridge, Mass., 1981) and Dianne Harris, 'Cultivating Power: The Language of Feminism in Women's Garden Literature, 1870–1920', *Landscape Journal*, 13 (1994) both detail contemporary resistance to the normative model. Hayden's *Redesigning the American Dream: The Future of Housing, Work, and Family Life* (New York, 1984) carries her story into the 1980s.

Elizabeth Collins Cromley, *Alone Together: A History of New York's Early Apartments* (Ithaca, NY, 1990) and Paul Groth, *Living Downtown: The History of Residential Hotels in the United States* (Berkeley and Los Angeles, 1994) correct another distortion of the traditional literature in demonstrating that Americans of all social classes have lived in multi-family housing since the early nineteenth century.

Chapter 2. Community

The Grand Federal Edifice and the Grand Federal Procession are discussed in Susan G. Davis, *Parades and Power: Street Theatre in Nineteenth-Century Philadelphia* (Philadelphia, 1986) while the recurrent image of the Edifice is treated in Robert L. Alexander, 'The Grand Federal Edifice', *Documentary Editing*, 9 (1987).

Authority

Ellen Weiss, *City in the Woods: The Life and Design of an American Camp Meeting on Martha's Vineyard* (Oxford, 1987); Dolores Hayden, *Seven American Utopias: The Architecture of Utopian Socialism, 1790–1975* (Cambridge, Mass., 1976); and Edward T. Price, 'The Central Courthouse Square in the American County Seat', in Upton and Vlach, eds., *Common Places*, collectively convey a sense of the traditional spaces of community and authority in the American landscape, and of the use of quasi-urban spatial models in all of them.

The political qualities of urban spaces in colonial America are evident in Dora P. Crouch, Daniel J. Garr, and Axel I. Mundingo, *Spanish City Planning in North America* (Cambridge, Mass., 1982) and in John Reps's many studies of American city plans, such as *The Making of Urban America: A History of City Planning in the United States* (Princeton, 1965). The best discussion of the evolution of New Orleans's plan is Samuel Wilson, Jr., *The Vieux Carré, New Orleans, Its Plan, Its Growth, Its Architecture* (New Orleans, 1968).

Indian Authority

William N. Morgan, *Prehistoric Architecture in the Eastern United States* (Cambridge, Mass., 1980), an architect's interpretive reconstructions of North American mound-builder sites, offers a good comparative starting-point for appreciating the number and variety of indigenous earthworks, but interested readers will also want to search out the still useful, visually delightful work by Cyrus Thomas, *Report on the Mound Explorations of the Bureau of Ethnology* (1894; repr. Washington, 1985).

The next step is to consult more detailed and more up-to-date (but also less analytical and harder-to-find) archaeological studies such as Jon L. Gibson, *Poverty Point: A Terminal Archaic Culture of the Lower Mississippi Valley* (2nd edn; Baton Rouge, La., 1996) and Robert S. Neitzel, *Archeology of the Fatherland Site: The Grand Village of the Natchez* (New York, 1965). A recent, and controversial, reinterpretation of one of the best-known Ohio Valley mounds is Robert V. Fletcher, Terry L. Cameron, Bradley T. Lepper, Dee Anne Wymer, and William Pickard, 'Serpent Mound: A Fort Ancient Icon?' *Midcontinental Journal of Archaeology*, 21 (1996).

The Iroquois longhouse has attracted comment and study since the seventeenth century. Mima Kapches, 'The Spatial Dynamics of Ontario Iroquoian Longhouses', *American Antiquity*, 55 (1990) reconstructs the early history of these distinctive buildings. On the Iroquois Confederacy and the evolution of the longhouse as metaphor and building type, see Daniel K. Richter, *The Ordeal of the Longhouse: The Peoples of the Iroquois League in the Era of European Colonization* (Chapel Hill, NC, 1992). The emergence of the Longhouse Religion is the subject of Anthony F. C. Wallace's classic *The Death and Rebirth of the Seneca* (New York, 1970); while contemporary Iroquois religious longhouses are discussed in Bruce G. Trigger, ed., *Handbook of North American Indians*, 15, *Northeast* (Washington, 1978).

Citizenship

Since Talbot F. Hamlin drew attention to its architectural importance in *Greek Revival Architecture in America* (Oxford, 1944), historians have looked to the United States Capitol as a laboratory and a source for the architectural imagery of civic life in the United States. Jeanne F. Butler, ed., 'Competition 1792: Designing a Nation's Capitol', *Capitol Studies*, 4 (1976) surveys the surviving entries to the original design competition. Hugh Honour, *Neo-Classicism* (Harmondsworth, 1968) is a brief, clear introduction to the symbolic premises that guided many of the competitors. For the later history of the Capitol, see Pamela Scott, *Temple of Liberty: Building the Capitol for the New Nation* (Oxford, 1995) and Vivian Green Fryd, 'Political Compromise in Public Art: Thomas Crawford's *Statue of Freedom*', in Harriet F. Senie and Sally Webster, eds., *Critical Issues in Public Art: Content, Context, and Controversy* (New York, 1992), which analyses the debate over the Crawford statue.

The plan of Washington, the symbolic landscape into which the Capitol was set, has been even more thoroughly documented than the Capitol building itself. National Capital Planning Commission and Frederick E. Gutheim, *Worthy of the Nation: The History of Planning for the National Capital* (Washington, 1977) and John W. Reps, *Monumental Washington: The Planning and Development of the Capital Center* (Princeton, 1967) are useful introductions, while Richard Longstreth, ed., *The Mall in Washington, 1791–1991* (Washington, 1991) treats the transformations of the ceremonial core over two centuries.

Since the time of the Capitol competition, the architectural representation of political values has been a constant topic of public debate. Lois Craig, *The Federal Presence: Architecture, Politics, and Symbols in United States Government Building* (Cambridge, Mass., 1978) catalogues significant federal efforts at political representation. Ron Robin's *Enclaves of America: The Rhetoric of American Political Architecture Abroad, 1900–1965* (Princeton, 1992) treats similar themes in embassies and military cemeteries. Outside the federal realm, Charles T. Goodsell, *The Social Meaning of Civic Space: Studying Political Authority through Architecture* (Lawrence, Kan., 1988) offers a political scientist's take on American political architecture. Howard Gillette, Jr., 'Philadelphia's City Hall: Monument to a New Political Machine', *Pennsylvania Magazine of History and Biography*, 97 (1973) is an exemplary study of the conflicts involved in creating one of the nation's most conspicuous civic buildings.

Ancestral Homelands
Ancestral homelands can best be understood as a kind of invented tradition, a term introduced in Eric Hobsbawm and Terence Ranger, eds., *The Invention of Tradition* (Cambridge, 1983) to refer both to long-standing cultural practices selected for increased emphasis and to those newly coined by national or ethnic groups to cultivate internal solidarity or to claim recognition and participation in diverse societies. Klara Bonsack Kelley and Harris Francis, *Navajo Sacred Places* (Bloomington, Ind., 1994) describe the ancestral homeland of the largest Native American nation, while Carol Herselle Krinsky, *Contemporary Native American Architecture: Cultural Regeneration and Creativity* (Oxford, 1996) treats imaginary ancestral homelands similar to those created by European-American and other immigrant groups.

The Colonial Revival, ongoing since the mid-nineteenth century, is the best-studied of the European-American ancestral homelands. William B. Rhoads, *The Colonial Revival* (New York, 1977) is the standard architectural history. Alan Axelrod, ed., *The Colonial Revival in America* (New York, 1985) juxtaposes architecture with other forms of material expression; the book contains an important theoretical introduction by Kenneth Ames. Karal Ann Marling, *George Washington Slept Here: Colonial Revivals and American Culture, 1876–1986* (Cambridge, Mass., 1988) and Robin Fleming, 'Picturesque History and the Medieval in Nineteenth-Century America', *American Historical Review*, 100 (1995) (on the Vikings) cast the net even wider, drawing the Colonial Revival into the realm of cultural history and connecting it to other forms of Anglo-American filiopietism, respectively.

The documentation and preservation of historic architecture has been indispensable to the Colonial Revival, and to the definition of ancestral homelands in general. Dell Upton, 'The Story of the Book', an introduction to Charles Morse Stotz's *Early Architecture of Western Pennsylvania* (1936; repr. Pittsburgh, 1995), one of many books of architectural documentation produced in the 1920s and 1930s, discusses the history of architectural fieldwork in the Colonial Revival. Margaret Henderson Floyd, 'Measured Drawings of the Hancock House by John Hubbard Sturgis: A Legacy to the Colonial Revival', in Abbott Lowell Cummings, ed., *Architecture in Colonial Massachusetts* (Charlottesville, Va., 1979) examines a pioneering recording project that inspired a generation of Colonial Revival architectural designs.

The history of historic preservation is

treated in two exhaustive but uncritical works by Charles B. Hosmer, Jr., *Presence of the Past: A History of the Preservation Movement in the United States Before Williamsburg* (New York, 1965) and *Preservation Comes of Age: from Williamsburg to the National Trust, 1926–1949* (Charlottesville, Va., 1981). The preservation movement's history and principles are treated more succinctly in William J. Murtagh, *Keeping Time: The History and Theory of Preservation in America* (New York, 1988). These works should be read in the context of Dolores Hayden, *The Power of Place: Urban Landscapes as Public History* (Cambridge, Mass., 1994) and Mike Wallace, *Mickey Mouse History and Other Essays on American Memory* (Philadelphia, 1996), important critiques of mainstream American preservation theory and practice that call for a more critical and inclusive approach to the past.

The practice of creating ancestral homelands through cultural synthesis and reinterpretation, epitomized by the Colonial Revival and historic preservation, is widespread among all ethnic groups in the United States. It is easiest to observe in African-American architecture and material culture because it has been the most closely studied of non-white American landscapes. John Michael Vlach, *The Afro-American Tradition in Decorative Arts* (Cleveland, 1978); Vlach, 'The Shotgun House: An African Architectural Legacy', in Upton and Vlach, eds., *Common Places*; and Jay D. Edwards, 'Cultural Syncretism in the Louisiana Creole Cottage', *Louisiana Folklore Miscellany*, 4 (1976–80) are key works. The Gulf Coast houses discussed by Vlach and Edwards share the same Afro-Caribbean sources as the contemporary *casitas* of the Puerto Ricans in New York; see Joseph Sciorra, 'Return to the Future: Puerto Rican Vernacular Architecture in New York City', in Anthony D. King, ed., *Re-Presenting the City: Ethnicity, Capital and Culture in the 21st-Century Metropolis* (New York, 1996).

Overseas Chinese traditions are less thoroughly documented, but Kay J. Anderson, *Vancouver's Chinatown: Racial Discourse in Canada, 1875–1980* (Montreal, 1991) and Christopher L. Yip, 'Association, Residence, and Shop: An Appropriation of Commercial Blocks in North American Chinatowns', in Elizabeth Collins Cromley and Carter L. Hudgins, eds., *Gender, Class, and Shelter: Perspectives in Vernacular Architecture, V* (Knoxville, Tenn., 1995) are helpful.

Cultural Authority

The exercise of cultural authority in colonial churches is treated in Upton, *Holy Things and Profane* and Robert J. Dinkin, 'Seating the Meetinghouse in Early Massachusetts', in St George, ed., *Material Life in America 1600–1860*.

Lawrence W. Levine's influential *Highbrow Lowbrow: The Emergence of Cultural Hierarchy in America* (Cambridge, Mass., 1988) examines the rise of cultural authority in the nineteenth century. Its architectural manifestations can be traced in studies of particular institutions such as Paul Turner, *Campus: An American Planning Tradition* (New York, 1984); Upton, 'Lancasterian Schools'; Kenneth Hafertepe, *America's Castle: The Evolution of the Smithsonian Building and Its Institution* (Washington, 1984); Morrison H. Hecksher, *The Metropolitan Museum of Art: An Architectural History* (New York, 1995); Abigail A. Van Slyck, *Free to All: Carnegie Libraries and American Culture, 1890–1920* (Chicago, 1996); Kenneth A. Breisch, *Henry Hobson Richardson and the Small Public Library: A Study in Typology* (Cambridge, Mass., 1997); and more broadly in Richard Guy Wilson, Dianne H. Pilgrim, and Richard N. Murray, *The American Renaissance 1876–1917* (New York, 1979). An indispensable dissection of the architecture of twentieth-century cultural authority is Alan Wallach and Carol Duncan, 'The Museum of Modern Art as Late Capitalist Ritual: An Iconographic Analysis', *Marxist Perspectives*, 1 (1978).

The few studies of North Easton, Mass., focus on Henry Hobson Richardson and Frederick Law Olmsted, virtually ignoring the Ames family's earlier development of the site. Robert F. Brown, 'The Aesthetic Transformation of an Industrial Community', *Winterthur Portfolio*, 12 (1977) offers a brief history of the town, while James F. O'Gorman, *H. H. Richardson: Architectural Forms for an American Society* (Chicago, 1987) considers the cultural and psychological implications of some of Richardson's works there.

Community

Community, representation, and inclusion are implicit issues underlying recent urban conflicts. Many of the most conspicuous have arisen over political and communal representations in monuments and works of public art. These conflicts extend to the beginnings of the republic and the design of the United States Capitol, which at one point was intended to contain a monument and mausoleum for George Washington. The century-long effort to create a suitable monument to Washington was the first of a series of difficult commemorative projects. Kirk Savage discusses the process in 'The Self-Made Monument: George Washington and the Fight to Erect a National Memorial', included in Senie and Webster, eds., *Critical Issues in Public Art*, an insightful collection of articles on public monuments ranging from the Washington Monument to the Vietnam Veterans' Memorial. Savage's *Standing Soldiers, Kneeling Slaves: Race, Art, and Monument in Nineteenth-Century America* (Princeton, 1997) is an important history of designers' attempts to come to terms with the representations of African-Americans in American public art. Erika Doss, *Spirit Poles and Flying Pigs: Public Art and Cultural Democracy in American Communities* (Washington, 1995) treats similar but more recent and more complex controversies in several American cities.

As Rosalyn Deutsche notes in her influential 'Uneven Development: Public Art in New York City', in Deutsche, *Evictions: Art and Spatial Politics* (Cambridge, Mass., 1996), public art projects (such as the Cincinnati Gateway discussed here) are often mounted in conjunction with redevelopment schemes and are consequently part of the larger issue of the power to control public space and public participation in the city. Margaret Crawford, 'Contesting the Public Realm: Struggles Over Public Space in Los Angeles', *Journal of Architectural Education*, 49 (1995) describes battles over the right to be in the streets and the ways landscape and architectural design are used as weapons in this bitter war. Crawford's essay touches on one aspect of the insidious privatization of public space in the contemporary city under the domination of revitalization and redevelopment. Others are treated in Michael Sorkin, ed., *Variations on a Theme Park: Scenes from the New American City and the End of Public Space* (New York, 1992) and William R. Taylor, ed., *Inventing Times Square: Commerce and Culture at the Crossroads of the World* (Baltimore, 1991). Neil Smith, *The New Urban Frontier: Gentrification and the Revanchist City* (London, 1996) examines the same issues as they impinge on the right to housing.

Communities

So far, the New Urbanism has been the subject of criticism and publicity, but not of history.

The most useful sources are tracts written by the movement's advocates, including Alex Krieger and William Lennertz, eds., *Andres Duany and Elizabeth Plater-Zyberk: Towns and Town-Making Principles* (New York, 1991); Peter Calthorpe, *The Next American Metropolis: Ecology, Community, and the American Dream* (Princeton, 1993); and Peter Katz's picture book, *The New Urbanism: Toward an Architecture of Community* (New York, 1994).

For the background to this latest round of urban-design theorizing, readers should consult Mel Scott, *American City Planning since 1890* (Berkeley and Los Angeles, 1969); William H. Wilson, *The City Beautiful Movement* (Baltimore, 1989); Robert Fishman, *Urban Utopias in the Twentieth Century: Ebenezer Howard, Frank Lloyd Wright, and Le Corbusier* (New York, 1977); M. Christine Boyer, *Dreaming the Rational City: The Myth of American City Planning* (Cambridge, Mass., 1983); and Kenneth Jackson, *Crabgrass Frontier: The Suburbanization of the United States* (Oxford, 1984), a historian's study.

Chapter 3. Nature

Conceptions of nature have been as diverse as the cultures who have inhabited the United States. Indigenous ideas and ecological practices are discussed in R. Douglas Hurt, *Indian Agriculture in America: Prehistory to the Present* (Lawrence, Kan., 1987); Robert F. Heizer and Albert B. Elsasser, *The Natural World of the California Indians* (Berkeley and Los Angeles, 1980); George F. MacDonald, *Haida Monumental Art: Villages of the Queen Charlotte Islands* (Vancouver, 1983); and in the *Handbook of North American Indians* series.

Euro-American notions can be traced in Clarence J. Glacken, *Traces on the Rhodian Shore: Nature and Culture in Western Thought from Ancient Times to the End of the Eighteenth Century* (Berkeley and Los Angeles, 1967) and Carolyn Merchant, *The Death of Nature: Women, Ecology, and the Scientific Revolution* (New York, 1980). These normative overviews should be supplemented by two comparative studies, William Cronon's paradigm-defining *Changes in the Land: Indians, Colonists, and the Ecology of New England* (New York, 1983) and Timothy Silver, *A New Face on the Countryside: Indians, Colonists, and Slaves in South Atlantic Forests, 1500–1800* (Cambridge, 1990). An older work, Roderick Nash, *Wilderness and the American Mind* (3rd edn; New Haven and London, 1982) carries the story to the late nineteenth century, while William Cronon, ed., *Uncommon Ground: Toward Reinventing Nature* (New York, 1995) is concerned primarily with recent decades.

On vernacular attitudes toward nature and the environment, see John R. Stilgoe, *Common Landscape of America, 1580 to 1845* (New Haven and London, 1982) and works on particular regions and ethnic groups, such as Richard Davisson, Jr., 'The Dragon and San Francisco', *Landscape*, 17 (1967–8); John Lehr, *Ukrainian Vernacular Architecture in Alberta* (Edmonton, 1976); and Marta Weigle and Peter White, *The Lore of New Mexico* (Albuquerque, NM, 1988).

Neo-classicism and Romanticism

Peter Collins's old but still useful *Changing Ideals in Modern Architecture, 1750–1950* (London, 1965) is the best introduction to neo-classicism and romanticism in Euro-American architecture. Associationism and the picturesque are explained most succinctly in George Hersey, *High Victorian Gothic: A Study in Associationism* (Baltimore, 1972).

R. W. B. Lewis, *The American Adam: Innocence, Tragedy, and Tradition in the Nineteenth Century* (Chicago, 1955) and Henry Nash Smith, *Virgin Land: The American Land in Myth and Symbol* (Cambridge, Mass., 1950) are classic studies of romantic ideas toward the landscape. They exemplify the 'myth and symbol' group of American studies, which sought to delineate a unitary American cultural temperament. In fact, these studies explored a small but conspicuous segment of nineteenth-century American literature that they wrongly assumed characterized the attitudes of all Americans. As it happens, though, the writers that Lewis and Nash treat deeply influenced some prominent nineteenth-century architects, notably Louis Sullivan and Frank Lloyd Wright: see Sherman Paul, *Louis Sullivan: An Architect in American Thought* (Englewood Cliffs, NJ, 1962); Narciso Menocal, *Architecture as Nature: The Transcendentalist Idea of Louis Sullivan* (Madison, 1981); and Carol R. Bolon, Robert S. Nelson, and Linda Seidel, eds., *The Nature of Frank Lloyd Wright* (Chicago, 1988).

Country Life

The history of the picturesque landscape tradition in the United States from its appearance in rural cemeteries through the creation of landscaped parks to its acceptance by middle-class householders is a favourite theme of architectural historians. Good starting-points include David C. Sloane, *The Last Great Necessity: Cemeteries in American History* (Baltimore, 1991); David Schuyler, *The New Urban Landscape: The Redefinition of City Form in Nineteenth-Century America* (Baltimore, 1986); and Handlin, *The American Home.* Virginia Scott Jenkins, *The Lawn: A History of an American Obsession* (Washington, 1994) carries the story into the twentieth century for ordinary houses. On twentieth-century landscape design, see Phoebe Cutler, *The Public Landscape of the New Deal* (New Haven and London, 1985); Peter Walker and Melanie Simo, *Invisible Gardens: The Search for Modernism in the American Landscape* (Cambridge, Mass., 1994), and Marc Treib, ed., *Modern Landscape Architecture: A Critical Review* (Cambridge, Mass., 1993).

Naturally, the story of the fantasy of country life is not as seamless as the standard account has it. Over time, notions of appropriate public recreation spaces have been challenged as tenaciously as they have been articulated. Daniel M. Bluestone, 'From Promenade to Park: The Gregarious Origins of Brooklyn's Park Movement', *American Quarterly*, 39 (1987) treats the clash of social classes in the informal recreational spaces of early-nineteenth-century Brooklyn. The contentious evolution of formal parks is the subject of Galen Cranz, *The Politics of Park Design: A History of Urban Parks in America* (Cambridge, Mass., 1982). Roy Rosenzweig and Elizabeth Blackmar, *The Park and the People: A History of Central Park* (Ithaca, NY, 1992) offer a major account of the continuous conflicts that have enveloped Central Park, New York, since it was first planned. Similarly, F. Herbert Bormann, Diana Balmori, and Gordon T. Geballe, *Redesigning the American Lawn: A Search for Environmental History* (New Haven and London, 1993) consider the problematic ecological legacy of the private landscape in the late twentieth century.

Place

The relationship of architecture to place is a continuing, if vaguely expressed, theme in American architecture. It has even spawned a journal, *Places.* California has been an especially popular testing-ground for ideas of place. Insiders and outsiders, writers and artists as well as architects have sought to identify some peculiar qualities of the state's landscape, climate, and ways of life that might distinguish its artistic production. Kevin Starr's perceptive history *Americans and the California Dream, 1850–1915* (Oxford, 1973) provides the cultural context. Sally

Woodbridge, ed., *Bay Area Houses* (rev. edn., Salt Lake City, 1988) illustrates the seductiveness of the idea of California as a distinctive place to architects and historians alike. Abigail A. Van Slyck, 'Mañana, Mañana: Racial Stereotypes and the Anglo Rediscovery of the Southwest's Vernacular Architecture, 1890–1920', in Cromley and Hudgins, eds., *Gender, Class, and Shelter*, uncovers the seamier side of regionalism, with particular attention to Charles Fletcher Lummis. Kenneth Frampton, 'Towards a Critical Regionalism: Six Points for an Architecture of Resistance', in Hal Foster, ed., *The Anti-Aesthetic: Essays on Postmodern Culture* (Port Townsend, Wash., 1983) has been influential in arguing for a regionalism that avoids the kinds of literalistic imagery and sentimental historic quotation that has characterized the celebration of place in much of American architecture, including California.

The Primitive
Marianna Torgovnick's *Primitive Passions: Men, Women, and the Quest for Ecstasy* (New York, 1996) explores some of the cultural roots of primitivism. Collins, *Changing Ideals in Modern Architecture* offers a succinct introduction to primitivism in high architectural theory. Primitivist interpretations of vernacular architecture derive from this theory and from late nineteenth-century anthropology; see Dell Upton, 'Outside the Academy: A Century of Vernacular Architecture Studies in America, 1890–1990', in Elisabeth Blair MacDougall, ed., *The Architectural Historian in America* (Washington, 1991). They also owe much to the literature of so-called 'folk art', explored in John Michael Vlach, *Plain Painters: Making Sense of American Folk Art* (Washington, 1988) and Michael D. Hall and Eugene W. Metcalf, eds., *The Artist Outsider: Creativity and the Boundaries of Culture* (Washington, 1994).

Perhaps no aspect of American architecture has been written about so badly for so long as log building. On the tenacious myth of log construction as a 'pioneer' technology, see Harold R. Shurtleff, *The Log Cabin Myth: A Study of the Early Dwellings of the English Colonies in North America* (Cambridge, Mass., 1939). Warren E. Roberts, 'The Tools Used in Building Log Houses in Indiana', in Upton and Vlach, eds., *Common Places*, conveys a sense of the technological sophistication of log construction. Fred B. Kniffen and Henry Glassie, 'Building in Wood in the Eastern United States: A Time-Place Perspective', in *Common Places*, offer the dominant reading of the Central European origins of log building in North America, while Terry G. Jordan, *American Log Buildings: An Old World Heritage* (Chapel Hill, NC, 1985) attempts to revive an older theory that American log construction derives from Scandinavia.

The Simple Life
The idea of the simple life has been a persistent one in American thought, as David E. Shi reveals in *The Simple Life: Plain Living and High Thinking in American Culture* (Oxford, 1985). Americans in the early national period touted 'republican simplicity'—a general sameness of lifestyle—as a recipe for political stability, an idea whose architectural implications Gwendolyn Wright touches on in *Building the Dream*. Contemporary ideals of simplicity in design and lifeways derive more directly from the aestheticized asceticism of the English Arts and Crafts movement. Eileen Boris, *Art and Labor: Ruskin, Morris, and the Craftsman Ideal in America* (Philadelphia, 1986) explores the movement's American fortunes.

The bungalow's history was implicated with, but not determined by, that of the Arts and Crafts movement. Anthony D. King's essential *The Bungalow: The Production of a Global Culture* (London, 1984) establishes the international cultural patterns that created this ubiquitous early-twentieth-century house type. Clay Lancaster, *The American Bungalow, 1880–1930* (New York, 1985) is a more popularly oriented treatment of the bungalow's American history. Alan Gowans, *The Comfortable House: North American Suburban Architecture, 1890–1930* (Cambridge, Mass., 1986) sets it among a variety of popular house forms of the turn of the century.

The aestheticized rusticity of the bungalow should also be contrasted with the domestic lives of rural Americans in the first half of the twentieth century. James N. Gregory, *American Exodus: The Dust Bowl Migration and Okie Culture in California* (Oxford, 1989) and Greg Hise, 'From Roadside Camps to Garden Homes: Housing and Community Planning for California's Migrant Work Force, 1935–1941', in Cromley and Hudgins, eds., *Gender, Class, and Shelter* offer a necessary context for understanding the bungalow.

Act Naturally
Contemporary ecological concerns have affected architecture and its history in two

ways: through the new field of 'environmental history', which examines the interaction of people and their surroundings, and through the movement for 'green' architectural design. Donald Worster, *The Wealth of Nature: Environmental History and the Ecological Imagination* (Oxford, 1993) is a helpful starting-point, enriched by 'A Round Table: Environmental History', a special section of the *Journal of American History*, 76 (1990). Christine Meisner Rosen and Joel Arthur Tarr, eds., 'The Environment and the City', a special issue of the *Journal of Urban History*, 20 (1994), add physical and public-policy dimensions to the story. The environmental history of individual buildings is much less advanced, but Handlin, *American Home*, touches on the subject.

On the pioneers of energy-efficient design in the 1930s and 1940s, readers must turn to the monographs by Robert Boyce, *Keck and Keck* (Princeton, 1993) and Doris Cole, *Eleanor Raymond, Architect* (Philadelphia, 1981).

There are many manifestos on sustainability, but no histories. Among the former, David W. Orr, *Ecological Literacy: Education and the Transition to a Post-Modern World* (Albany, NY, 1992) is representative and eloquent. Martin W. Lewis, *Green Delusions: An Environmental Critique of Radical Environmentalism* (Durham, NC, 1992) is a sharp, perceptive critique of the ideas to which Orr and others subscribe.

Sam Davis, *Designing for Energy Efficiency: A Study of Eight California State Office Buildings* (Berkeley, 1981) reports on the late 1970s programme of California's Office of the State Architect that created the Bateson Building, as well as the other seven experimental structures. Hayden, *Redesigning the American Dream* describes several attempts to build sustainable houses during the same years. More recent ecological design is discussed in Michael J. Crosbie, *Green Architecture: A Guide to Sustainable Design* (Rockport, Mass., 1994), a picture-book.

Chapter 4. Technology
David E. Nye, *American Technological Sublime* (Cambridge, Mass., 1994) reveals the origins of the word *technology*. I have benefited greatly from Nye's arguments in shaping the first portions of this chapter. Sigfried Giedion, *Mechanization Takes Command: A Contribution to Anonymous History* (New York, 1948) is a brilliant, ground-breaking statement of the principle that technological development follows social demand. For the

industrial context of American architectural technology, see Brooke Hindle and Steven Lubar, *Engines of Change: The American Industrial Revolution 1790–1860* (Washington, 1986) and Robert B. Gordon and Patrick M. Malone, *The Texture of Industry: An Archaeological View of the Industrialization of North America* (Oxford, 1994).

Work
Carl W. Condit, *American Building Art: Materials and Techniques from the Beginning of the Colonial Settlements to the Present* (2nd edn; Chicago, 1982), a condensed version of his encyclopaedic *American Building Art* (2 vols.; Oxford, 1960–1), is an old, whiggish survey that remains the most convenient source for much of the technological history of high-end American architecture. Smaller-scale, and particularly vernacular, building technologies have no similar survey, although Charles E. Peterson, ed., *Building Early America: Contributions toward the History of a Great Industry* (Radnor, Penn., 1976) and H. Ward Jandl, ed., *The Technology of Historic American Buildings: Studies of the Materials, Craft Processes, and the Mechanization of Building Construction* (Washington, 1983) fill in some of the blanks.

For Anglo-American vernacular timber-framing, start with Dell Upton, 'Traditional Timber Framing', in Brooke Hindle, ed., *Material Culture of the Wooden Age* (Tarrytown, NY, 1981). Add Cary Carson, Norman F. Barka, William M. Kelso, Garry Wheeler Stone, and Dell Upton, 'Impermanent Architecture in the Southern American Colonies', *Winterthur Portfolio*, 16 (1981), a major rethinking of building construction in the early South; Cummings, *Framed Houses of Massachusetts Bay*, the best and most recent of many studies of classic New England timber building; and John F. Fitchen, *The New World Dutch Barn: A Study of Its Characteristics, Its Structural System, and Its Probable Erectional Procedures* (Syracuse, NY, 1968) for Netherlandish construction. Native American building technology has been almost entirely neglected, but in addition to the Nabokov and Easton survey, see Robert H. Lowie, *Indians of the Plains* (New York, 1954).

The industrial transformation of work, is discussed in the title essay in Herbert G. Gutman, *Work, Culture and Society in Industrializing America: Essays in American Working-Class and Social History* (New York, 1976), Daniel T. Rodgers, *The Work Ethic in Industrial Society, 1850–1920* (Chicago, 1974);

and Ruth Schwartz Cowan, *A Social History of American Technology* (Oxford, 1997). Catherine W. Bishir, Charlotte V. Brown, Carl R. Lounsbury, and Ernest H. Wood III, *Architects and Builders in North Carolina: A History of the Practice of Building* (Chapel Hill, NC, 1990) is a wide-ranging study with importance to all of American architectural history.

The most recent works on the balloon frame are Paul. E. Sprague, 'Chicago Balloon Frame: The Evolution During the 19th Century of George W. Snow's System for Erecting Light Frame Buildings from Dimension Lumber and Machine-Made Nails', in Jandl, ed., *The Technology of Historic American Buildings* and Upton, 'Traditional Timber Framing', which presents a different point of view from Sprague's.

Gilbert Herbert, *Pioneers of Prefabrication: The British Contribution in the Nineteenth Century* (Baltimore, 1978) discusses some early schemes to supply prefabricated buildings to the United States. There is no specifically American history, except for the fragments Charles E. Peterson assembled in many instalments of his 'American Notes' column, scattered through the *Journal of the Society of Architectural Historians* in the 1950s and 1960s. Donald Albrecht, ed., *World War II and the American Dream: How Wartime Building Changed a Nation* (Cambridge, Mass., 1994) discusses the drive to industrialize domestic construction in the 1940s and the invention of the Quonset hut.

Ventilation

On ventilation in American houses, see Handlin, *American Home* and Elizabeth Collins Cromley, 'A History of American Beds and Bedrooms', in Thomas Carter and Bernard L. Herman, eds., *Perspectives in Vernacular Architecture, IV* (Columbia, Mo., 1991). John D. Thompson and Grace Goldin, *The Hospital: A Social and Architectural History* (New Haven and London, 1975) is a detailed study that is useful for understanding the history of ventilation in many types of institutional buildings.

Gender, Sex, and Filth

Reyner Banham, *The Architecture of the Well-Tempered Environment* (Chicago, 1969) is the standard and nearly the only history of HVAC (heating, ventilating, and air-conditioning) technology in the United States. It has been supplemented, but not replaced, by Cecil D. Elliott, *Technics and Architecture: The Development of Materials and Systems for Buildings* (Cambridge, Mass., 1992). To understand the Larkin Building's technology, readers should also consult Banham's addendum, 'The Services of the Larkin "A" Building', *Journal of the Society of Architectural Historians*, 37 (1978) and Jack Quinan's monograph *Frank Lloyd Wright's Larkin Building: Myth and Fact* (New York, 1987). The American obsession with dirt is the subject of Suellen Hoy, *Chasing Dirt: The American Pursuit of Cleanliness* (Oxford, 1995), while Gwendolyn Wright has analysed the idea of the homelike world in *Moralism and the Model Home*.

On the domestic front, Maureen Ogle, *All the Modern Conveniences: American Household Plumbing, 1840–1890* (Baltimore, 1996) is a rare extended analysis of household hygienic technology. Ellen Lupton and J. Abbott Miller, *The Bathroom, The Kitchen, and the Aesthetics of Waste* (Cambridge, Mass., 1992) and Elizabeth Collins Cromley, 'Transforming the Food Axis: Houses, Tools, Modes of Analysis', *Material History Review*, 44 (1996) discuss the connections between the laboratory and the kitchen.

The Technological Sublime

For bridges, see Nye, *American Technological Sublime*, and David P. Billington, *The Tower and the Bridge: The New Art of Structural Engineering* (Princeton, 1983), the sources of many of the ideas and data that I have used in this section. The theoretical bases of large engineering structures are discussed in T. M. Charlton, *A History of Theory of Structures in the Nineteenth Century* (Cambridge, 1982), while Raymond H. Merritt, *Engineering in American Society, 1850–1875* (Lexington, Ky., 1969) examines the history of the profession. In contrast to these traditional histories, many of the essays in Margaret Latimer, Brooke Hindle, and Melvin Kranzberg, eds., *Bridge to the Future: A Centennial Celebration of the Brooklyn Bridge* (New York, 1984); along with Eugene S. Ferguson, *Engineering and the Mind's Eye* (Cambridge, Mass., 1992) treat engineering design as an aesthetic more than a scientific process.

Leo Marx, *The Machine in the Garden: Technology and the Pastoral Ideal in America* (Oxford, 1964); John F. Kasson, *Civilizing the Machine: Technology and Republican Values in America, 1776–1900* (New York, 1976); and Alan Trachtenberg, *Brooklyn Bridge: Fact and Symbol* (2nd edn; Chicago, 1979) are classic studies of the cultural impact of hubristic technology in America.

Producers and Consumers

The aesthetic appreciation of technology is an enduring theme in twentieth-century American culture, as Cecilia Tichi describes in *Shifting Gears: Technology, Literature, Culture in Modernist America* (Chapel Hill, NC, 1987). Richard Guy Wilson, Dianne H. Pilgrim, and Dickran Tashjian, *The Machine Age in America, 1918–1941* (New York, 1986) is a catalogue of essays that focus on one period of intense interest in machine-inspired design, which was celebrated architecturally in Henry-Russell Hitchcock and Philip Johnson, *The International Style: Architecture Since 1922* (New York, 1932). Esther McCoy, *Case Study Houses, 1945–1962* (2nd edn; Los Angeles, 1977) carries the story into postwar California.

Consuming Architecture

Historians rediscovered industrial design in the 1970s. Jeffrey L. Meikle, *Twentieth-Century Limited: Industrial Design in America, 1935–1939* (Philadelphia, 1979) is the best introduction to the origins and goals of the profession. Arthur J. Pulos, *American Design Ethic: A History of Industrial Design to 1940* (Cambridge, Mass., 1983) and his *The American Design Adventure, 1940–1975* (Cambridge, Mass., 1988) are more detailed chronicles. The advertising roots of industrial design are evident in Roland Marchand, *Advertising the American Dream: Making Way for Modernity, 1920–1940* (Berkeley and Los Angeles, 1985) and T. J. Jackson Lears, *Fables of Abundance: A Cultural History of Advertising in America* (New York, 1994).

On technological futurism, consult Joseph J. Corn and Brian Horrigan, *Yesterday's Tomorrows: Past Visions of the American Future* (New York, 1984), an exhibition catalogue, and the proceedings of an associated symposium, Joseph J. Corn, ed., *Imagining Tomorrow: History, Technology, and the American Future* (Cambridge, Mass., 1986). William J. Mitchell, *City of Bits: Space, Place, and the Infobahn* (Cambridge, Mass., 1995) demonstrates that while the technology changes, the promises and metaphors that cluster around it do not.

The literature of twentieth-century world's fairs is copious but selective (there has been little written about Chicago's Century of Progress, for example) and it tends to be more popular and celebratory than analytical.

Robert W. Rydell has become the leading scholar of American world's fairs. His *World of Fairs: The Century-of-Progress Exhibitions* (Chicago, 1993) probes the social roots of the 1930s expositions, while Helen A. Harrison, ed., *Dawn of a New Day: The New York World's Fair, 1939/40* (New York, 1980) is one of the more insightful studies of an individual Depression-era technofair.

Chapter 5. Money

The Political Economy of Architecture

Kendrick Frazier, *People of Chaco: A Canyon and Its Culture* (New York, 1986) is a good popular introduction to Chaco Canyon. The recent work on the political economy of the Anasazi community there can be followed in Linda S. Cordell, *Prehistory of the Southwest* (Orlando, Fla., 1984); Stephen H. Lekson, Thomas C. Windes, John R. Stein, and W. James Judge, 'The Chaco Canyon Community', *Scientific American*, 259 (July 1988); and Patricia A. Crown and W. James Judge, eds., *Chaco and Hohokam: Prehistoric Regional Systems in the American Southwest* (Santa Fe and Seattle, 1991).

Proximity

For the early history of Philadelphia, see two significant, often overlooked, articles: Gary B. Nash, 'City Planning and Political Tensions in the Seventeenth Century: The Case of Philadelphia', *Proceedings of the American Philosophical Society*, 112 (1968) and Hannah Benner Roach, 'The Planting of Philadelphia: A Seventeenth-Century Real Estate Development', *Pennsylvania Magazine of History and Biography*, 92 (1968). Greg Hise, *Magnetic Los Angeles: Planning the Postwar Metropolis* (Baltimore, 1997) brilliantly analyses the development of Los Angeles after 1945.

System and Flow

Joyce O. Appleby, *Economic Thought and Ideology in Seventeenth-Century England* (Princeton, 1978) describes the growth of popular ideas of the systematic nature of economic life. She follows its eighteenth-century dissemination to North America in her essays collected in *Liberalism and Republicanism in the Historical Imagination* (Cambridge, Mass., 1992). The application of these ideas to the city is discussed in Dell Upton, 'Another City: The Urban Cultural Landscape in the Early Republic', in Catherine E. Hutchins, ed., *Everyday Life in the Early Republic* (Winterthur, Del., 1994).

For the grid, also see Peter Marcuse, 'The Grid as City Plan: New York City and Laissez-Faire Planning in the Nineteenth Century', *Planning Perspectives*, 2 (1987) and Paul Groth, 'Streetgrids as Frameworks for Urban Variety', *Harvard Architectural Review*, 2 (1981).

Sam Bass Warner, Jr.'s classic *Streetcar Suburbs: The Process of Growth in Boston, 1870–1900* (Cambridge, Mass., 1962) demonstrates the ways that systems of transportation reorganized the proximate city. It is nicely complemented by William Cronon, *Nature's Metropolis: Chicago and the Great West* (New York, 1991), a model study of the systematic connections between a major city and its hinterland. In contrast to systems such as these that emerged from the actions of many politicians, builders, merchants, and ordinary citizens one might set planners' efforts to create artificially ordered cities, detailed in Boyer, *Dreaming the Rational City*. Too often, planners' efforts attempt to suppress messy or unpleasant, but necessary elements of the city, such as those sketched in J. B. Jackson's 1957 essay 'The Stranger's Path', reprinted in Ervin H. Zube, ed., *Landscapes: Selected Writings of J. B. Jackson* (Amherst, Mass., 1970).

The Social Life of Work

To understand office buildings, one must understand corporate organization, as well as the quotidian routines and material demands of office work. The standard work on corporate structure is Alfred D. Chandler, Jr., *The Visible Hand: The Managerial Revolution in American Business* (Cambridge, Mass., 1977). On office work, see Elyce J. Rotella, 'The Transformation of the American Office: Changes in Employment and Technology', *Journal of Economic History*, 41 (1981), an early essay that has been considerably extended by Angel Kwolek-Folland, *Engendering Business: Men and Women in the Corporate Office, 1870–1930* (Baltimore, 1994). Kwolek-Folland discusses the architecture and material culture of work, but these are treated in more detail in Adrian Forty, *Objects of Desire: Design and Society 1750–1980* (London, 1986) and JoAnne Yates, *Control Through Communication: The Rise of System in American Management* (Baltimore, 1989).

The Public Life of Business

Architectural critics and historians have been obsessed with the relationship between structural technology and the appearance of the tall office building almost since the type became an object of public scrutiny in the late nineteenth century. Carl W. Condit, *The Chicago School of Architecture: A History of Commercial and Public Building in the Chicago Area, 1875–1925* (Chicago, 1964) is a classic study in this traditional mode, and is now complemented by Sarah Bradford Landau and Carl Condit, *Rise of the New York Skyscraper, 1865–1913* (New Haven and London, 1996). Cervin Robinson and Rosemarie Haag Bletter, *Skyscraper Style: Art Deco New York* (Oxford, 1975) and Ada Louise Huxtable, *The Tall Office Building Reconsidered: The Search for a Skyscraper Style* (New York, 1984) carry the aesthetic appreciation of skyscrapers into the 1930s and the 1980s respectively.

However, Daniel M. Bluestone, *Constructing Chicago* (New Haven and London, 1991), has pointedly delineated the discrepancy between those aspects of the office building that contemporaries thought were important and those that architectural historians care about. The appearance of the skyscraper, for example, has as much to do with corporate visibility and distinction in the landscape as it does with the abstractions of architectural art. Carol Willis's *Form Follows Finance: Skyscrapers and Skylines in New York and Chicago* (Princeton, 1995) goes even farther. In this highly original work, Willis reduces exterior appearance to a minor element of tall-office-building design, one that lagged behind such paramount concerns as office-work patterns, real-estate calculations, and zoning regulations in shaping skyscrapers.

Business corporations use architectural design to assert their public presence in many other settings, most notably in retail outlets of all sorts. These other manifestations of corporate aesthetics are explored in Barbara Rubin, 'Aesthetic Ideology and Urban Design', in Upton and Vlach, eds., *Common Places*; Daniel M. Bluestone, 'Roadside Blight and the Reform of Commercial Architecture', in Jan Jennings, ed., *Roadside America: The Automobile in Design and Culture* (Ames, Ia., 1990); Daniel I. Vieyra, *Fill 'er Up: An Architectural History of America's Gas Stations* (New York, 1979); and Chester H. Liebs, *Main Street to Miracle Mile: American Roadside Architecture* (Boston, 1985).

The Moral Authority of Capitalism

In contrast to twentieth-century world's fairs, nineteenth-century fairs, particularly the World's Columbian Exposition, have been the objects of intense scholarly scrutiny and popular celebration. Robert W. Rydell, *All the World's a Fair: Visions of Empire at American International Expositions, 1876–1916* (Chicago, 1984) focuses most closely on the moral relationship between fairs and the capitalist order. Among the most useful works on the 1893 fair are R. Reid Badger, *The Great American Fair: The World's Columbian Exposition and American Culture* (Chicago, 1979); Rydell, 'The World's Columbian Exposition of 1893: The Racist Underpinnings of a Utopian Artifact', *Journal of American Culture*, 1 (1978); and James Gilbert, *Perfect Cities: Chicago's Utopias of 1893* (Chicago, 1991), which places the World's Columbian Exposition in the context of Chicago's commercial downtown and its model worker suburb at Pullman.

The Spatial Economy of Consumption
Architectural historians are just beginning to acknowledge the landscapes of retail consumption. For the nineteenth century, Meredith L. Clausen's brief 'The Department Store—Development of the Type', *Journal of Architectural Education*, 39 (1985) can be augmented with Susan Porter Benson, *Counter Cultures: Saleswomen, Managers, and Customers in American Department Stores 1890–1940* (Champaign, Ill., 1986), a social history. For the business and retailing imperatives that helped to shape one famous department store building, see Joseph Siry, *Carson Pirie Scott: Louis Sullivan and the Chicago Department Store* (Chicago, 1988).

William S. Worley, *J. C. Nichols and the Shaping of Kansas City: Innovation in Planned Residential Communities* (Columbia, Mo., 1990) and Richard W. Longstreth's important *City Center to Regional Mall: Architecture, the Automobile, and Retailing in Los Angeles, 1920–1950* (Cambridge, Mass., 1997), are essential for understanding twentieth-century retailing. Meredith L. Clausen, 'Northgate Regional Shopping Center—Paradigm from the Provinces', *Journal of the Society of Architectural Historians*, 43 (1984); Howard Gillette, Jr, 'The Evolution of the Planned Shopping Center in City and Suburb', *Journal of the American Planning Association*, 51 (1985); and the 'AHR Forum' on postwar shopping centres, *American Historical Review*, 101 (1996) outline the history of postwar shopping centres and malls. It should be noted that most histories of the postwar period rely heavily on an important primary source that is worth consulting directly: Geoffrey Baker and Bruno Funaro, *Shopping Centers: Design and Operation* (New York, 1951). On the culture of the contemporary shopping mall and the retailing imperatives that shape it, see Margaret Crawford, 'The World in a Shopping Mall', in Sorkin, ed., *Variations on a Theme Park*.

Consuming Architecture
Since the early nineteenth century American architects, planners, and cultural critics have pondered the problem of supplying cheap well-made houses of 'good' design to ordinary Americans. Among the first to do anything about the issue were industrial corporations, who were impelled by the desire for a stable, docile work force, and who believed that good housing would attract and hold such employees (as well as binding them economically to the company in ways that would make it difficult to leave or to strike). The classic example is Pullman, Illinois; see Stanley Buder, *Pullman: An Experiment in Industrial Order and Community Planning, 1880–1930* (Oxford, 1967). John S. Garner, *The Model Company Town* (Amherst, Mass., 1984) and Margaret Crawford, *Building the Workingman's Paradise: The Design of American Company Towns* (London and New York, 1995) explore company housing more broadly.

Beginning with the campaign to build war-worker housing during World War I, public agencies took up the quest. Richard M. Candee, *Atlantic Heights: A World War I Shipbuilders' Community* (Portsmouth, NH, 1985) describes one such war-housing project. Richard Pommer, 'The Architecture of Urban Housing in the United States during the Early 1930s', *Journal of the Society of Architectural Historians*, 37 (1978); Hise, 'From Roadside Camps to Garden Homes'; and Gail Radford, *Modern Housing for America: Policy Struggles in the New Deal* (Chicago, 1996) continue the story into the Depression years.

During World War II, government housers and speculative builders collaborated, as Albrecht, ed., *World War II and the American Dream* and some of the essays in Marc Treib, ed., *An Everyday Modernism: The Houses of William Wurster* (Berkeley and Los Angeles, 1995) show. The classic speculative suburbs produced by this collaboration are treated in Ned Eichler, *The Merchant Builders* (Cambridge, Mass., 1982) and Barbara M. Kelly, *Expanding the American Dream: Building and Rebuilding Levittown* (New York, 1993).

At the same time, it is important to acknowledge that, visible as public and philanthropic housing has been, for-profit builders have always provided most of the shelter for middle- and working-class Americans. Wright, *Moralism and the Model Home* discusses the struggle between architects and developers for control of this market in turn-of-the-century Chicago. Her work is complemented nicely by the more economically directed analysis of Marc A. Weiss, *The Rise of the Community Builders: The American Real Estate Industry and Urban Land Planning* (New York, 1987).

The ordinary Americans who occupied these 'market' houses had their own domestic standards and desires that were not always consonant with those of reformers or developers. A sense of these alternative viewpoints can be found in Groth, *Living Downtown*; James Borchert, *Alley Life in Washington: Family, Community, Religion, and Folklife in the City, 1850–1970* (Champaign, Ill., 1980); Guy A. Szuberla, '*Dom, Namai, Heim*: Images of the New Immigrant's Home', *Prospects: An Annual of American Cultural Studies*, 10 (1985); Lizabeth Cohen, 'Embellishing a Life of Labor: Interpretation of the Material Culture of American Working-Class Homes, 1885–1915', in Upton and Vlach, eds., *Common Places*; Cohen, *Making a New Deal: Industrial Workers in Chicago, 1919–1939* (Cambridge, 1990); and a fascinating and revealing early twentieth-century sociological study, Margaret Byington, *Homestead: The Households of a Mill Town* (Pittsburgh, 1910).

Housing Non-Consumers
The difficult history of housing for the poorest Americans is directly connected with the political nation's ambivalent moral attitudes towards them, eloquently chronicled in Michael B. Katz, *In the Shadow of the Poorhouse: A Social History of Welfare in America* (2nd edn.; New York, 1996), and its more generalized fears of social chaos, treated in Paul Boyer, *Urban Masses and Moral Order in America, 1820–1920* (Cambridge, Mass., 1978) and Carl Smith, *Urban Disorder and the Shape of Belief: The Great Chicago Fire, the Haymarket Bomb, and the Model Town of Pullman* (Chicago, 1995).

Studies of the history of public housing are fewer than critiques of its putative failures. Among the former, Devereux Bowly, Jr., *The Poorhouse: Subsidized Housing in Chicago 1895–1976* (Carbondale, Ill., 1978) and John F. Bauman, *Public Housing, Race, and Renewal: Urban Planning in Philadelphia, 1920–1974* (Philadelphia, 1987), which discusses the

programmes that led to the construction of Guild House, stand out. Among the latter, Eugene J. Meehan, *The Quality of Federal Policymaking: Programmed Failure in Public Housing* (Columbia, Mo., 1979) is a detailed critique focusing on St Louis. Katharine G. Bristol, 'The Pruitt–Igoe Myth', *Journal of Architectural Education*, 44 (1991), which lays that notorious project's shortcomings at the door of planners, legislators, and downtown businessmen rather than architects, is an important corrective to the view that Pruitt–Igoe represented the 'failure of modernism'. Marta Gutman, 'Housers and Other Architects: Pragmatism and Aesthetics in Recent Competitions', *Journal of Architectural Education*, 46 (1993) treats the impediments that continue to confront those who would design for the poor.

Chapter 6. Art
Architects and Builders
The best study of the structure of the architectural and building trades and their evolving relationship over the past three hundred years is Bishir, Brown, Lounsbury, and Wood, *Architects and Builders in North Carolina*. Roger W. Moss, Jr, summarizes his dissertation on the Carpenters' Company in 'The Origins of the Carpenters' Company of Philadelphia', in Peterson, ed., *Building Early America*. Ian M. G. Quimby, ed., *The Craftsman in Early America* (New York, 1984) sets builders in the broader context of early American artisanry.

Why Architects?
The history and structure of the architectural profession is much more complex than it has been made to appear by historians. A better history would start with an understanding of the sociology and culture of professionalism. I have relied on Magali Sarfatti Larson, *The Rise of Professionalism: A Sociological Analysis* (Berkeley and Los Angeles, 1977), from which I have borrowed the concepts of the market profession and cognitive exclusiveness. It would also take account of the history of professionalism in America. Gerald L. Geison, ed., *Professions and Professional Ideologies in America* (Chapel Hill, NC, 1983) and an older anthology, Kenneth S. Lynn and the editors of *Daedalus*, eds., *The Professions in America* (Boston, 1967) are useful in this regard.

For the prehistory of the American architectural profession, see Barrington Kaye, *The Development of the Architectural Profession in Britain* (London, 1960) and Spiro Kostof, ed., *The Architect: Chapters in the History of the Profession* (Oxford, 1977), which also treats the American architectural profession.

Benjamin Latrobe epitomized early American architectural professionalism. His aspirations are illuminatingly discussed in two brief essays: J. Meredith Neil, 'The Precarious Professionalism of Latrobe', *AIA Journal*, 53 (May 1970) and Edward C. Carter II, *Benjamin Henry Latrobe and Public Works: Professionalism, Private Interest, and Public Policy in the Age of Jefferson* (Chicago, 1976). For the profession in the first half of the nineteenth century generally, see Dell Upton, 'Pattern Books and Professionalism: Aspects of the Transformation of American Domestic Architecture, 1800–1860', *Winterthur Portfolio*, 19 (1984).

Andrew Saint, *The Image of the Architect* (New Haven and London, 1983) focuses on the British and American professions between the mid-nineteenth and the mid-twentieth centuries. Among the flurry of recent books on the contemporary architectural profession, Judith Blau, M. E. La Gory, and J. S. Pipkin, eds., *Professionals and Urban Form* (New York, 1983); Robert Gutman, *Architectural Practice: A Critical View* (Princeton, 1988); and Magali Sarfatti Larson, *Behind the Postmodern Façade: Architectural Change in Late Twentieth-Century America* (Berkeley and Los Angeles, 1993) stand out.

Architecture as a Business
In addition to the works in the previous section, see Harry Braverman's classic *Labor and Monopoly Capital: The Degradation of Work in the Twentieth Century* (New York, 1974) for the reorganization of head and hand labour under industrial capitalism.

Architecture and Social Class
Daniel H. Calhoun, *Professional Lives in America: Structure and Aspiration 1750–1850* (Cambridge, Mass., 1965) treats profession-alism as a road to social advancement. On collegiate education and professional status, see Burton J. Bledstein, *The Culture of Professionalism: The Middle Class and the Development of Higher Education in America* (New York, 1976). Other than an old dissertation, Arthur Clason Weatherhead, *The History of Collegiate Education in Architecture in the United States* (Los Angeles, 1941) and Kostof, ed., *The Architect*, there are no studies of architectural education in the United States. Information must be dug out of the anniversary histories published by many schools, as well as biographies and monographs of individual architects.

Style
Style is a concept as elusive as it is central to the literature of architectural history. Most architectural historians employ a definition derived from art history. Meyer Schapiro, 'Style', in A. L. Kroeber, ed., *Anthropology Today: An Encyclopedic Inventory* (Chicago, 1953) is the basic modern text. Margaret Finch, *Style in Art History* (Metuchen, NJ, 1974) is a more recent treatment, while Berel Lang, ed., *The Concept of Style* (rev. edn.; Ithaca, NY, 1987) treats a variety of literary and visual art forms. George Kubler, *The Shape of Time: Remarks on the History of Things* (New Haven and London, 1962) is a notable, if idiosyncratic, essay on formal change.

Although Carroll L. V. Meeks, *The Railroad Station: An Architectural History* (New Haven and London, 1956) attempted to adapt art historian Heinrich Wölfflin's theories of style in painting to the history of architecture, architectural historians have for the most part been content to borrow art-historical models unmodified. In other cases, they conflate the various levels of style, and use the word simply to mean visual appearance. This is the sense in which the word is employed in the many popular guides to the styles of American architecture. Richard Longstreth warns against this habit in a brief but cogent essay, 'The Problem with "Style" ', in *The Forum: Bulletin of the Committee on Preservation*, Society of Architectural Historians 6 (1985), included in *SAH Newsletter*, 29 (June 1985).

Anthropological and sociological approaches to style have much to offer to architectural historians. Dick Hebdige, *Subculture, The Meaning of Style* (London, 1979) treats style from the perspective of British cultural studies. Among anthropo-logists, J. L. Fischer, 'Art Styles as Cultural Cognitive Maps', *American Anthropologist*, 63 (1961) is a classic, widely reprinted essay from a structuralist perspective. James R. Sackett, 'The Meaning of Style in Archaeology: A General Model', *American Antiquity*, 42 (1977) and Robert C. Dunnell, 'Style and Function: A Fundamental Dichotomy', *American Antiquity*, 43 (1978) are more recent theoretical statements. Many of the case studies included in Margaret Conkey and Christine Hastorf, eds., *The Uses of Style in Archaeology* (Cambridge, 1990) offer provocative models for architectural historians. Dell Upton, 'Form and User: Style, Mode, Fashion and the Artifact', in Gerald L. Pocius, ed., *Living in a Material World: Canadian and American Approaches to Material Culture* (St John's, Newfoundland, 1991) applies anthropological concepts of style to architecture in this manner.

The relationship between architectural form and ethnic identity is difficult to sort out. For efforts to do so from disparate perspectives, see Dell Upton, 'Ethnicity, Authenticity, and Invented Traditions', *Historical Archaeology*, 30 (1996); Chappell, 'Rhenish Houses' and Vlach, 'The Shotgun House', in Upton and Vlach, eds., *Common Places*; and Krinsky, *Contemporary Native American Architecture*.

Styles of the Self

Howard S. Becker, *Art Worlds* (Berkeley and Los Angeles, 1982) illuminates the social role of the contemporary artist. Larson, *Behind the Postmodern Façade*; Roxanne Kuter Williamson, *American Architects and the Mechanics of Fame* (Austin, Tex., 1991); and especially Robert Twombly, *Power and Style: A Critique of Twentieth-Century Architecture in the United States* (New York, 1996) are important for understanding the ways in which artistic self-presentation promotes the architect's professional advancement.

Who Is an Architect?

In the past twenty years, the place of women and minorities in architecture has been the focus of more interest than real scholarship. Typically, early efforts were devoted simply to recovering forgotten names and chronicling obscure careers. Doris Cole, *From Tipi to Skyscraper: A History of Women in Architecture* (Boston, 1973); Susana Torre, ed., *Women in American Architecture: A Historic and Contemporary Perspective* (New York, 1977); and Doris Cole and Karen Cord Taylor, *The Lady Architects: Lois Lilley Howe, Eleanor Manning and Mary Almy, 1893–1937* (New York, 1990) are examples. More recent and more sophisticated efforts have been less interested in names than in institutions, ideas, and social structures. Among the best are Gwendolyn Wright's essay on the professional and personal relationship of Catherine Bauer and William Wurster in Treib, ed., *An Everyday Modernism*; her 'On the Fringe of the Profession: Women in American Architecture' (to which I am particularly indebted in this section), in Kostof, ed., *The Architect*; Ellen Perry Berkeley, ed.,

Architecture: A Place for Women (Washington, 1989); and Debra Coleman, Elizabeth Danze, and Carol Henderson, eds, *Architecture and Feminism* (Princeton, 1996).

Non-professional women's roles in shaping architecture are less well known, but see Katherine C. Grier, *Culture and Comfort: People, Parlors, and Upholstery 1850–1930* (Rochester, NY, 1988); Sally McMurry, 'Women in the American Vernacular Landscape', *Material Culture*, 20 (1989); McMurry, *Families and Farmhouses in Nineteenth-Century America: Vernacular Design and Social Change* (Oxford, 1988); and Jessica H. Foy and Karal Ann Marling, eds., *The Arts and the American Home, 1890–1930* (Knoxville, Tenn., 1994).

For African-American builders, the opposite is true. Much more is known about vernacular builders than about professionals. Catherine W. Bishir, 'Black Builders in Antebellum North Carolina', *North Carolina Historical Review*, 61 (October 1984) is a classic essay that dispels all the pernicious but persistent myths about the minor role of African-Americans in antebellum architecture. John Michael Vlach, ' "Us Quarters Fixed Fine": Finding Black Builders in Southern History', in Vlach, *By the Work of Their Hands: Studies in Afro-American Folklife* (Charlottesville, Va., 1991) will help readers to know where to conduct their own research. Ellen Weiss, *An Annotated Bibliography on African-American Architects and Builders* (Philadelphia, 1993) conveniently lists the scholarly publications on African-American architects issued to that date. Most are name-recovery pieces, such as her own 'Robert R. Taylor of Tuskegee: An Early Black American Architect', *Arris: Journal of the Southeast Chapter of the SAH*, 2 (1991), which returns a significant designer at an important African-American institution to historical memory.

Beyond Art

In the 1960s and 1970s popular architectural design seemed like pure fun or populist exuberance. Rubin, 'Aesthetic Ideology and Urban Design'; Liebs, *Main Street to Miracle Mile*; Karal Ann Marling, *The Colossus of Roads: Myth and Symbol on the American Highway* (Minneapolis, 1984); John Chase, *Exterior Decoration: Hollywood's Inside-Out Houses* (Los Angeles, 1982); and Chase, *Unvernacular Vernacular: Contemporary American Consumerist Architecture*, special issue (131) of *Design Quarterly* (1986) interpret the popular in this manner while offering analyses that transcend the usual purely celebratory tone of most publications. Robert Venturi, Denise Scott Brown and Steven Izenour, *Learning from Las Vegas: The Forgotten Symbolism of Architectural Form* (Cambridge, Mass., 1977) is in a class by itself, at once a treatise, an advertisement, and a scholarly study. Reyner Banham's *Los Angeles: The Architecture of Four Ecologies* (Harmondsworth, 1971), which embraces the pop design sensibility at the scale of the megalopolis, is slightly dated and equally idiosyncratic, but still provocative.

The wacky and appealing image of popular architecture derives mostly from one-off products of individual entrepreneurs built in the early days of automobile travel. Current studies find the commodified consumerist imagery of multinational corporate design more troublesome. The idiosyncratic exuberance of the early years of roadside architecture has been replaced by a carefully contrived imagery that seems to stifle, rather than encourage, popular expression. Compare the appreciative tone of Paul Hirshorn and Steven Izenour, *White Towers* (Cambridge, Mass., 1979) with Stan Luxenberg, *Roadside America: How the Chains Franchised America* (New York, 1986) and Diane Ghirardo's discussion of the Disney empire in *Architecture after Modernism* (London and New York, 1996).

	10000 BCE	2000 BCE	1000 BCE	0 CE	500 CE

Architectural/ Urban

● *c.*1000 Poverty Point

● *c.*500 BCE–900 CE Hopewellian Culture
● *c.*200 Newark Earthworks

● *c.*800–1500 Cahokia
● *c.*900 Early Iroquoian longhouse at Eldorado Site (Ontario)
● 910 Pueblo Bonito

Cultural

Socio-political

● *c.*10,000 Humans arrive in the Americas

● *c.*2000–700 Poverty Point Culture

● *c.*700–1300 Pueblo-building phase of Anasazi Culture
● *c.*700–1800 Mississippian Culture
● *c.*800–present Iroquoian Culture

Technological

Dates of settlements and institutions are dates of their founding; dates of buildings and sociopolitical events are dates of their commencement.

1000 CE   1050 CE   1100 CE   1150 CE   1200 CE   1250 CE

● *c.*1000 Norse settlement at L'Anse aux Meadows (Newfoundland)

● *c.*1000 Monk's Mound

● *c.*1070 Great Serpent Mound

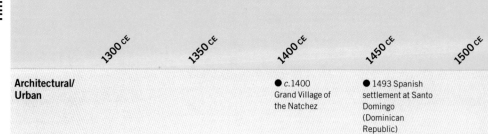

	1300 CE	1350 CE	1400 CE	1450 CE	1500 CE
Architectural/ Urban			● *c.*1400 Grand Village of the Natchez	● 1493 Spanish settlement at Santo Domingo (Dominican Republic)	
Cultural					
Socio-political	● *c.*1300 Navajo enter present homeland in Southwest		● *c.*1400–1600 Iroquois Confederation formed		● 1519 Spanish invasion of Mexico
Technological					

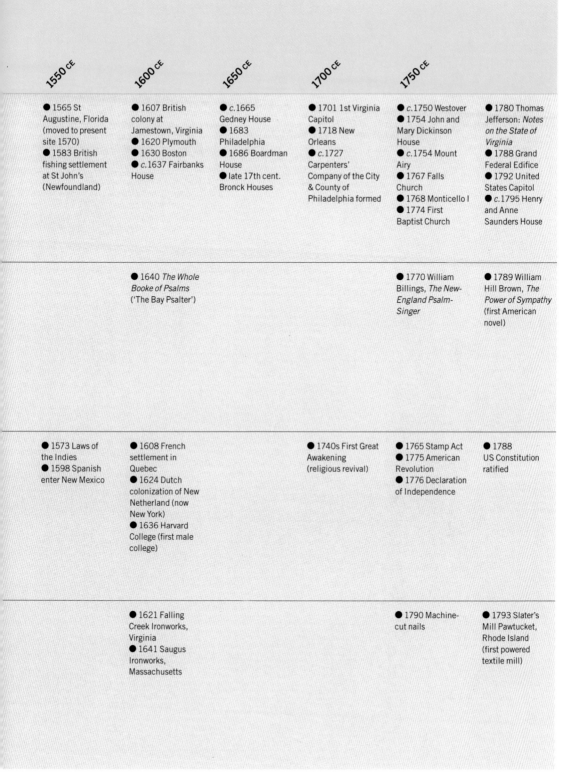

1550 CE	1600 CE	1650 CE	1700 CE	1750 CE	
● 1565 St Augustine, Florida (moved to present site 1570) ● 1583 British fishing settlement at St John's (Newfoundland)	● 1607 British colony at Jamestown, Virginia ● 1620 Plymouth ● 1630 Boston ● c.1637 Fairbanks House	● c.1665 Gedney House ● 1683 Philadelphia ● 1686 Boardman House ● late 17th cent. Bronck Houses	● 1701 1st Virginia Capitol ● 1718 New Orleans ● c.1727 Carpenters' Company of the City & County of Philadelphia formed	● c.1750 Westover ● 1754 John and Mary Dickinson House ● c.1754 Mount Airy ● 1767 Falls Church ● 1768 Monticello I ● 1774 First Baptist Church	● 1780 Thomas Jefferson: *Notes on the State of Virginia* ● 1788 Grand Federal Edifice ● 1792 United States Capitol ● c.1795 Henry and Anne Saunders House
	● 1640 *The Whole Booke of Psalms* ('The Bay Psalter')			● 1770 William Billings, *The New-England Psalm-Singer*	● 1789 William Hill Brown, *The Power of Sympathy* (first American novel)
● 1573 Laws of the Indies ● 1598 Spanish enter New Mexico	● 1608 French settlement in Quebec ● 1624 Dutch colonization of New Netherland (now New York) ● 1636 Harvard College (first male college)		● 1740s First Great Awakening (religious revival)	● 1765 Stamp Act ● 1775 American Revolution ● 1776 Declaration of Independence	● 1788 US Constitution ratified
	● 1621 Falling Creek Ironworks, Virginia ● 1641 Saugus Ironworks, Massachusetts			● 1790 Machine-cut nails	● 1793 Slater's Mill Pawtucket, Rhode Island (first powered textile mill)

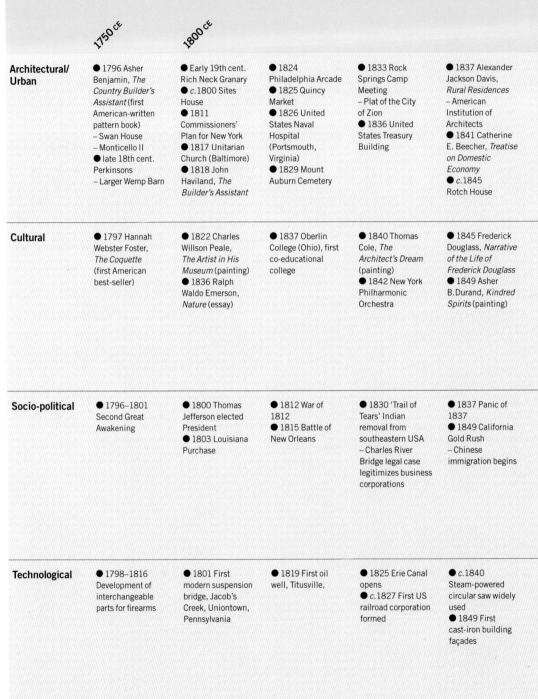

1750 CE   1800 CE

Architectural/ Urban	● 1796 Asher Benjamin, *The Country Builder's Assistant* (first American-written pattern book) – Swan House – Monticello II ● late 18th cent. Perkinsons – Larger Wemp Barn	● Early 19th cent. Rich Neck Granary ● c.1800 Sites House ● 1811 Commissioners' Plan for New York ● 1817 Unitarian Church (Baltimore) ● 1818 John Haviland, *The Builder's Assistant*	● 1824 Philadelphia Arcade ● 1825 Quincy Market ● 1826 United States Naval Hospital (Portsmouth, Virginia) ● 1829 Mount Auburn Cemetery	● 1833 Rock Springs Camp Meeting – Plat of the City of Zion ● 1836 United States Treasury Building	● 1837 Alexander Jackson Davis, *Rural Residences* – American Institution of Architects ● 1841 Catherine E. Beecher, *Treatise on Domestic Economy* ● c.1845 Rotch House
Cultural	● 1797 Hannah Webster Foster, *The Coquette* (first American best-seller)	● 1822 Charles Willson Peale, *The Artist in His Museum* (painting) ● 1836 Ralph Waldo Emerson, *Nature* (essay)	● 1837 Oberlin College (Ohio), first co-educational college	● 1840 Thomas Cole, *The Architect's Dream* (painting) ● 1842 New York Philharmonic Orchestra	● 1845 Frederick Douglass, *Narrative of the Life of Frederick Douglass* ● 1849 Asher B. Durand, *Kindred Spirits* (painting)
Socio-political	● 1796–1801 Second Great Awakening	● 1800 Thomas Jefferson elected President ● 1803 Louisiana Purchase	● 1812 War of 1812 ● 1815 Battle of New Orleans	● 1830 'Trail of Tears' Indian removal from southeastern USA – Charles River Bridge legal case legitimizes business corporations	● 1837 Panic of 1837 ● 1849 California Gold Rush – Chinese immigration begins
Technological	● 1798–1816 Development of interchangeable parts for firearms	● 1801 First modern suspension bridge, Jacob's Creek, Uniontown, Pennsylvania	● 1819 First oil well, Titusville,	● 1825 Erie Canal opens ● c.1827 First US railroad corporation formed	● c.1840 Steam-powered circular saw widely used ● 1849 First cast-iron building façades

1850 CE

- mid-19th cent. Balls Creek Camp Meeting
- 1850 Andrew Jackson Downing, *The Architecture of Country Houses*
- 1853 Andrew Jackson Downing: *Rural Essays*
- 1855 Tower Hall
- 1856 Central Park

- 1857 American Institute of Architects
 –Richard Morris Hunt opens architectural atelier on École des Beaux-Arts model
- 1865 First collegiate school of architecture at Massachusetts Institute of Technology

- 1868 Riverside
- 1869 Catherine E. Beecher and Harriet Beecher Stowe, *The American Woman's Home*
 – East River (Brooklyn) Bridge
- 1870s Sour Springs Longhouse
- 1872 Pennsylvania Academy of

Fine Arts
- 1876 Johns Hopkins Hospital
- 1877 Oliver Ames Memorial Library
- 1879 Oakes Ames Memorial Hall
 – Ames Monument
- 1880 Ames Gate Lodge
- c.1885 Henry R. Mallory House

- 1885 James Hopkins Smith House
- 1890 Wainwright Building
- 1892 Winslow House
- 1893 World's Columbian Exposition
 – Massachusetts Building
 – Women's Building

- 1896 Louis H. Sullivan, *The Tall Office Building Artistically Considered*
 – Blackfeet tipi circle
- 1897 First architectural licensing law
 – El Alisal
- c.1900 Kenton Hotel

- 1850 Nathaniel Hawthorne, *The Scarlet Letter*
 – Harriet Beecher Stowe, *Uncle Tom's Cabin*
 – Susan Warner, *The Wide, Wide World*

- 1851 Herman Melville, *Moby–Dick*
- 1854 Henry David Thoreau, *Walden*
- 1855 Walt Whitman, *Leaves of Grass* (poems)

- 1876 Thomas Eakins, *The Gross Clinic* (painting)

- 1885 William Dean Howells, *The Rise of Silas Lapham*
 – Mark Twain, *Huckleberry Finn*

- 1888 Edward Bellamy, *Looking Backward, 2000–1888*
- 1890 First commercial sound recording

- 1893 Henry B. Fuller, *The Cliff Dwellers*
- 1895 Henry B.Fuller, *With the Procession*
- 1896 *The Yellow Kid* (first comic strip)

- 1851 Mary Sharp College (Tennessee), first women's college
- 1854 Ashmun Institute, first collegiate/theological school for blacks

- 1861–5 Civil War
- 1863 Emancipation Proclamation

- 1872 Yellowstone National Park, Wyoming (first national park)
- 1876 Centennial Exhibition, Philadelphia

- 1881 Tuskegee Institute
- 1882 Chinese Exclusion Act
- 1884 Haskell Institute

- 1890 Battle of Little Big Horn
 – *Plessy v. Ferguson* legitimizes racial segregation
- c.1890 Japanese immigration to mainland USA begins

- c.1890–1910 Jim Crow laws
- 1893 Panic of 1893

- 1854 Otis passenger elevator
- 1854–6 Bessemer steel-making process

- c.1868 Typewriter patented

- c.1871 Portland cement patented in US
- 1872 Terracotta cladding introduced for metal framing

- c.1876 Telephone
 – Bicyles introduced to US
- 1877 Phonograph

- 1879 Electric light
- 1884 First use of steel in tall-building framing
- 1889 First hydroelectric dam

- 1890s Wire nails in common use
- 1892 Escalator

	1900 CE			1910 CE	
Architectural/ Urban	● 1901–16 *The Craftsman* (magazine) ● 1902 Collis P. Huntington Memorial Academic Building – Hearst Memorial Mining Building – Edith Wharton and Ogden Codman Jr, *The Decoration of Houses*	● 1903 Cleveland Group Plan – Larkin Company Administration Building ● 1905 Shaker Heights ● 1906 Country Club District ● 1907 Gamble House – St Rita of Cescia Church	● 1908 Robie House ● 1909 Daniel H. Burnham and Edward H. Bennett, *The Plan of Chicago* – Chinese Telephone Exchange/Bank of Canton – Metropolitan Life Insurance Tower	● 1911 Henry H. Saylor *Bungalows* ● 1915 Palace of the Fine Arts	● 1916 Terminal Tower Complex ● 1919 San Simeon ('Hearst Castle')
Cultural	● 1902 First commercial black-gospel music recording	● 1903 W. E. B. DuBois, *The Souls of Black Folk* – First commercial European ethnic music recording	● 1906 Charles Ives, *The Unanswered Question* (music)	● 1913 The Armory Show (paintings) ● 1915 Panama-Pacific International Exposition ● 1915 Charlotte Perkins Gilman, *Herland*	● 1917 First commercial jazz music recording ● 1918 Henry Adams, *The Education of Henry Adams*
Socio-political				● 1910 Margaret Byington, *Homestead: The Households of a Mill Town* ● 1911 Frederick Winslow Taylor, *The Principles of Scientific Management* ● 1913 Income tax instituted in USA	● 1916 New York Zoning Law – Federal Road Aid Act – National Park Service founded ● 1917 USA enters World War I – Large-scale emigration of southern blacks to northern cities begins – Prohibition
Technological	● 1903 Wright Brothers' first flight	● 1906 Willis Carrier patents his air-conditioning system	● 1908 Ford Model T car introduced	● 1913 First assembly line at Ford plant, Highland Park, Michigan	

● 1922 Country Club Plaza
– Nebraska State Capitol and World War I Memorial
● 1923 Regional Planning Association of America founded

● 1926 Haskell Institute Stadium Arch
– Lovell Beach House
– Rockefeller Center
● 1927 Lovell 'Health' House
– George Washington Bridge

● 1928 4-D Utility Unit/Dymaxion House
– Radburn, NJ
● 1929 Philadelphia Saving Fund Society
– Shaker Square
– Berkeley Women's City Club
– Empire State Building

● 1930 Carew Towers
● 1932 Norman Bel Geddes, *Horizons*
● 1933 Century of Progress
– House of Tomorrow
– Carl Mackley Houses
– Historic American Buildings Survey

● 1934 Catherine Bauer, *Modern Housing*
● 1935 Fallingwater (Kauffman House)
● 1936 Chandler Farms Housing
– S. C. Johnson & Son Administration Building

● 1937 Jacobs House No. 1
● 1939 Azurest South (Meredith–Colson House)
– New York World's Fair
– Tacoma Narrows Bridge

● 1920 First commercial blues recording
– Joseph Stella, *The Bridge* (painting)
● 1922 T. S. Eliot, *The Waste Land* (poem)

● 1923 First commercial hillbilly (country music) recording
● 1924 George Gershwin, *Rhapsody in Blue* (music)

● 1925 Alain Locke, ed., *The New Negro*
– F. Scott Fitzgerald, *The Great Gatsby*
● 1929 *The Jazz Singer* (first talking motion picture)

● 1933 *King Kong* (film)
● 1935 Works Progress Administration and Resettlement Administration/ Farm Security Administration employ photographers such as Walker Evans, Dorothy Lange, Ansel Adams

● 1938 Aaron Copeland, *Billy the Kid* (ballet)

● 1939 John Steinbeck, *The Grapes of Wrath*
– *Gone with the Wind* (film)
– *Spirituals to Swing* concert (Carnegie Hall, New York)

● 1920 Women's suffrage
● 1923 Revised Chicago Zoning Law

● 1924 National Origins (Johnson–Reed) Act severely restricts immigration and establishes ethnic quotas

● 1929 Great Depression begins

● 1933 New Deal begins with inauguration of Franklin D. Roosevelt as president

● 1935 Works Progress Administration gives employment to artists, architects, and writers

– Resettlement Administration founded; reorganized as Farm Security Administration 1937

● 1920 First electrical sound recording
– First commercial radio broadcast

● 1926 Home air-conditioning units patented
– First liquid-fuel rocket flight

● 1928 First television broadcast

● 1934 First divided, limited-access highway: Meadowbrook Parkway, New York City

● 1939 Fluorescent lighting

1940 CE   1950 CE   1960 CE

Architectural/ Urban	● 1940 Baldwin Hills Village ● 1941 Carquinez Heights – Duncan House – Quonset Hut ● 1943 Chabot Terrace ● 1944 Elizabeth Mock, *Built in USA Since 1932* (exhibition; book 1945)	● 1947 Northgate Regional Shopping Center – First Unitarian Church (Madison, Wisconsin) ● 1948 Sun–Heated House – Donnell Garden ● 1949 Glass House (Johnson)	● 1950 J. C. Nichols Memorial Fountain – Pruitt–Igoe Houses – Bavinger House – Bay Street Public Housing ● 1953 Schuylkill Falls Public Housing ● 1954 Northland Shopping Center	● 1956 'City X' plan – Southdale Shopping Center ● 1957 Clarence S. Stein, *Toward New Towns for America* – Richards Medical Research Laboratory ● 1959 Kalamazoo Pedestrian Mall – Salk Institute for Biological Studies	● 1960 Guild House ● 1962 Vanna Venturi House – Governor Nelson A. Rockefeller Empire State Plaza ● 1964 Fresno Pedestrian Mall ● 1965 Smith House
Cultural			● 1952 Ralph Ellison, *The Invisible Man* – John Cage, *4'33"* (music) ● 1954 Elvis Presley, 'That's Alright Mama' (song)	● 1956 Allen Ginsberg, *Howl* (poem) ● 1959 Robert Frank, *The Americans* (photography)	● 1962 Rachel Carson, *Silent Spring* – Tillie Olsen, *Tell Me a Riddle*
Socio-political	● 1941 USA enters World War II	● 1945 Atomic bombing of Hiroshima and Nagasaki	● 1954 American involvement in Vietnam begins – *Brown v. Board of Education* strikes down racial segregation	● 1955 Montgomery Bus Boycott brings Civil Rights Movement to national attention ● 1956 Federal Interstate Highway Act ● 1957 Little Rock integration crisis	● 1960 Greensboro NC, civil rights sit-in ● 1963 March on Washington –John F. Kennedy assassinated ● 1964 Berkeley Free Speech Movement
Technological	● 1940 Collapse of Tacoma Narrows Bridge	● 1942 Penicillin introduced ● 1947 Transistor invented	● 1954 First transistor radio	● 1957 Birth-control pill introduced	● 1961 First US manned space flight

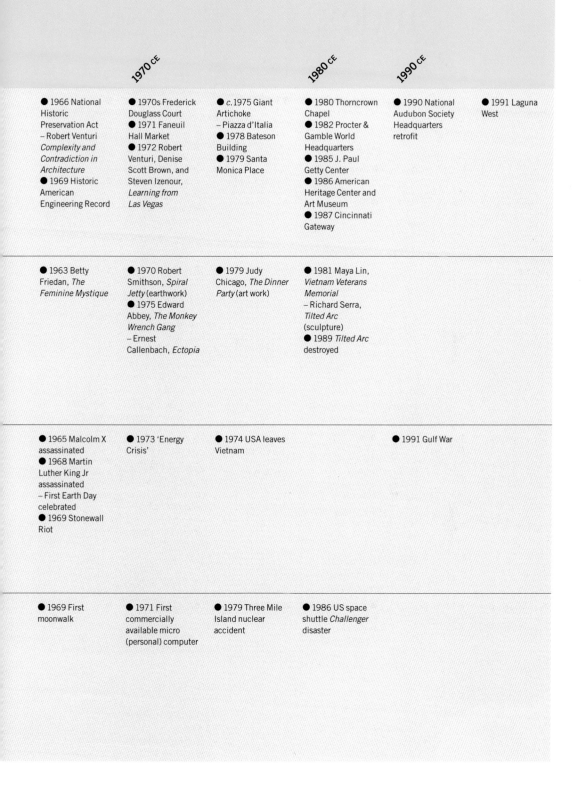

1970 CE **1980 CE** **1990 CE**

● 1966 National Historic Preservation Act – Robert Venturi *Complexity and Contradiction in Architecture*
● 1969 Historic American Engineering Record

● 1970s Frederick Douglass Court
● 1971 Faneuil Hall Market
● 1972 Robert Venturi, Denise Scott Brown, and Steven Izenour, *Learning from Las Vegas*

● c.1975 Giant Artichoke – Piazza d'Italia
● 1978 Bateson Building
● 1979 Santa Monica Place

● 1980 Thorncrown Chapel
● 1982 Procter & Gamble World Headquarters
● 1985 J. Paul Getty Center
● 1986 American Heritage Center and Art Museum
● 1987 Cincinnati Gateway

● 1990 National Audubon Society Headquarters retrofit

● 1991 Laguna West

● 1963 Betty Friedan, *The Feminine Mystique*

● 1970 Robert Smithson, *Spiral Jetty* (earthwork)
● 1975 Edward Abbey, *The Monkey Wrench Gang* – Ernest Callenbach, *Ectopia*

● 1979 Judy Chicago, *The Dinner Party* (art work)

● 1981 Maya Lin, *Vietnam Veterans Memorial* – Richard Serra, *Tilted Arc* (sculpture)
● 1989 *Tilted Arc* destroyed

● 1965 Malcolm X assassinated
● 1968 Martin Luther King Jr assassinated – First Earth Day celebrated
● 1969 Stonewall Riot

● 1973 'Energy Crisis'

● 1974 USA leaves Vietnam

● 1991 Gulf War

● 1969 First moonwalk

● 1971 First commercially available micro (personal) computer

● 1979 Three Mile Island nuclear accident

● 1986 US space shuttle *Challenger* disaster

Index

Oxford History of Art

Titles in the Oxford History of Art series are up-to-date, fully-illustrated introductions to a wide variety of subjects written by leading experts in their field. They will appear regularly, building into an interlocking and comprehensive series.